IMAGES
of America

TIPPAH COUNTY

On the Cover: A scene of the square in Ripley, Mississippi, where "First Monday" was held for years. Looking east, the white house in the background was the home of Ira Leander Clayton and Nancy McCord Clayton. The house was built on a lot from W. W. Robinson around 1909 and burned in 1921. The white frame building facing the east side of the square housed the *Southern Sentinel* newspaper, edited by A.C. Anderson. (Courtesy of Tommy Covington.)

IMAGES
of America

TIPPAH COUNTY

Duane Bullard

ARCADIA
PUBLISHING

ISBN 978-0-7385-8784-4

Published by Arcadia Publishing
Charleston, South Carolina

Printed in the United States of America

Library of Congress Control Number: 2011924176

For all general information, please contact Arcadia Publishing:
Telephone 843-853-2070
Fax 843-853-0044
E-mail sales@arcadiapublishing.com
For customer service and orders:
Toll-Free 1-888-313-2665

Visit us on the Internet at www.arcadiapublishing.com

This book is dedicated to the memory of my parents, Bonnie and Herman Bullard, and in honor of my wife and daughter, Sherri and Natalie Bullard. Thanks to all who have preserved their memories so that we can share this medium of expression.

Contents

ACKNOWLEDGMENTS

Many individuals and organizations have helped in making this book possible. The author would like to especially thank Tommy Covington, retired librarian at the Ripley Public Library, for his love of history and his knowledge of the region's history. Mr. Covington has spent his entire life learning the history and facts about public buildings, people, and houses throughout Tippah County. He also has had many family collections of photographs given to him that he allowed the Tippah County Development Foundation to scan for inclusion in the Tippah County Treasures.

This series of photographs comes from a collection of more than 12,000 photos from the 1850s to the 1960s. These photographs came via collections from the Rainey Estate, Andrew Brown, Mauldin Studios, and McKnight Studios. It must also be noted that Ray Sartor, retired county agent for Tippah County, made many photographs during his work life from 1950 to the early 1990s.

The Tippah County Development Foundation began to scan and document all available photographs that we could find in 2006, and have since scanned and documented almost 12,000 photographs from Tippah County. Together, Duane Bullard, Tommy Covington, and Deborah Hurt have put together a great collection that will withstand the generations to come.

Brinkley Taliaferro, the author's editor at Arcadia, began the process of approving the pictures and book writing process, and we wish to thank her for her patience and being available to answer our questions along the way. Thanks also to Tommy Covington and Anna Quinn for proofreading Tippah County prior to production. Unless otherwise noted, all images in this book are courtesy of Tippah County Treasures and Tommy Covington.

Introduction

Tippah County is one of Northern Mississippi's original counties with a distinguished history that spans the periods of time with the Chickasaw Indians, early white settlers, Civil War, the Reconstruction Era, and the industrial modernization in later years.

On February 14, 1836, more than a year before the removal of the Chickasaws to the west began, the Mississippi Legislature divided the Chickasaw Cession into 10 counties, of which Tippah was one. The name "Tippah" is a Chickasaw word meaning "cut off," and is taken from the creek of the same name that flows across much of the original county from north to south before emptying into the Tallahatchie River. The creek was probably named because it, and the ridges on either side, cut off the western part of the region from the eastern portion.

When Northeast Mississippi was opened to white settlement, it presented an aspect far different from that of today. The entire region was covered by a dense growth of timber, broken only by the few small patches that the Chickasaws had cleared for cultivation. Streams were clear at most times and their flow more constant than in later years after the removal of timber and the cutting of drainage canals. From 1836 to the Civil War in 1861, much of the bottomland in Tippah County was cleared and put into cultivation. Timber still covered the majority of the land until the War Between the States.

Tippah County's prime character in our history was Col. W.C. Falkner. Colonel Falkner was a war veteran of the Mexican War and the Civil War. He was a lawyer, large landowner, and owner of the railroad that helped Tippah County grow and prosper. But it was his death in 1889 that changed the history of Tippah County. He and his longtime friend and business partner, R.J. Thurmond, became embroiled in personal battles later in life until it culminated with R.J. Thurmond shooting and killing Col. W.C. Falkner after Colonel Falkner had just been elected to the State House of Representatives. Colonel Falkner is also noted as having been the great grandfather of the famous writer William Faulkner. Colonel Falkner was also a good writer in his own right and known the most for his writing of the novel, *The White Rose of Memphis*.

In the 1850s, every business house, church, and residence in Ripley, except the courthouse and "Falkner's brick building" on the north side of the square, was of frame construction. Add the universal lighting by candles and it is easy to see why fire was a constant menace. Many of the Ripley businesses were burned from this period until the early 1900s. An excerpt from Orlando Davis' diary says: "On July 9, 1884, at 7 a.m., the Federal Army under Gen. A.J. Smith commenced arriving on the LaGrange Road, and were until 3 p.m. passing through Ripley. The scenes of this visitation were the most terrible we have ever experienced in Ripley. The Yankees were infuriated because of their defeat here and swearing vengeance on the town. Thirty-five stores, dwellings, and churches, including the courthouse, were burned. The cavalry fired the south side of the square in the morning, the rest by Negroes in the evening. Mrs. Price's, Col. Falkner's, and Mrs. Ford's dwellings were burned. The courthouse, Cumberland Presbyterian Church, the Methodist Church, and the Female Academy shared the same fate. My own dwelling was saved by the exertions by a guard left by Col. McMillen." Much of Ripley was built with bricks by 1909. Before the courthouse was burned in 1864, Tippah County's Chancery Clerk placed some of the courthouse records in a trunk and hid it out in the county away from danger. Today, those records are very valuable to Tippah County in the research of land records.

In September 1873, Gen. Mark Perrin Lowrey started Blue Mountain College. It remained in the Lowrey family and was run by them until the 1950s. There have only been seven presidents to serve Blue Mountain College in its 138 years. The present-day president, Dr. Bettye Coward, is the first woman president.

First Monday Trade Days began on July 4, 1893, and has never missed a first Monday weekend since it began. It was first the tax sale day on the Ripley Square when farmers also swapped livestock and other items. Over the years, it became transformed into a flea market. Finally in the mid-1970s, the flea market migrated from the Tippah County Fairgrounds across the highway to property owned by Wayne Windham. The Windham family became the owners of the flea market and it hosted crowds of up to 75,000 people per weekend, and as many as 500,000 per year.

In 1901, Paul J. Rainey who was just 24 years old began purchasing property in Tippah County, and within a few years owned around 10,000 acres. He inherited great wealth from his father. Rainey bought a small farmhouse near Cotton Plant and he enlarged and remodeled it until it included an indoor heated pool and a large game and billiard room. Being a sportsman who hunted worldwide, that game room became decorated with his wild game trophies. In the early days of the development of motion pictures, Rainey was the first to make movies of hunting in Africa. Some of those films were edited into movies shown in New York City, New Orleans, and London. They were also shown at community Fourth of July picnics at his Tippah Farms when up to a thousand county residents would show up for barbecue and entertainment. The W.C. Handy Band from Memphis entertained small parties for his visiting friends at times. Paul Rainey was a very generous man with his tenants and others who he came in contact with. Rainey bought a large amount of land in Nairobi, British East Africa, just to have a place to hunt without being restricted by the British government. While onboard a ship headed to his property in Africa on his 46th birthday, Rainey died of a stroke on September 18, 1923. In less than 50 years, the Rainey Estate had gone full circle when it was finally sold out of the family in 1947.

Tippah County has constantly been changing and has had its share of great residents and citizens to hang its heritage on. This book shares photographs of some of the people who have been a part of Tippah County's past. The North Mississippi County of Tippah is proud of its past and excited about its future.

One

Blue Mountain College

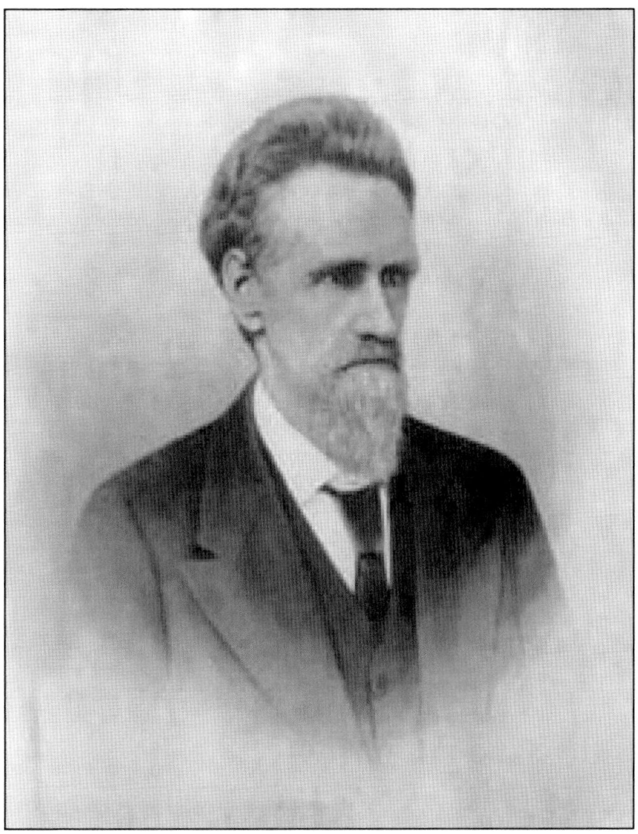

Civil War Brig. Gen. Mark Perrin Lowrey founded Blue Mountain College in 1873. As a village preacher before the war, General Lowrey was a man of vision who saw the importance of providing a thorough education for women. He and his two oldest daughters Modena and Margaret comprised the first faculty at what was then Blue Mountain Female Institute. Fifty students were enrolled for the first session.

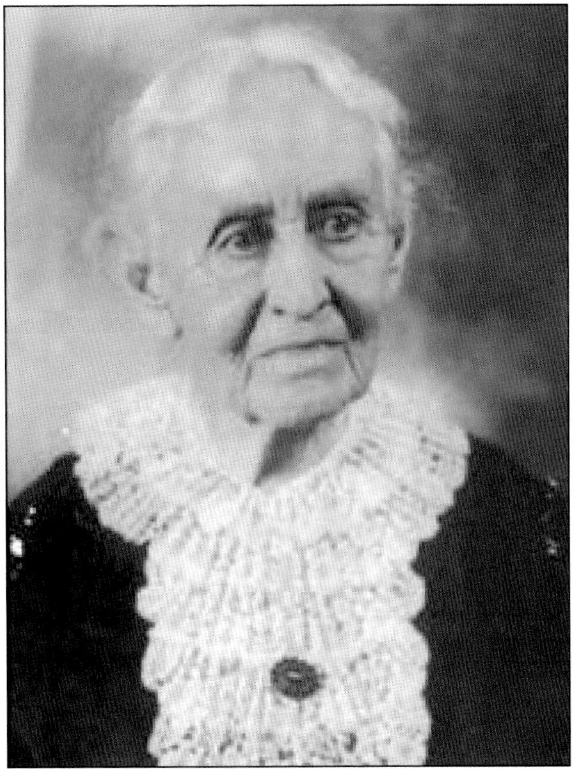

This photograph is of Modena Lowrey Berry, affectionately known as "Mother Berry." She was the daughter of the founder of Blue Mountain College, and the long leader of the faculty from the 1870s through to 1934. Mother Berry served as "Lady Principal" and then as vice president from 1873 to 1934, a tenure perhaps unequaled by a woman as a major college official. She was the second woman in Mississippi's history to be named to the Mississippi Hall of Fame. Mother Berry passed away in 1942, after a 92-year life of service to Blue Mountain College.

This Blue Mountain College faculty picture was taken in the 1894 to 1895 school year and shows Mother Berry, the long time vice president (sitting in chair in front of door), Rev. W.E. Berry, her husband and co-owner of the college (with long beard), and many of the children of Gen. M.P. Lowrey that helped run the college.

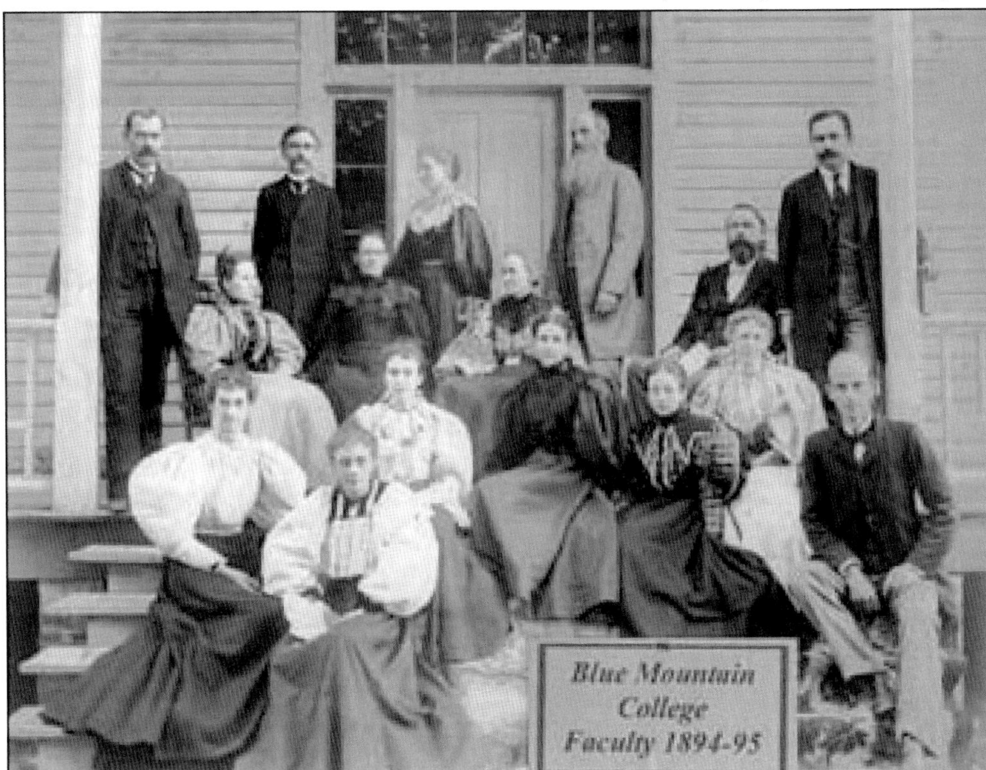

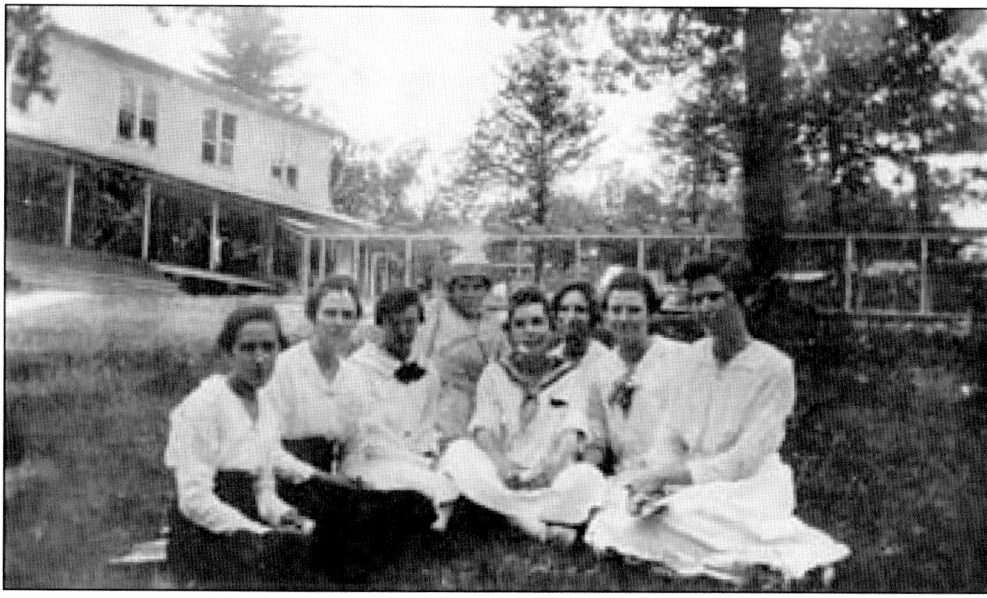

Pictured is a group of eight lady students sitting in the grass on the north side of the administration building. During this early 1900s photograph, it is noted that all buildings were connected via covered walkways for the girls to be protected during rain, snow, and even direct sunlight.

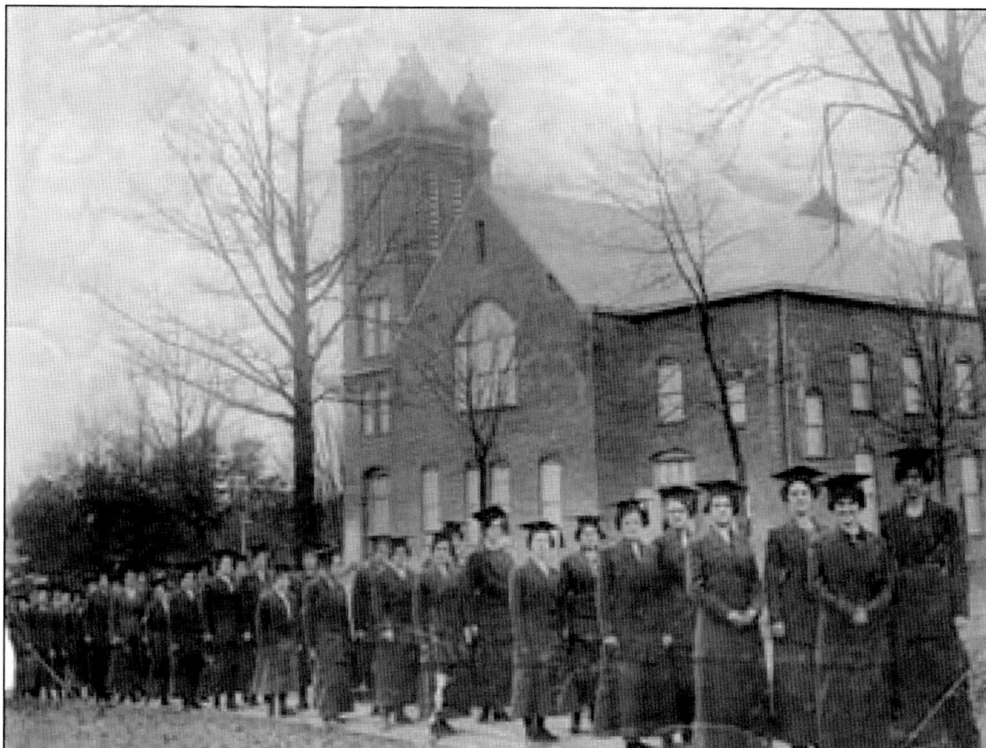

This photograph is of a graduating class of young women making their walk from the Lowrey Baptist Church via a wooden plank walkway to the administration building where the ceremonies were held.

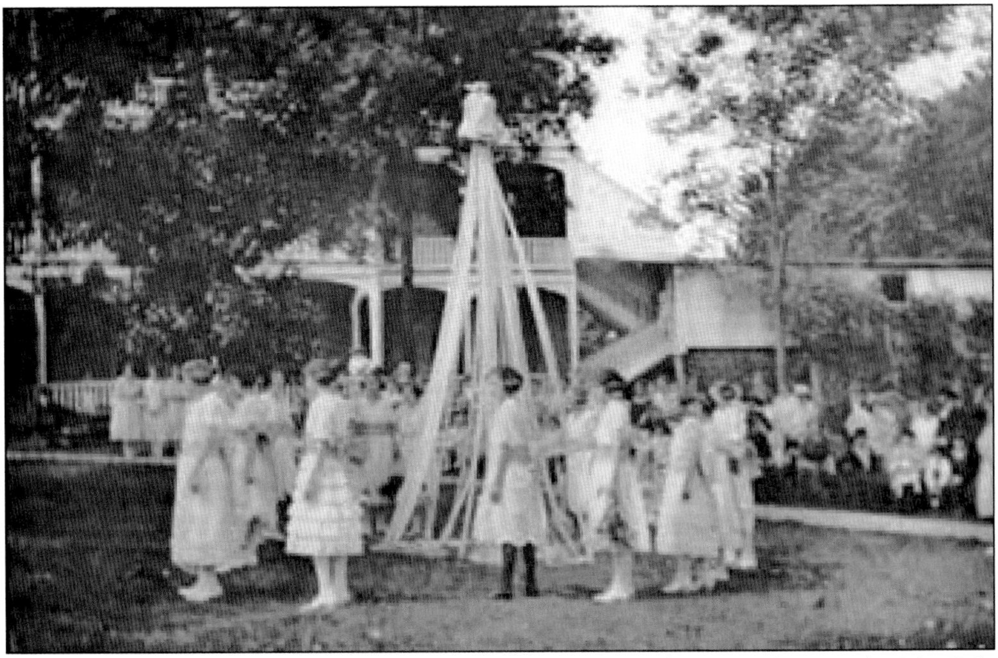

This is the Blue Mountain College May Day Festival in the early 1900s, showing the May Pole where students would grab a ribbon and dance around the flagpole in celebration. The honor of having a part with the dance around the May Pole was very important in the lives of the female students at Blue Mountain College. This event lasted until the mid-1900s. Students wore their white dresses all day for the festival.

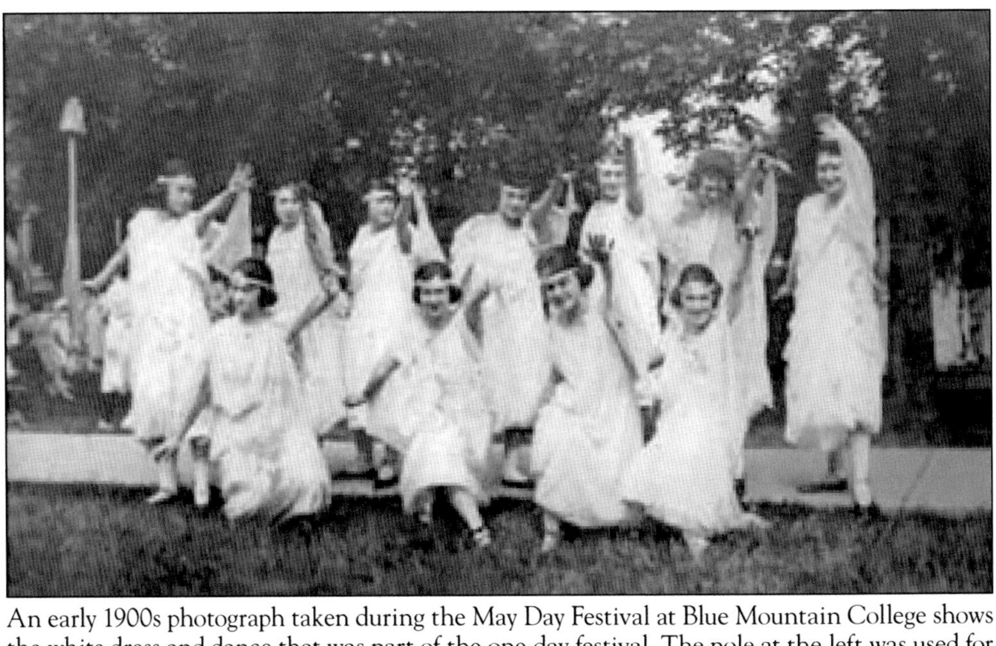

An early 1900s photograph taken during the May Day Festival at Blue Mountain College shows the white dress and dance that was part of the one-day festival. The pole at the left was used for the dance around the May Pole. All who participated enjoyed a very spiritual day.

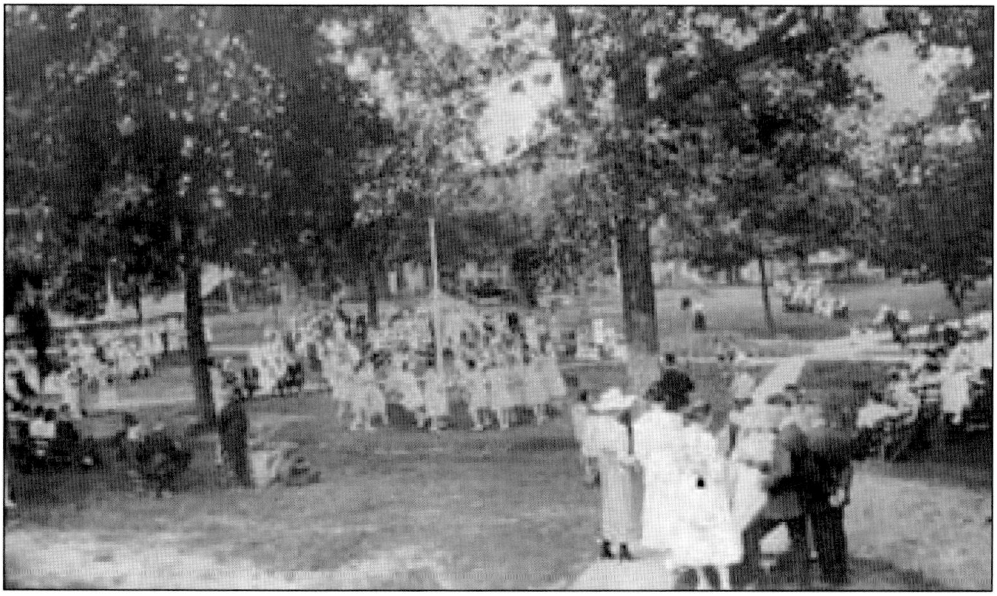

An elaborate May Day Festival takes place with students adorned with white dresses playing around the May Pole. Male students were invited from Mississippi Heights Academy to enjoy the fun. With parents and faculty, May Day was a highlight of the year for most students.

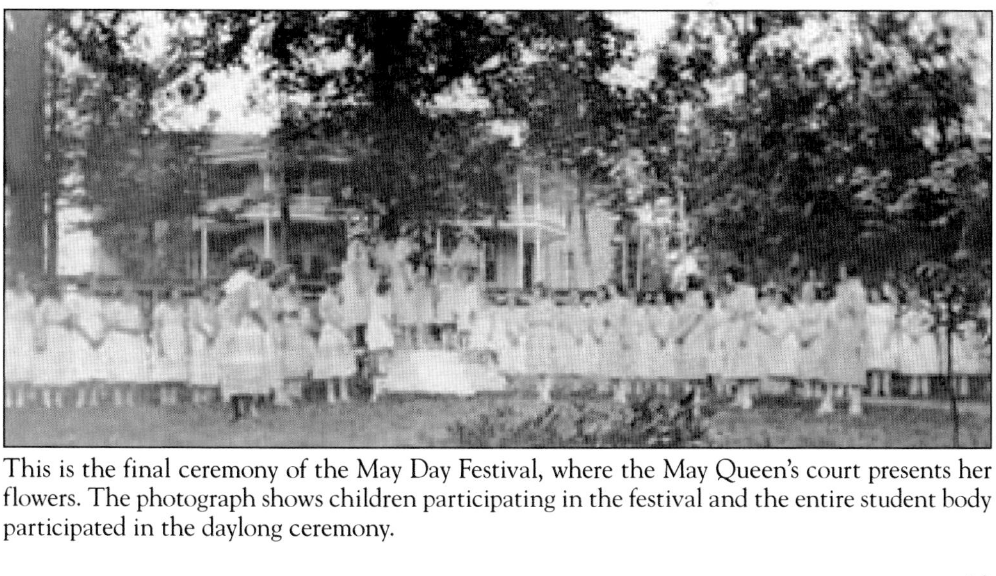

This is the final ceremony of the May Day Festival, where the May Queen's court presents her flowers. The photograph shows children participating in the festival and the entire student body participated in the daylong ceremony.

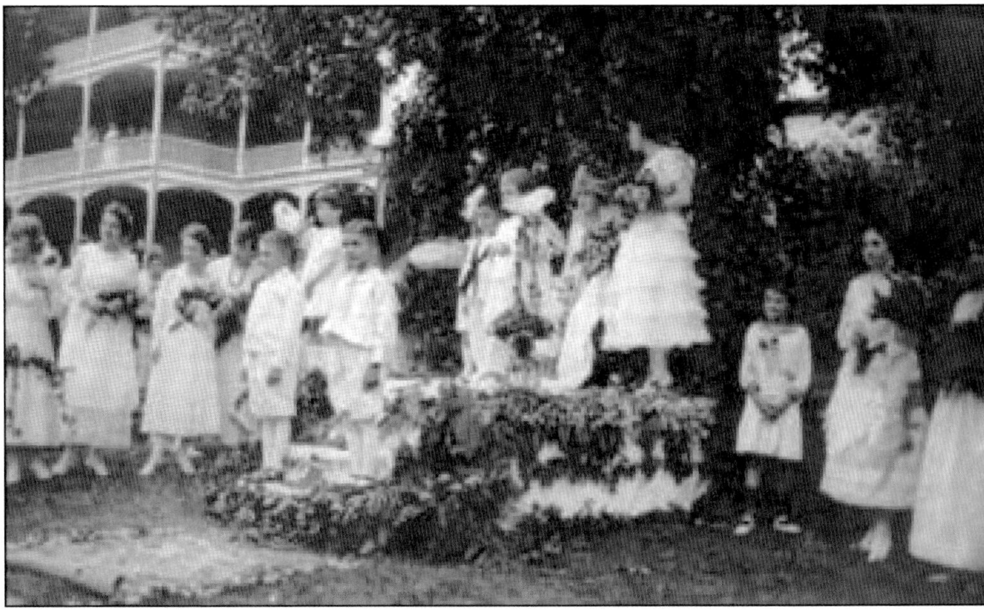

The presentation of the May Queen is about to be made with the help of a number of youth, both male and female. Many flowers and decorations are a large part of the ceremonial day. Activities took place in front of the campus dormitories.

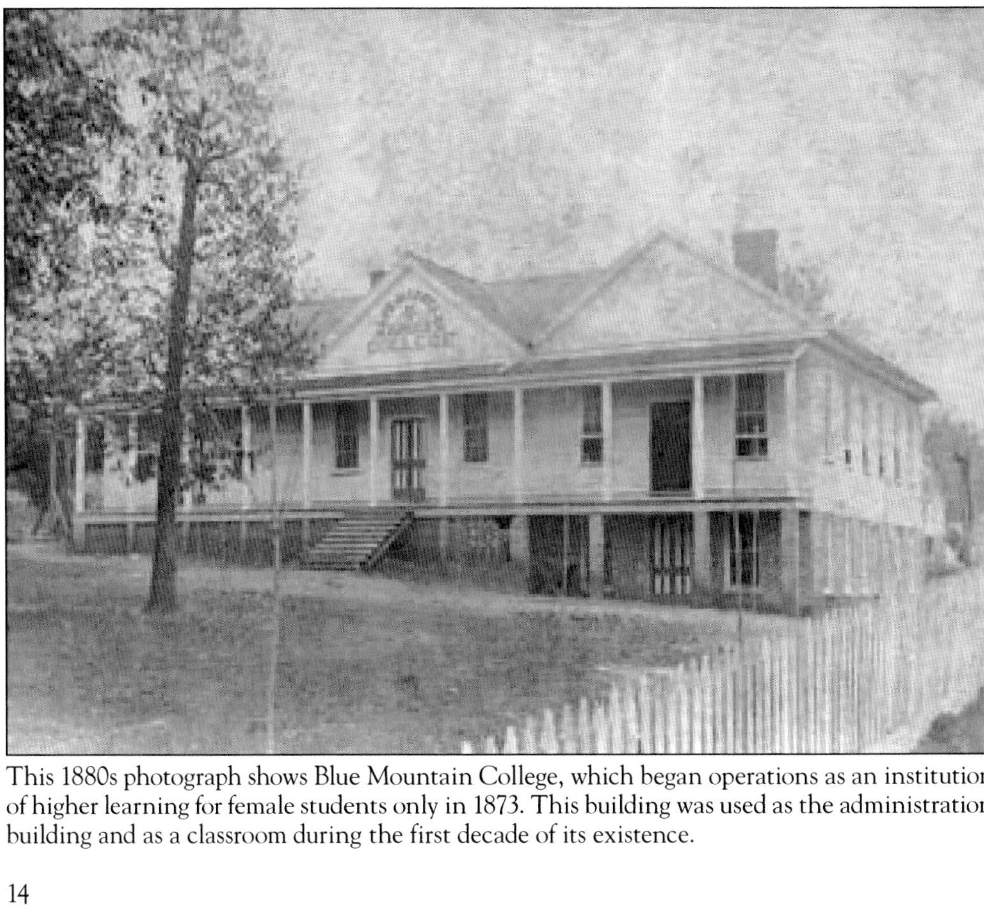

This 1880s photograph shows Blue Mountain College, which began operations as an institution of higher learning for female students only in 1873. This building was used as the administration building and as a classroom during the first decade of its existence.

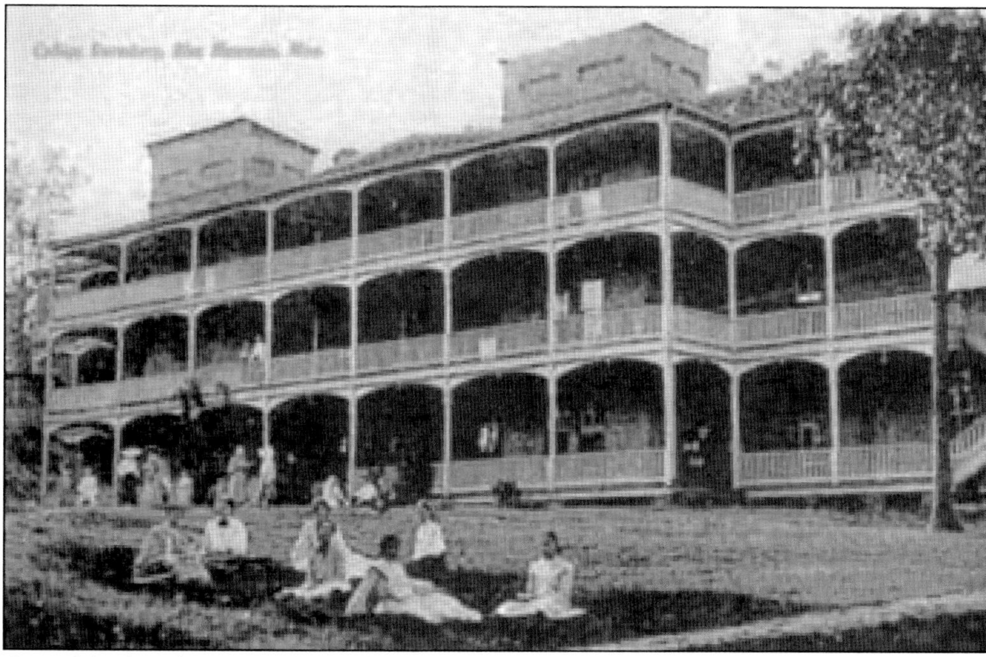

One of the first dormitories located on the Blue Mountain College campus was this three-story structure. It had the finest materials this region had seen with marble floors and countertops and elaborate fireplaces. This photograph was taken near the turn of the century and this dormitory burned during the early 1900s.

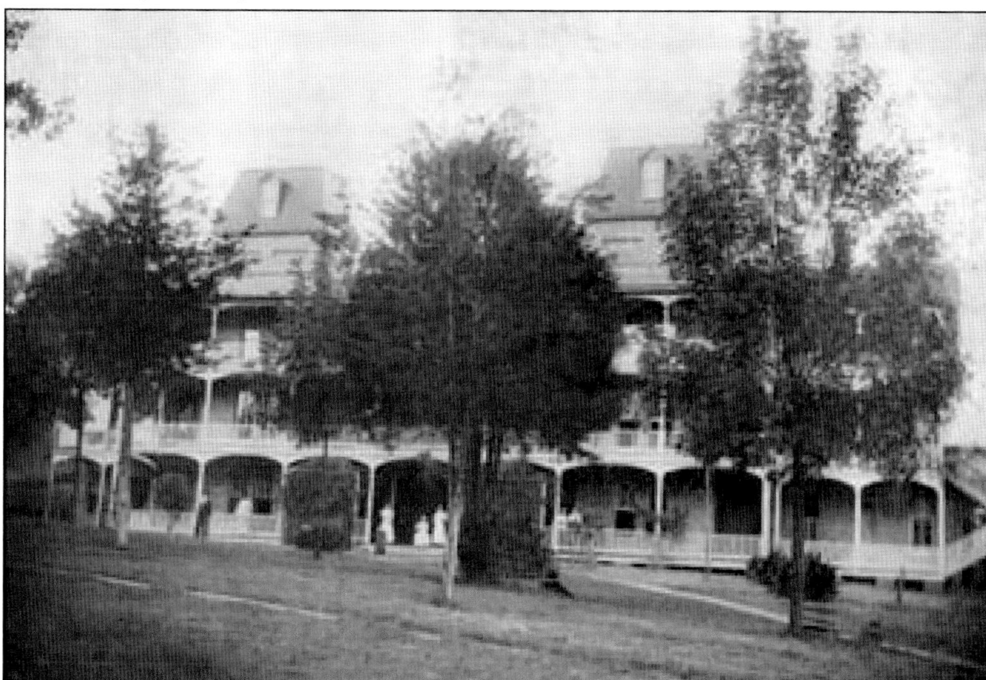

This early 1900 picture is showing another brick dormitory that was built to house the growing population at the all-girl college in Blue Mountain, Mississippi.

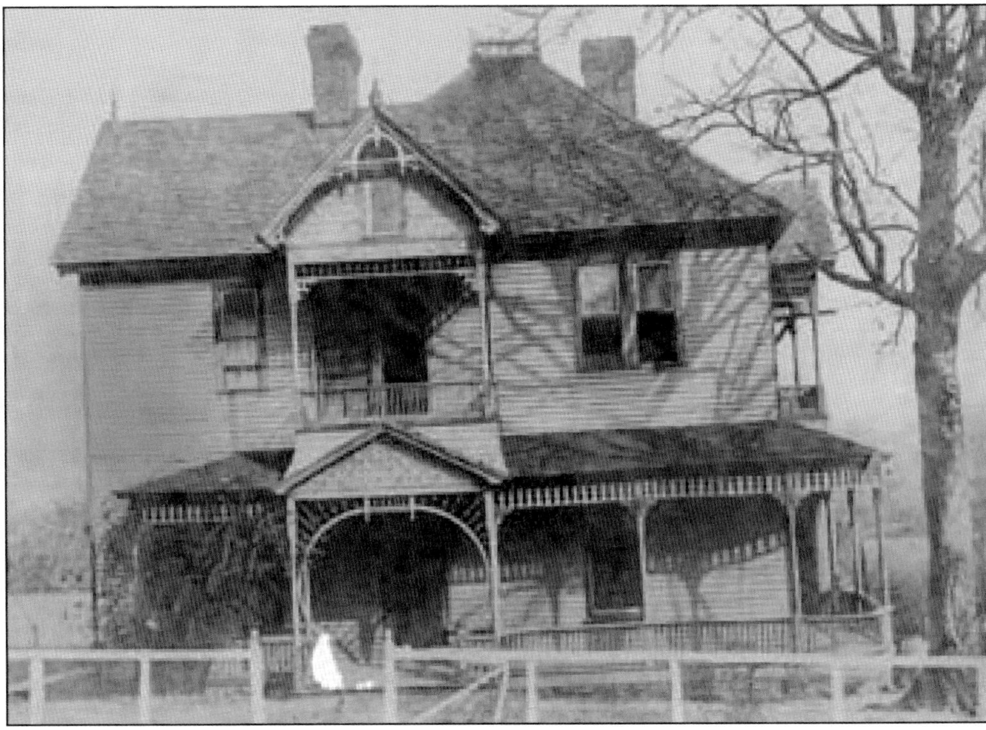

Anderson House at Blue Mountain College, seen in this photograph, was once used as the president's home during the early 1900s.

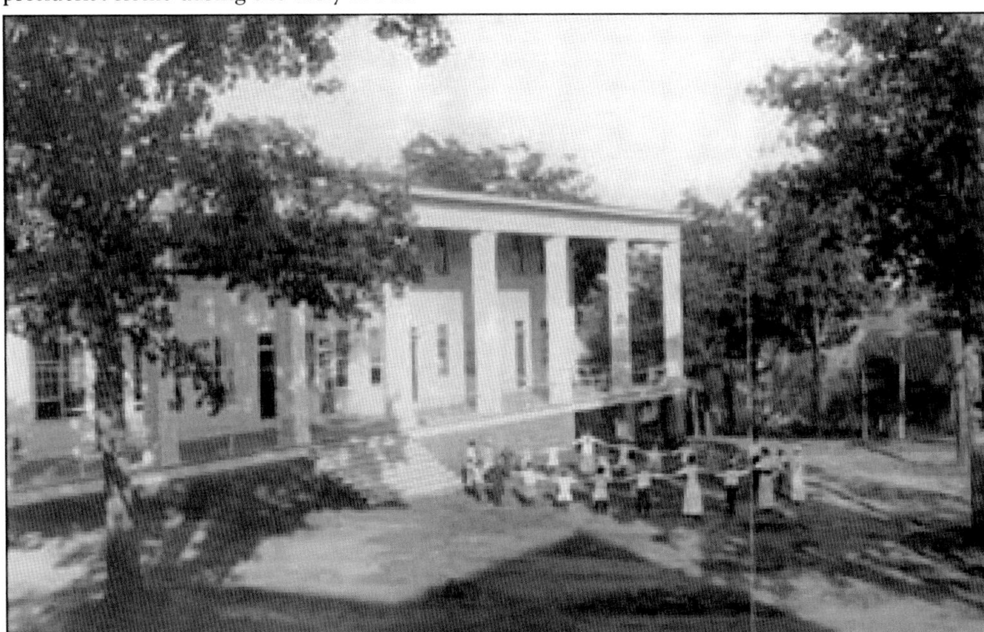

This photograph is of the Blue Mountain College Administration Building as it looked in 1915. The building was built in the early 1900s, and remained until the new administration building was completed in 1928. Teachers and students worked with children in learning how to train teachers for education degrees.

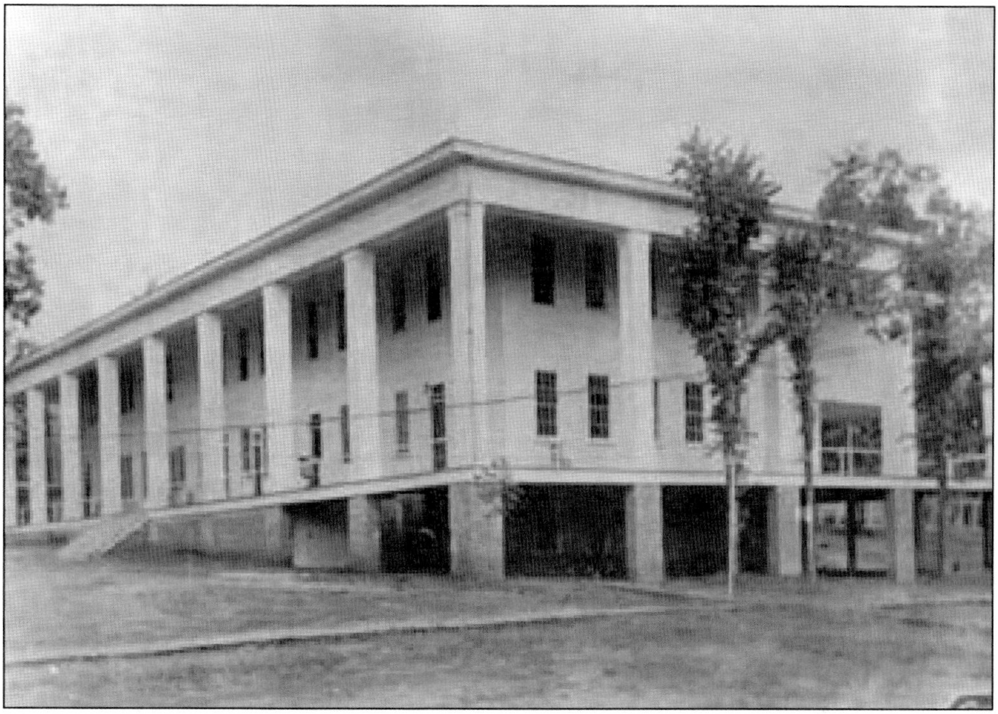

This northeast corner view of the Blue Mountain College Administration Building was a beautiful southern structure made from a wooden frame. It served the college for more than 25 years until it was torn down for a new modern building in 1928.

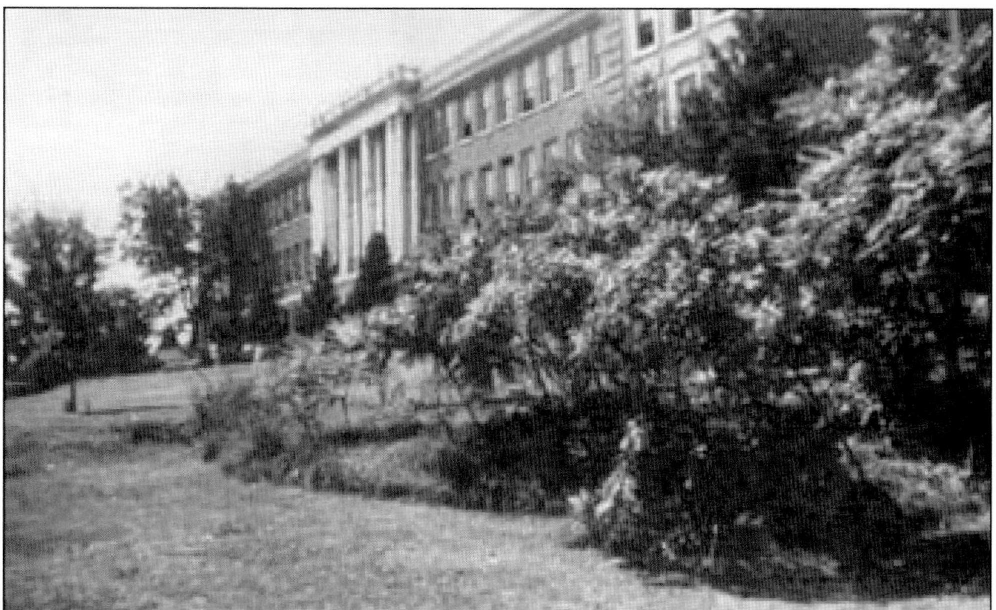

This 1928 large administration building constructed of bricks held the classrooms that were needed for this period, as well as all of the administrative offices for the college. A large auditorium was also added on the back of the building for church meetings and large gatherings. This was a very elaborate building for Tippah County, even today.

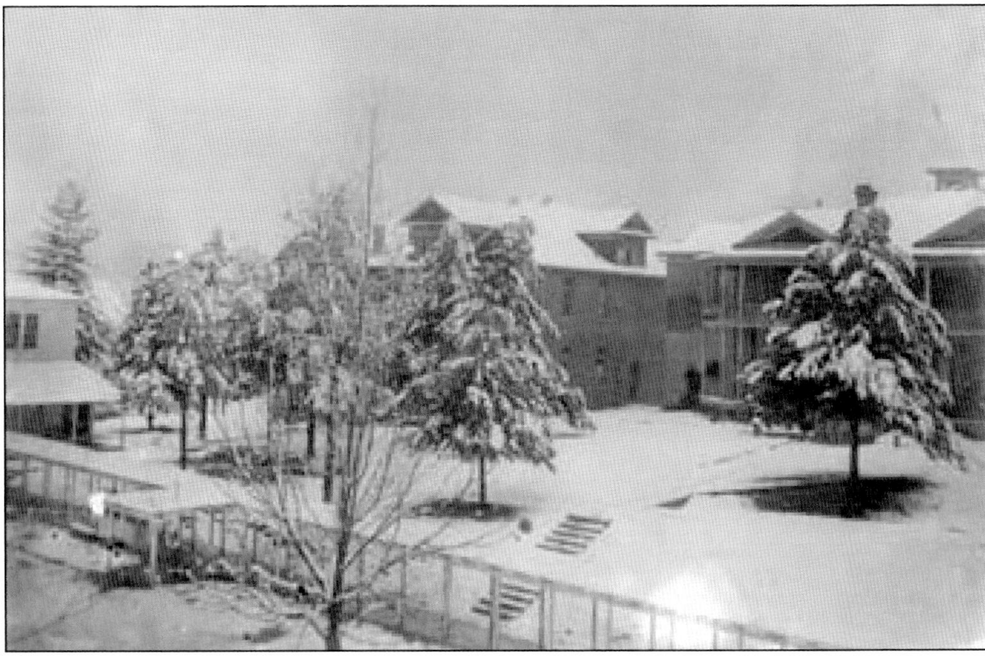

Pictured here is an early 1900s Blue Mountain College wintry snow scene on the campus. Snow only happens every few years in this area, so this was a welcome change on campus. This photograph is looking west behind the administration building.

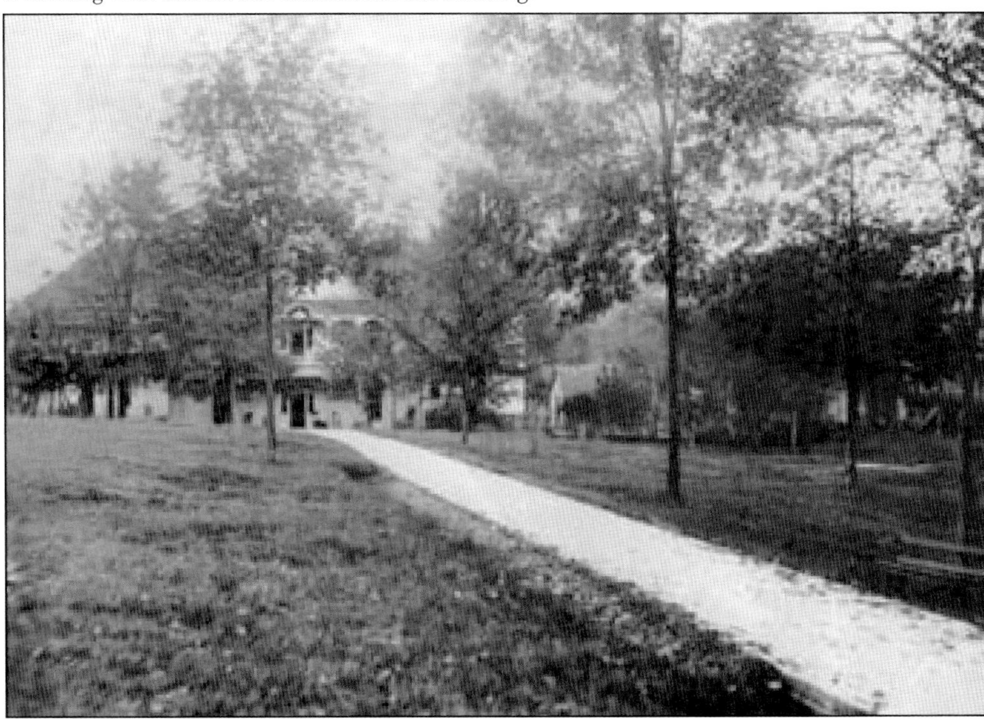

This is one of the faculty houses located on the campus of Blue Mountain College. The large grassy hillsides drop off toward a concrete walkway, protected with a drainage ditch that emptied into a culvert that led under the sidewalk.

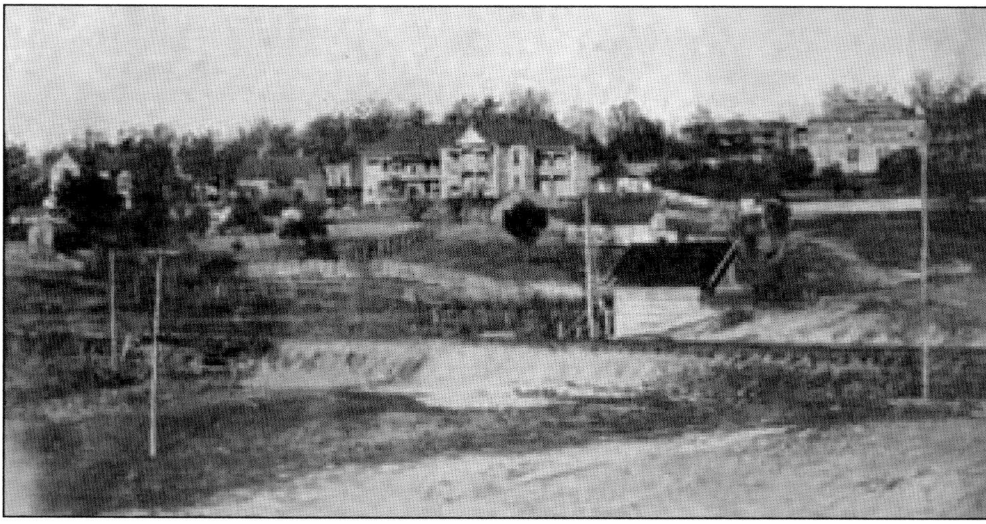

This photograph shows a northeast to southwest view of the campus of Blue Mountain College. The college was very hilly and became Blue Mountain College after someone suggested to Gen. M.P. Lowrey that the hills had a blue hue to them in the mornings. That is when he named the college Blue Mountain Female Academy and later changed it to Blue Mountain College. The Town of Blue Mountain incorporated a year or so after the college was named.

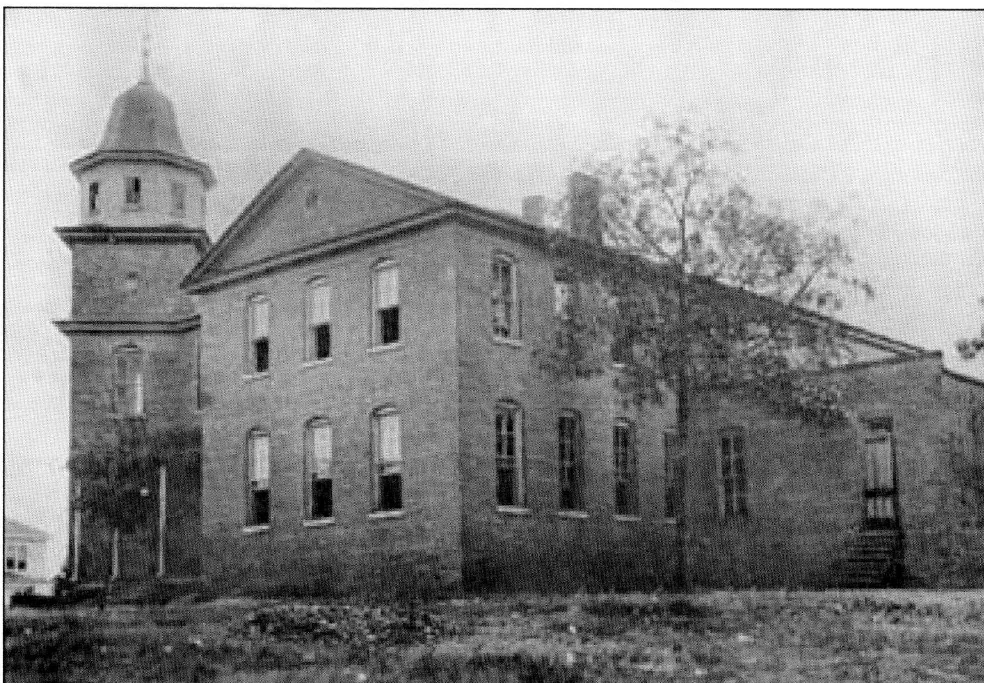

Mississippi Heights Academy was started by Dr. B.G. Lowrey of Blue Mountain College as a school for boys to be prepared adequately for college. The school was formed by organizing a stock company to raise funds and the school was built in 1904. The Board of Directors, of which Dr. Lowrey was president, obtained the services of Prof. J.E. Brown as headmaster. In 1914, the trustees sold the property to Professor Brown, who operated it until it closed in 1943. The boarding school topped out in 1910 with 229 students. The building was torn down in 1957.

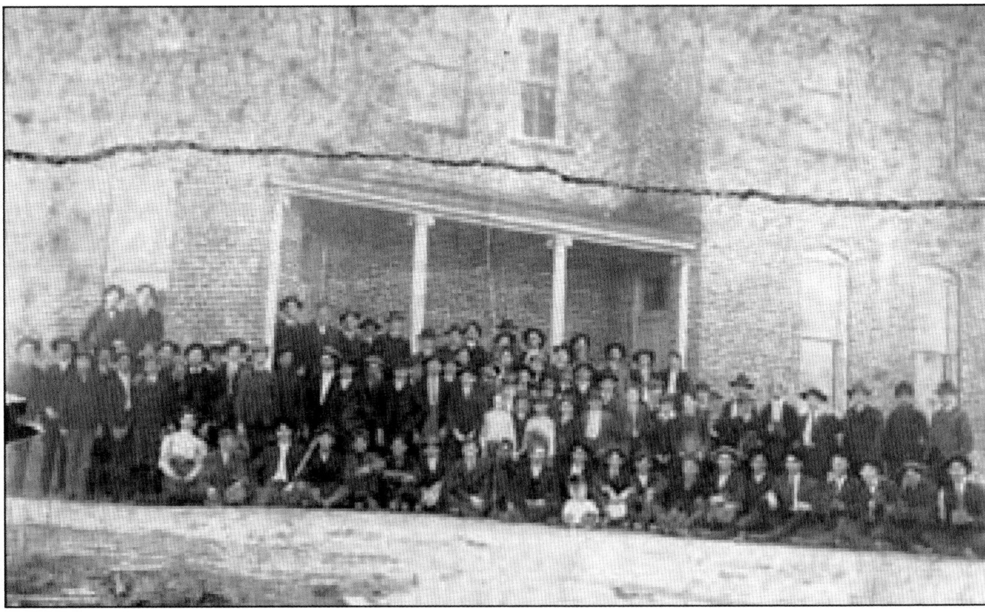

In the early 1900s, the Mississippi Heights Academy in Blue Mountain, Mississippi, was a thriving boarding school for promising young men. Prof. J.E. Brown led the school; a man that had the rare ability to inspire not only respect, but also affection. Professor Brown administered thrashings to rowdy youths that acted in ways they should not have, and he went fishing with his boys, played baseball with them, and stood by them as long as they were right and sometimes when they were not. This photograph shows a number of students behind the school posing in their Sunday best. Charles Collins is the second person from the left on the back row. Students came from as far away as a 100-mile radius.

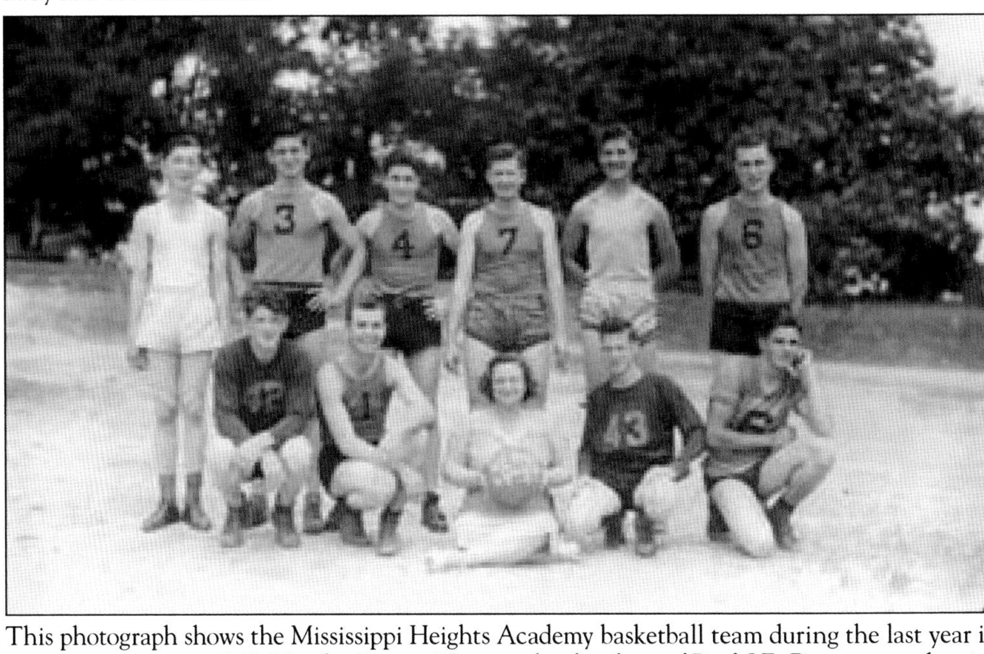

This photograph shows the Mississippi Heights Academy basketball team during the last year it was in operation in 1943. Natalie Brown Watson, the daughter of Prof. J.E. Brown, was the girl holding the ball.

Two

Col. W.C. Falkner

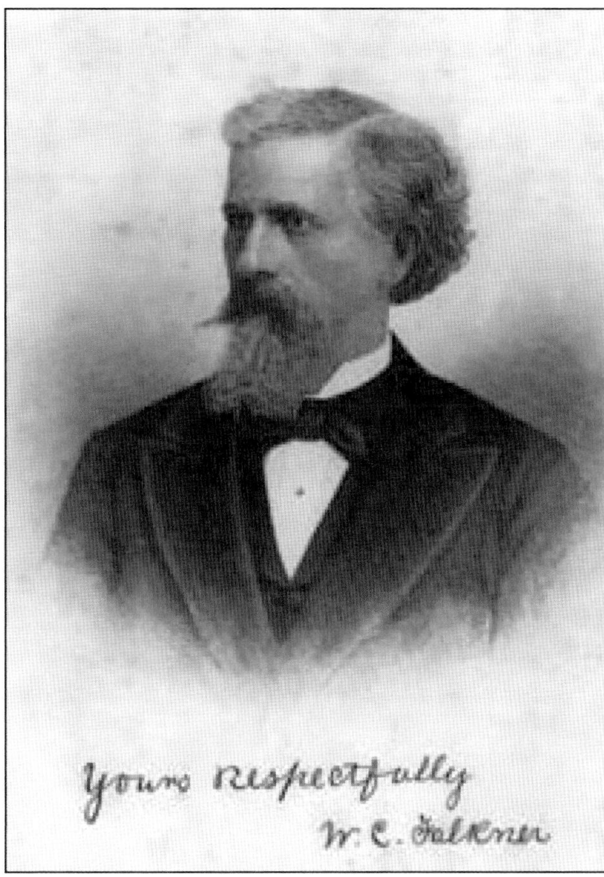

Col. W.C. Falkner had this photograph made and he autographed it and used it in his correspondence. A small person, about 5'6" tall with a nasty tempered spirit, Colonel Falkner was a very colorful and wealthy man that was successful in business, war, politics, and even an accomplished writer. He was born in 1825 and died on November 6, 1889, the day following being shot.

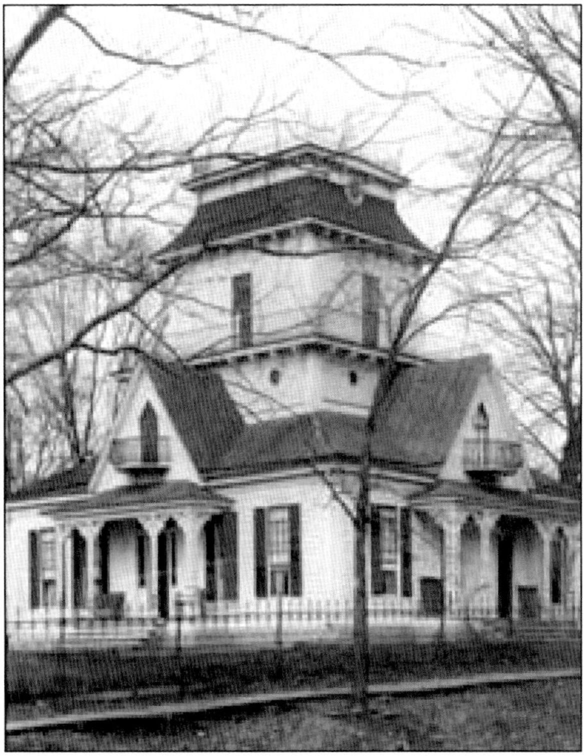

Mrs. W.C. Falkner purchased Col. W.C. Falkner's house, known as "Warwick Place," from Richard Jackson Thurmond in 1865. It was a smaller house until Colonel Falkner took an extended tour of Europe in 1883, which influenced him to have the house remodeled with the central tower, iron balconies, and gingerbread work added. The house was torn down in 1937 to make way for a new post office, but materials from the house were used to build an apartment house. In 1941, it became Dr. John Tate's hospital, Ripley Medical Clinic in the early 1960s, and the Dixie-Net, Inc. headquarters in 2001.

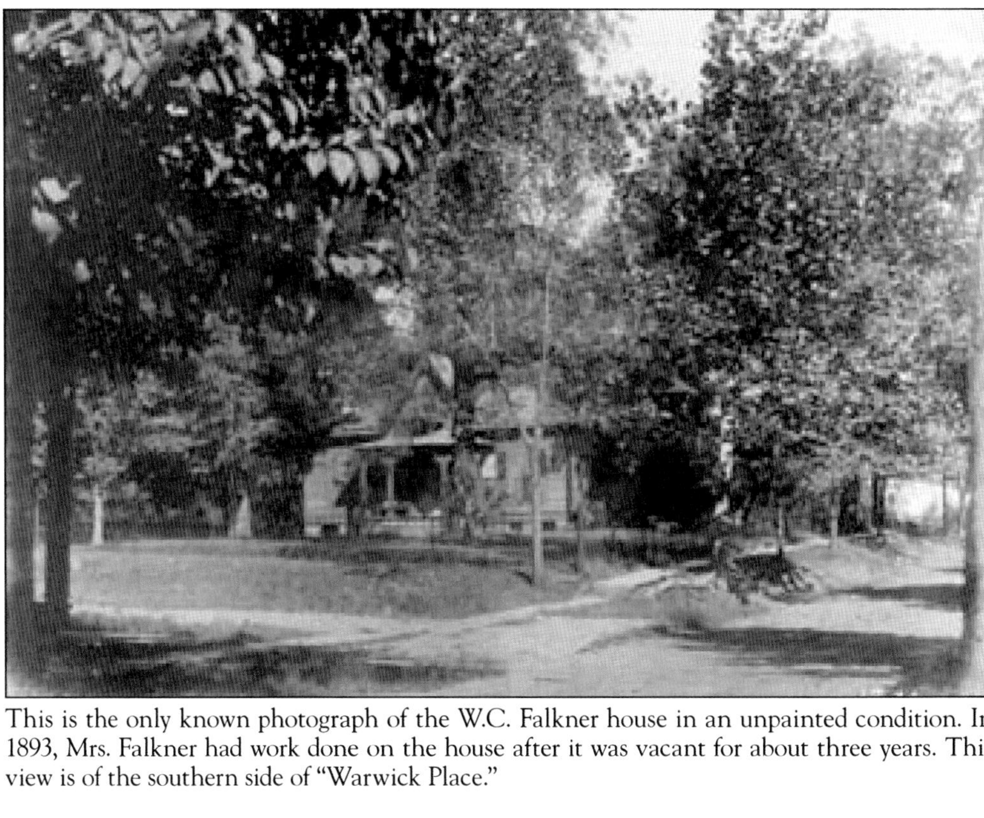

This is the only known photograph of the W.C. Falkner house in an unpainted condition. In 1893, Mrs. Falkner had work done on the house after it was vacant for about three years. This view is of the southern side of "Warwick Place."

This is Col. W.C. Falkner's statue as it looked near the turn of the century in 1900. It was said he had his left hand in his pocket to hide that he was missing three fingers that he lost during the Mexican War in 1848. It was also rumored that a member of the Thurmond family shot off the fingers on the right hand of the statue in years following its placement in the cemetery.

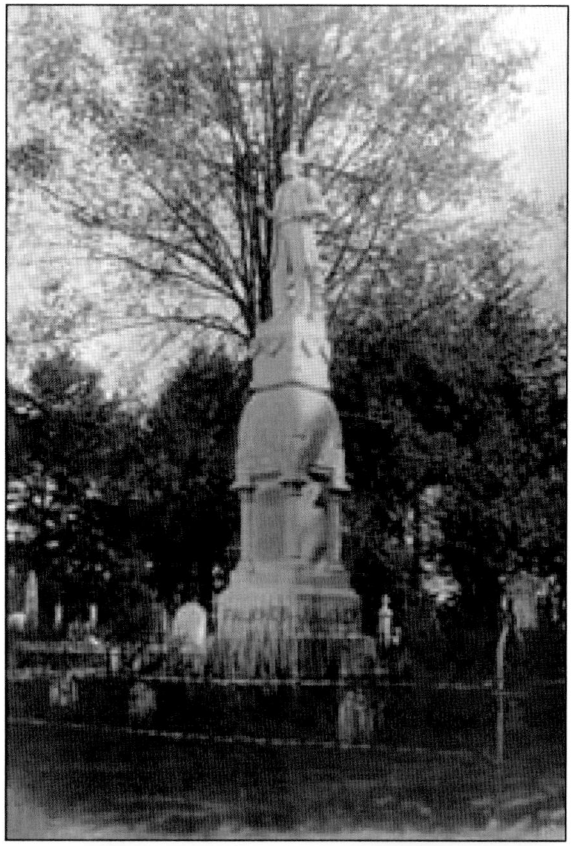

This home was built by Col. W.C. Falkner for his daughter Willie Falkner Carter and her husband, Dr. N.G. Carter. Colonel Falkner was carried to this house after being shot by R.J. Thurmond on the west side of the town square. Colonel Falkner died on the next day from his wounds. The home was located just north of Cooper Street and just east of the railroad. It stood across the railroad from Capt. Thomas Spight's home. Many know it as the William Hines home. The Carter home passed into the possession of William Hines, whose wife, Mattie, was the daughter of Capt. Thomas Spight.

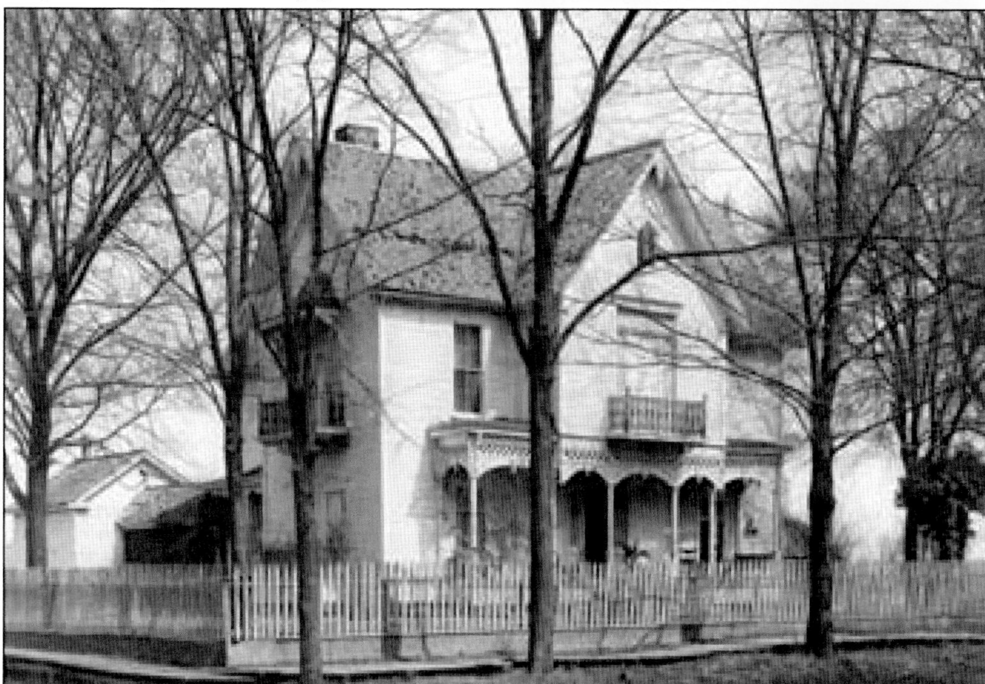

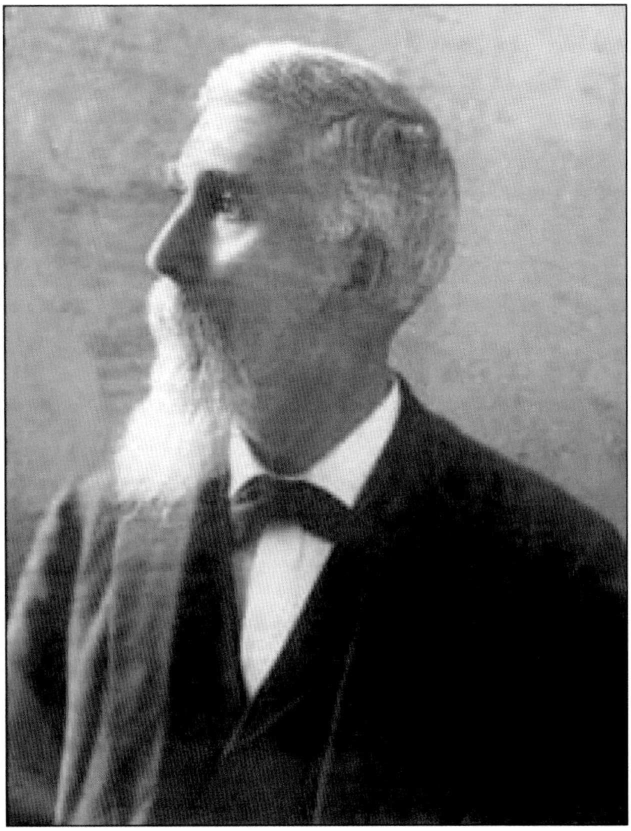

This is a portrait of R.J. Thurmond, the man known to have shot Col. W.C. Falkner on the streets of Ripley just after Colonel Falkner had won an election to the office of state representative to the legislature. R.J. Thurmond was acquitted of all charges in the shooting of his longtime friend and business partner that had gone sour in later years. R.J. Thurmond was born in 1828 and died in 1907. Sometime after 1900, he moved from Ripley to Elkin, North Carolina.

This building was the C.M. Thurmond-Harris law office at one time, and later became the dental office of Dr. Jeff D. Burns. In later years, it has become known as the site of Renfrow's Café, a popular eating establishment for breakfast and lunch.

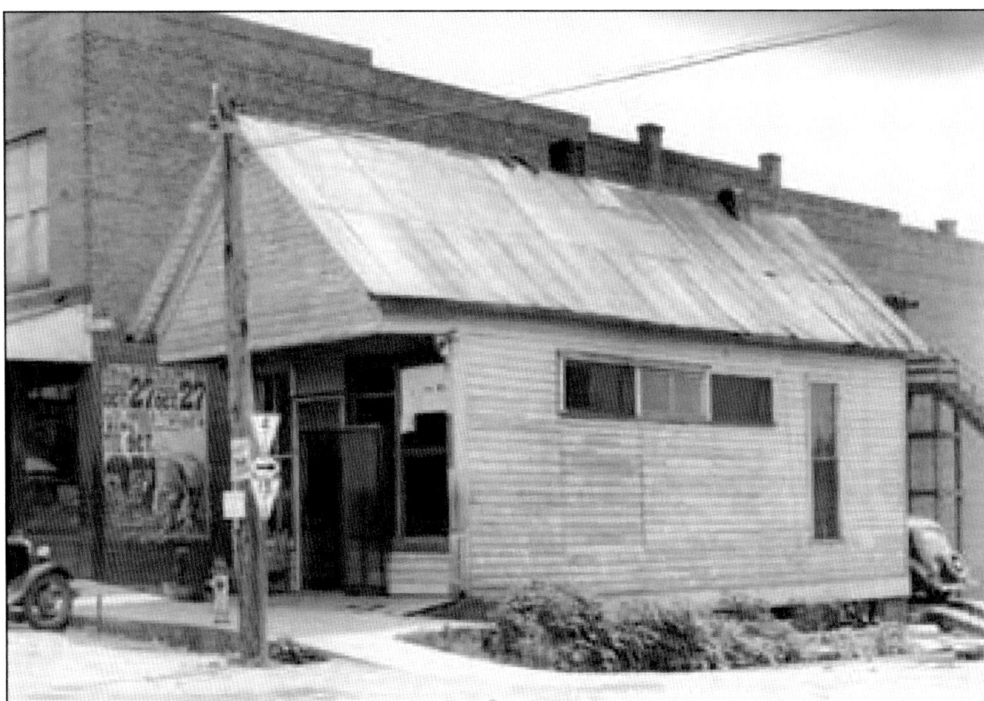

Three

First Monday Trade Days

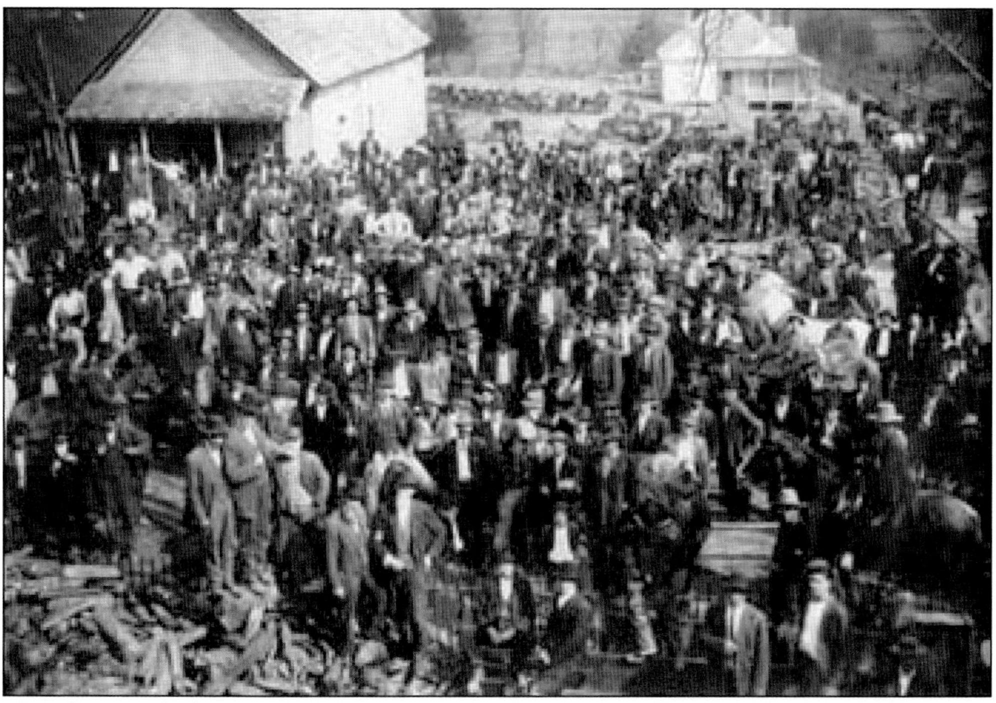

This photograph shows a scene of the Ripley square on which "First Monday" was held for years. Looking east, the white house in the background was the home of Ira Leander Clayton and Nancy McCord Clayton. The house was built around 1909 on a lot from W.W. Robinson, and later burned in 1921. The white frame building facing the east side of the square housed the *Southern Sentinel* newspaper, edited by A.C. Anderson.

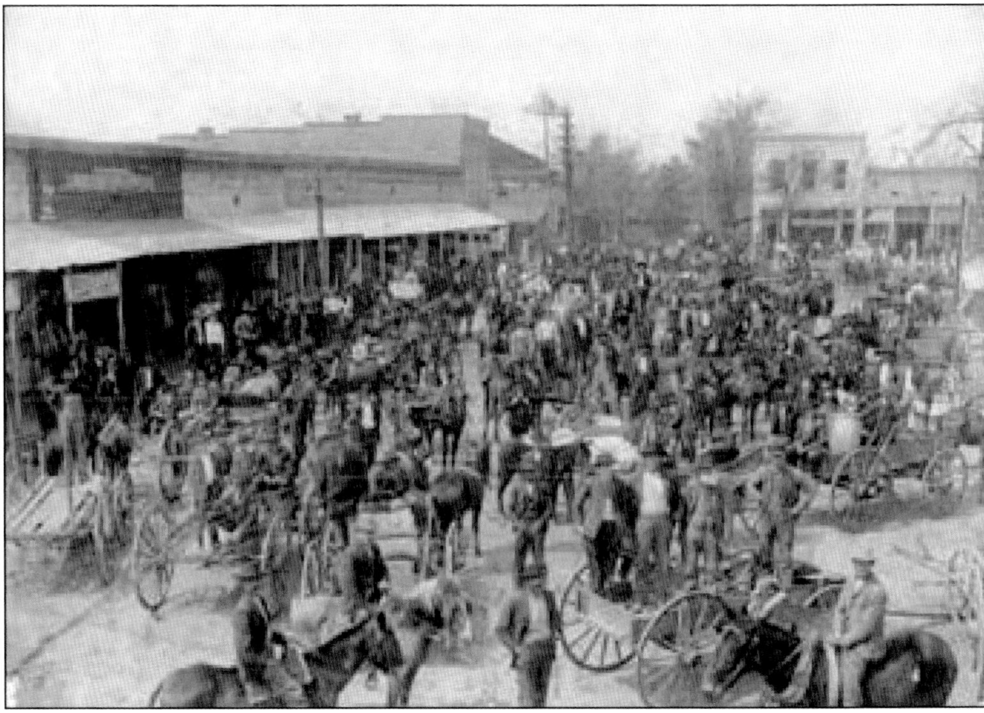

Pictured is a street scene in Ripley on April 5, 1909. It shows Jefferson Street looking west from the store of A.N. Clayton and Company.

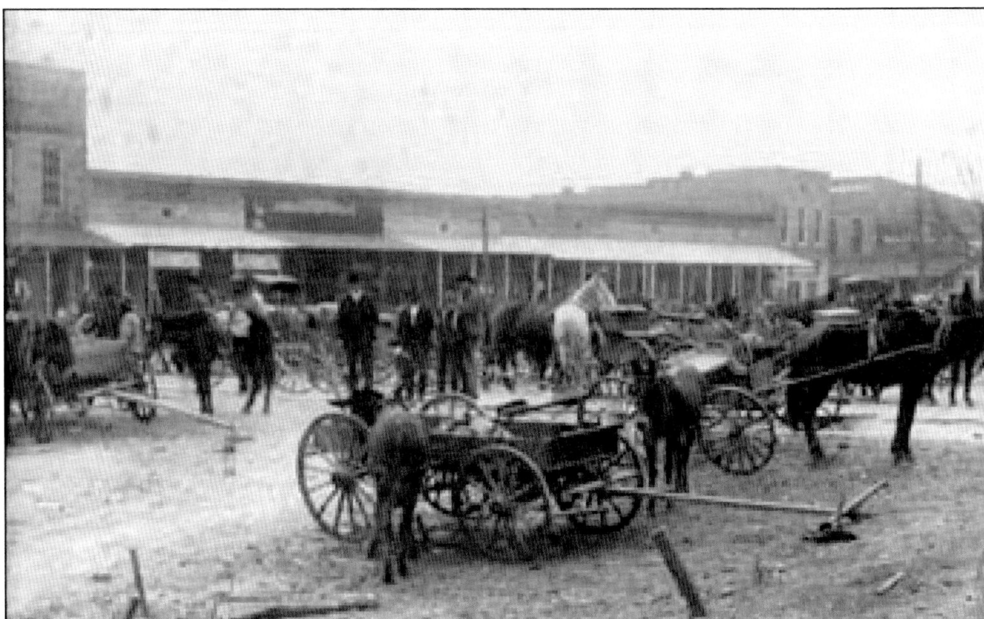

This 1906 photograph of the south side of the square shows traffic building for a large first Monday crowd. Wagons of all sizes with mules, donkeys, and horses are brought to the square and tied off to the poles driven into the ground. The businesses in the background were rebuilt in the early 1900s and still look much the same today.

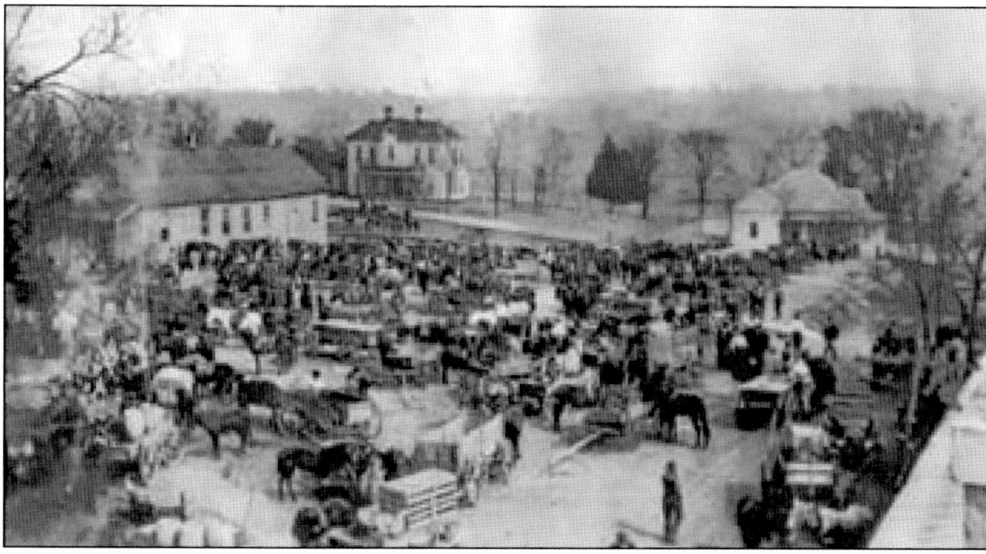

This is a view of the east side of the square in Ripley on a First Monday in 1916. The building on the left is the *Southern Sentinel,* the house left of center is the W.W. Robinson house that now serves as the Tippah County Historical Museum, and the home on the right sits where the Peoples Bank is now located.

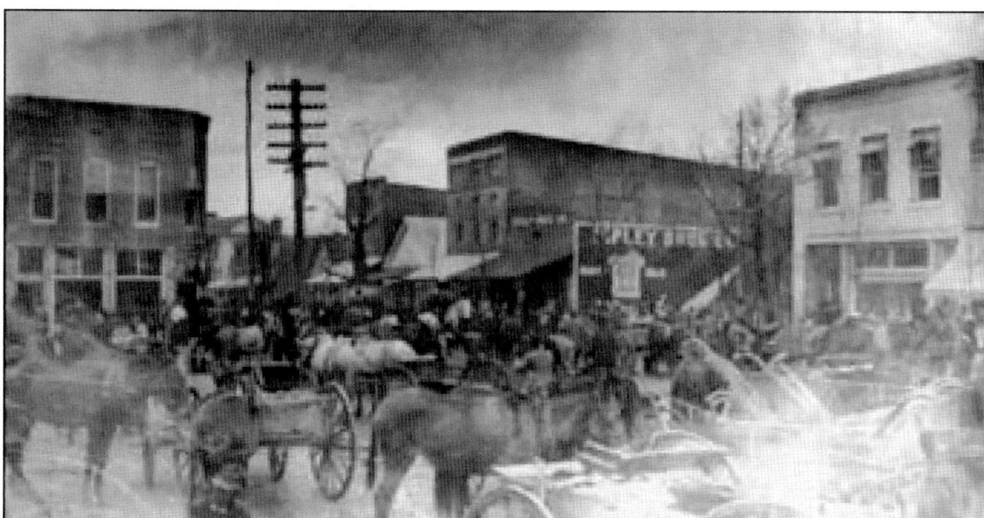

This is a typical First Monday scene on the square in Ripley, with the southwest corner of the square at the center of the picture. Notice the many wagons and mules that brought in the crowds of farmers to First Monday Trade Day in the early days.

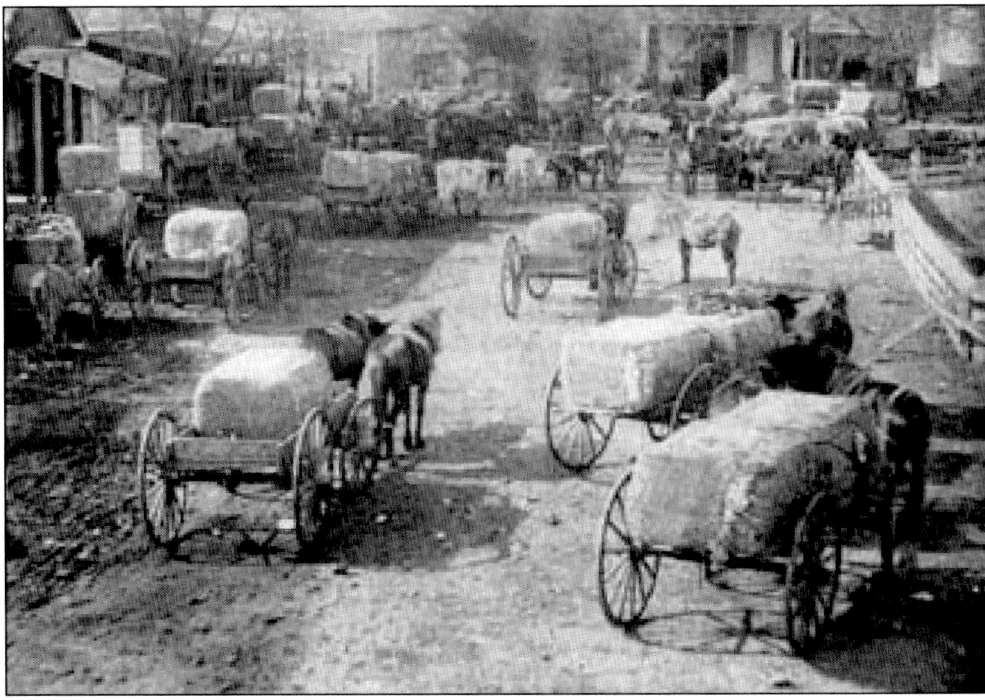

This is an 1890 photograph that shows the west side of the square looking north. Bales of cotton are loaded onto the wagons during a First Monday. The fence to the courthouse is located on the right.

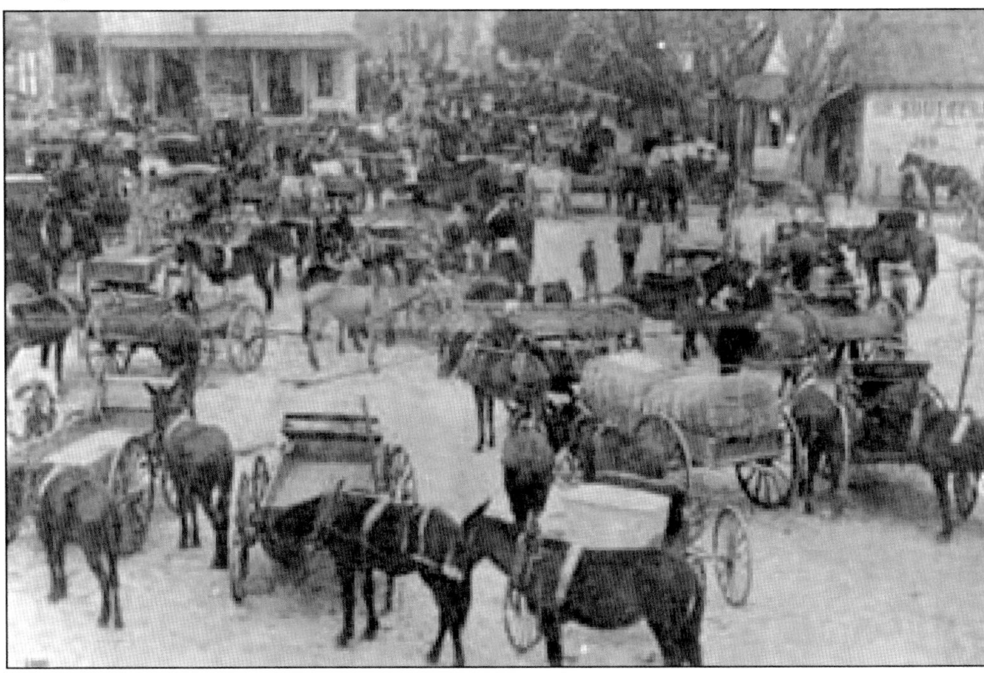

This is First Monday on March 1, 1909, on the courthouse square in Ripley. This is on the east side of the square looking north. Wagons with their mules staked out surround the square. The old Southern Sentinel office is on the right and Fingers is located at the top left of the photograph.

Four

Paul J. Rainey Estate

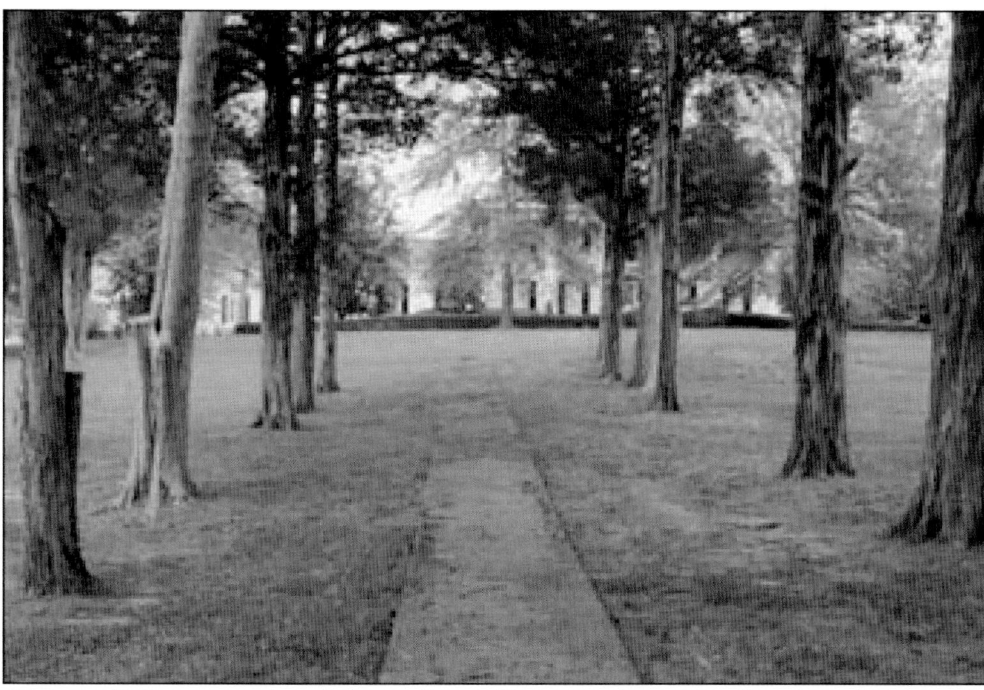

When Paul J. Rainey purchased the small Ratliff home, Highway 15 had not been built yet. The rambling Tippah Lodge that Rainey built faced east where the road south to New Albany was located at that time. There would have been a private road coming west from the house down to the railroad. In later years, another owner of the house planted cedar trees along a path down to Highway 15.

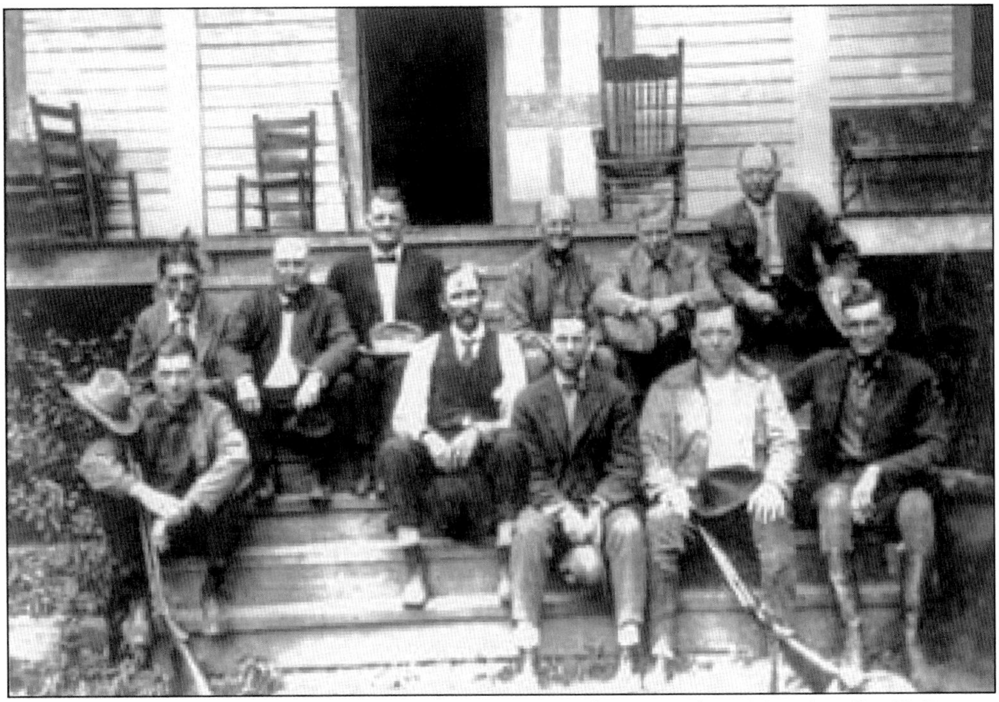

The Rainey Estate was a well-known hunting plantation that started in 1901, when Paul J. Rainey began purchasing land near Cotton Plant. Rainey (bottom right) was a wealthy sportsman. He eventually had acquired around 10,000 acres of land where he hunted birds, trained dogs, and hosted many Fourth of July picnics with up to 1,000 regional residents that came for barbecue and entertainment. This photograph shows a group of businessmen after a day of bird hunting.

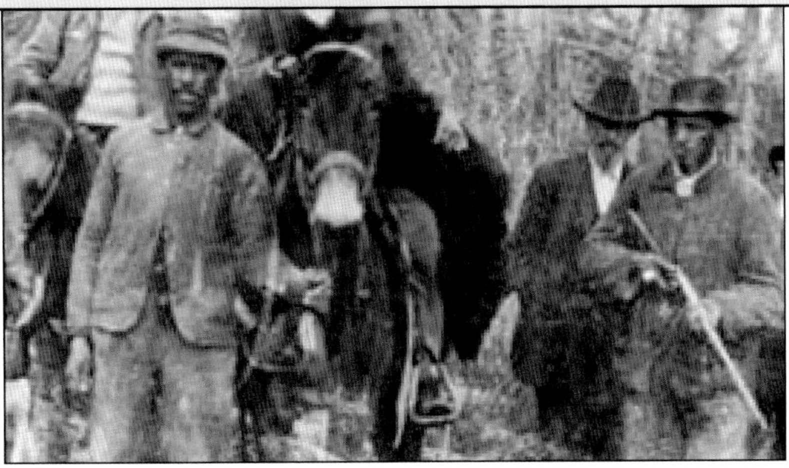

This photograph is of some of Paul J. Rainey's help, who helped him train his dogs that hunted birds, bear, and lions. Large field trials were held on the Rainey Estate where he also hosted groups from all over the country.

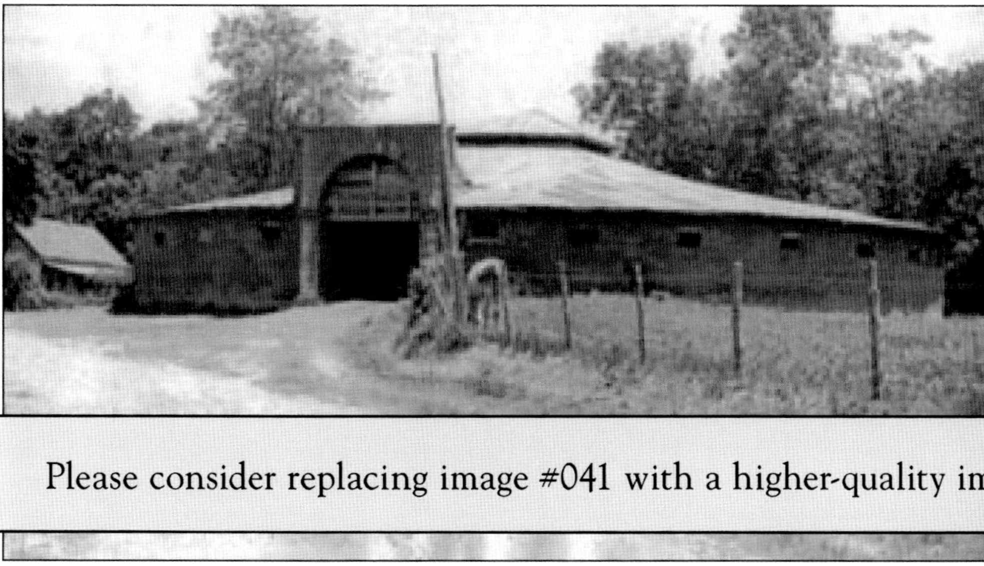

Paul J. Rainey built this round polo barn in 1906, during his early years in Tippah County to house his many horses. This barn was circular and held up to 50 horses in individual stalls. Mr. Rainey was an avid sportsman and a master polo player that brought the game to Tippah County. The barn has since been renovated to its original glory with a brick exterior and brick floors.

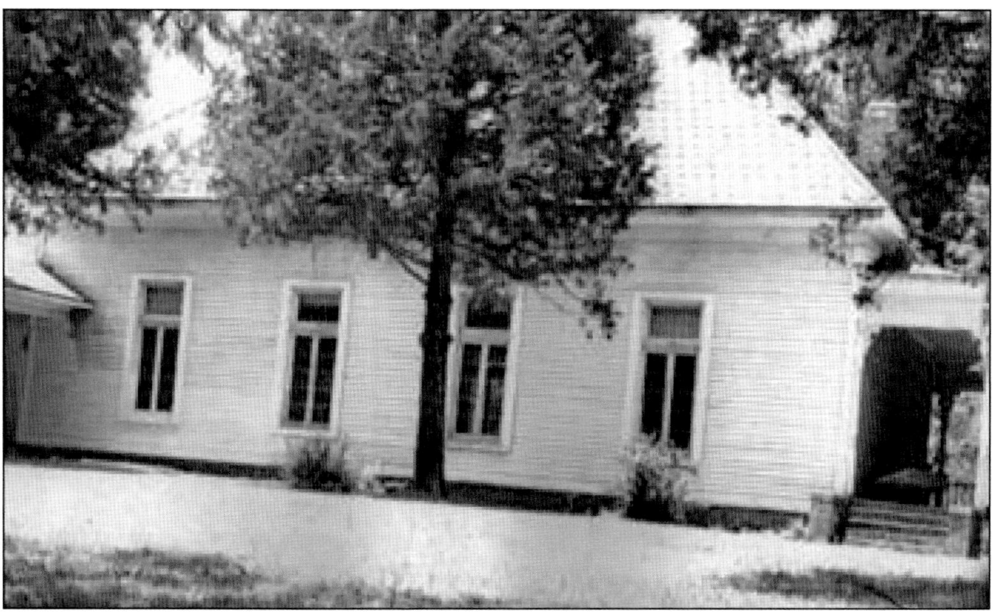

This photograph shows the trophy room of the Rainey Estate in its heyday. The trophy room contained hundreds of wild animal skins and displays that Paul J. Rainey had amassed from his years of safari hunting in Africa and the southern part of the United States.

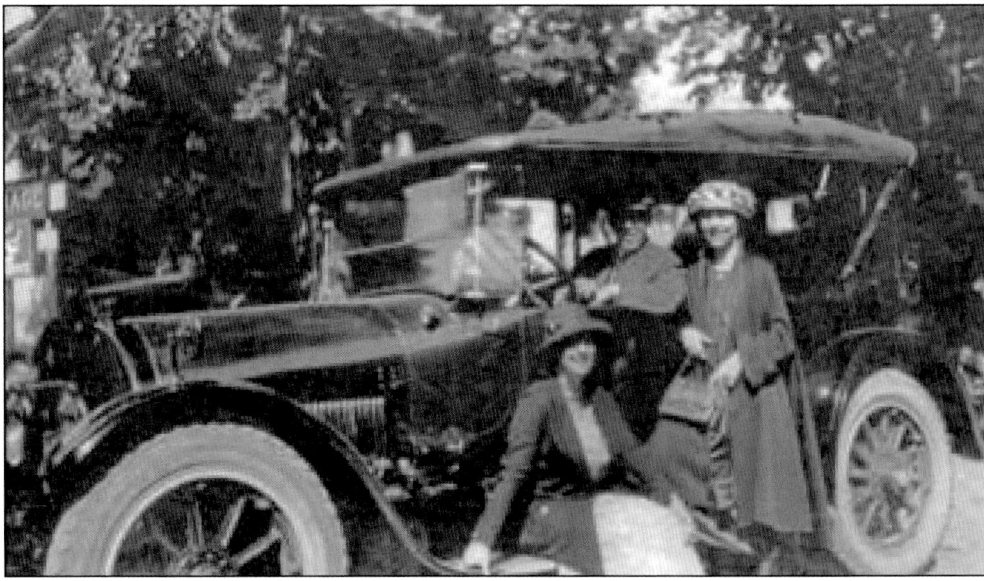

This photograph shows Paul J. Rainey sitting in the car and May Peters Graham, a longtime friend of Rainey's. The other person is thought to be Rainey's sister, Grace Rainey Rogers. Rainey was known to be very generous with his friends and loved to spend time with his lady friends. He never wanted to get married during his lifetime of 46 years.

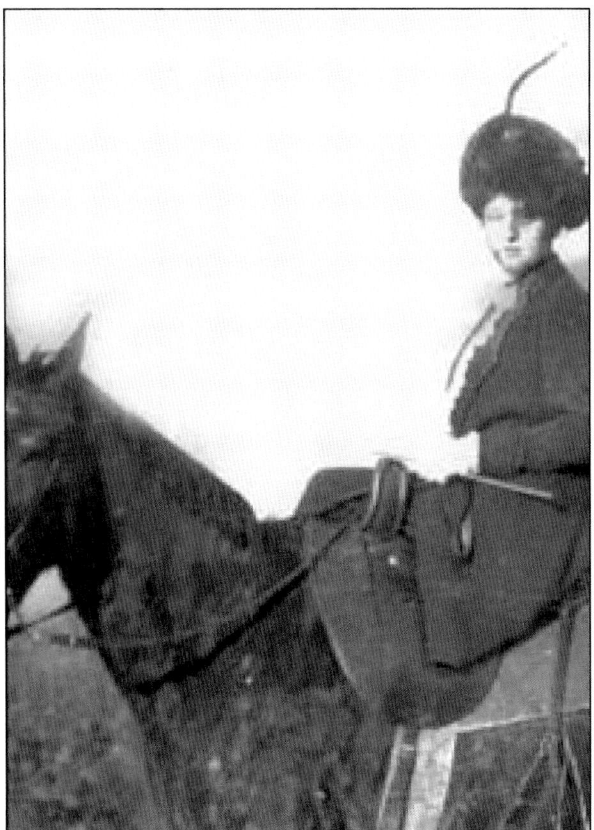

Pictured here is May Peters Graham, the longtime friend of Paul J. Rainey, riding a horse in Tippah County in the early 1900s. When Paul J. Rainey died on September 18, 1923, his fortune was given to his sister Grace Rainey Rogers, who never spent much time at the estate and held no interest in it. She sold around 471 acres to May Graham, who built a home that she dwelled in until her death in 1959.

Five

SCHOOLS

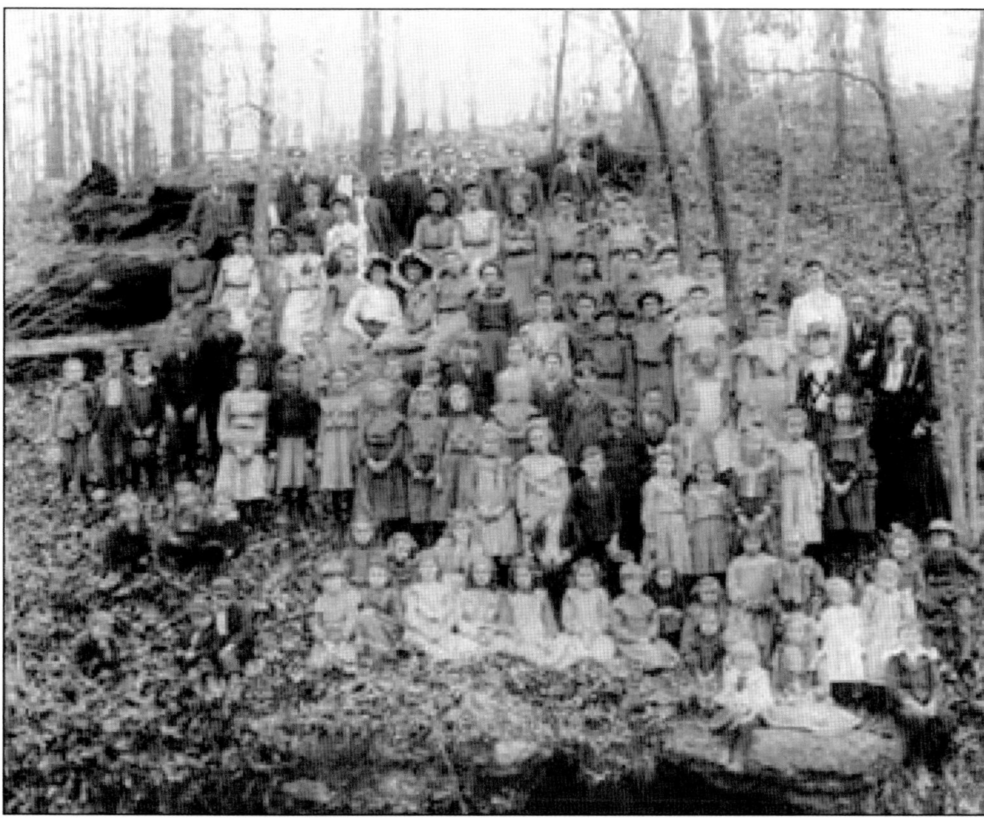

This 1900 photograph of school kids and teachers overlooking the Chalybeate Springs is a wonderful depiction of life, dress, and discipline at the turn of the 20th century. This was a great place for the kids to swim and go for a picnic.

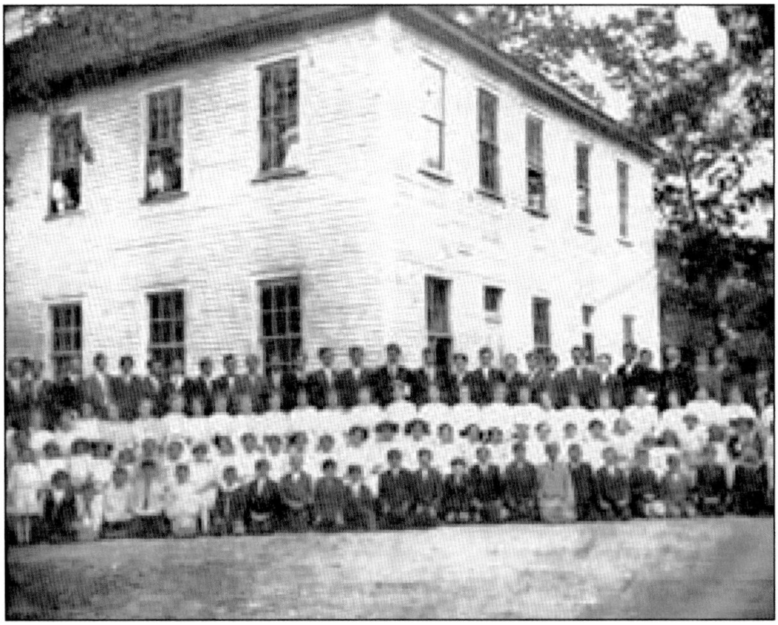

Seen here is a school picture of the student body of the Chalybeate Springs School in 1904, showing proper attire and a large class of students. This was a very large school in the late 1800s and early 1900s, with some students living as boarding students.

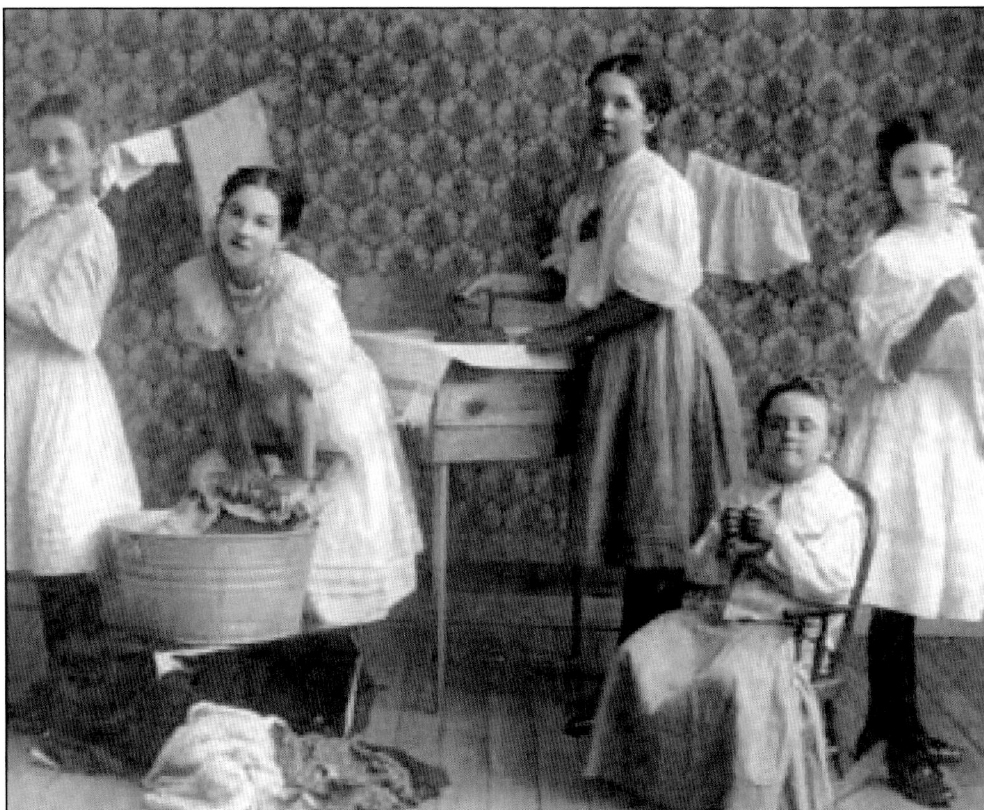

In this photograph are girls from Chalybeate Springs Institute doing laundry at the girls' dormitory. Mary Davidson is on the far left. Everyone had a job to do at the dormitory to keep things operating.

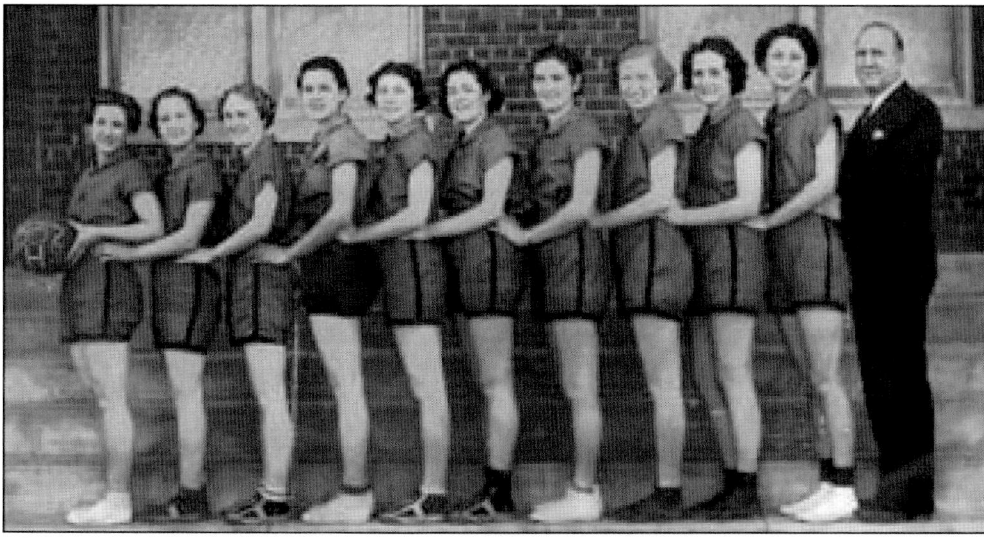

The 1937 basketball team at Chalybeate High School became the first sports team in Tippah County to capture a Mississippi state championship. Coached by B.L. Mercer, the team was led in scoring by Willard Cranford and was played with the court divided in thirds with guards on one end, centers in the middle, and forwards that shot the ball.

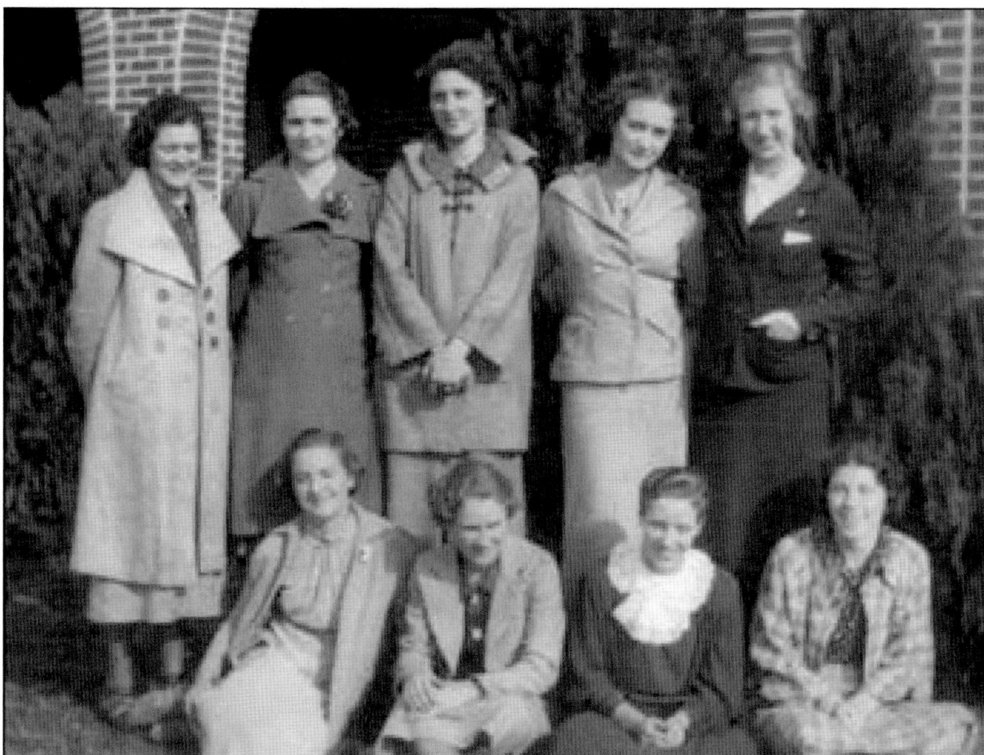

The 1937 Chalybeate girls' basketball team won the state championship. This photograph was taken of the basketball team just after winning the title game in Decatur, Mississippi. The team was honored with a dinner in Jackson, Mississippi, before returning to Chalybeate. There were four McCoy family members on the team.

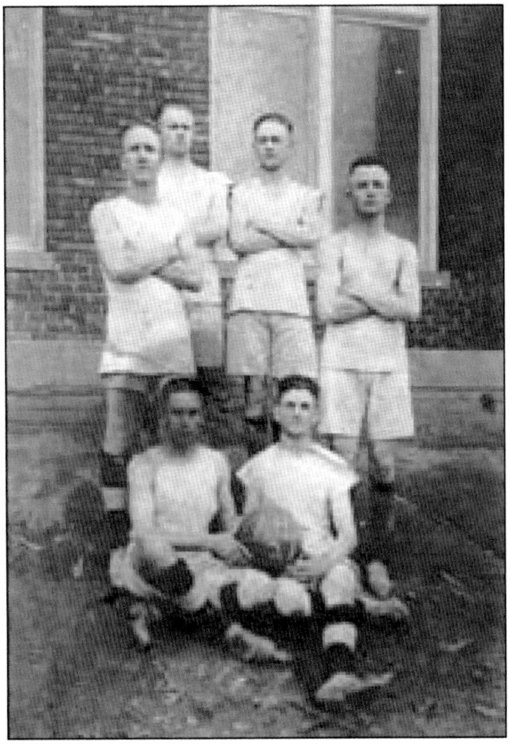

This is a photograph of the basketball team of 1921 at the Chalybeate Agricultural High School, a boarding school located in the northern part of Tippah County. The only player known in the picture is B.L. Mercer, standing on the left. He is also known as the coach of the state championship girls' basketball team in 1937. Mr. Mercer kept teaching until the late 1960s, and lived until he was more than 100 years old in Tishomingo County.

The 1923 Tippah County Agricultural High School football team located in Chalybeate is pictured here. The coach on the top left is George "Duke" Humphrey, later to become the president of Mississippi State University from 1934 to 1945, and the president of the University of Wyoming from 1945 to 1964. In 1994, he was inducted into the Wyoming Athletic Hall of Fame.

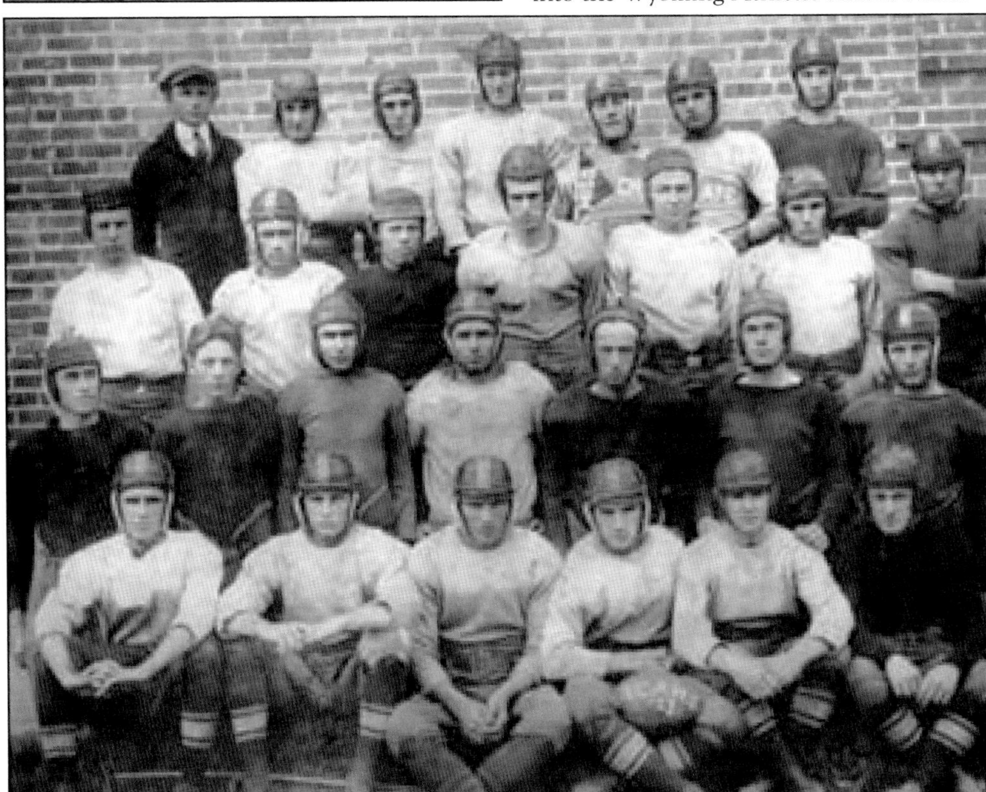

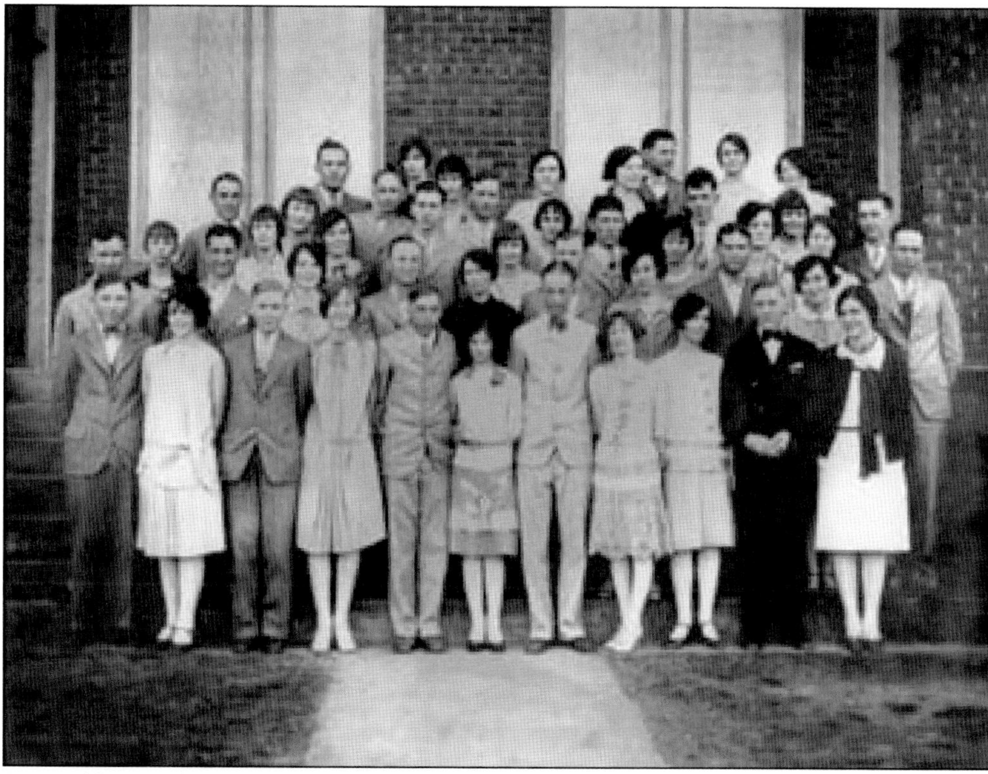

Pictured here is the Tippah County Agricultural High School on April 12, 1928. Among those pictured are Berlin Cross, Howard Luna, Oleta Rutherford, Palmer Harrison, and Oscar Shannon. Oscar Shannon is on the back row, third from the right.

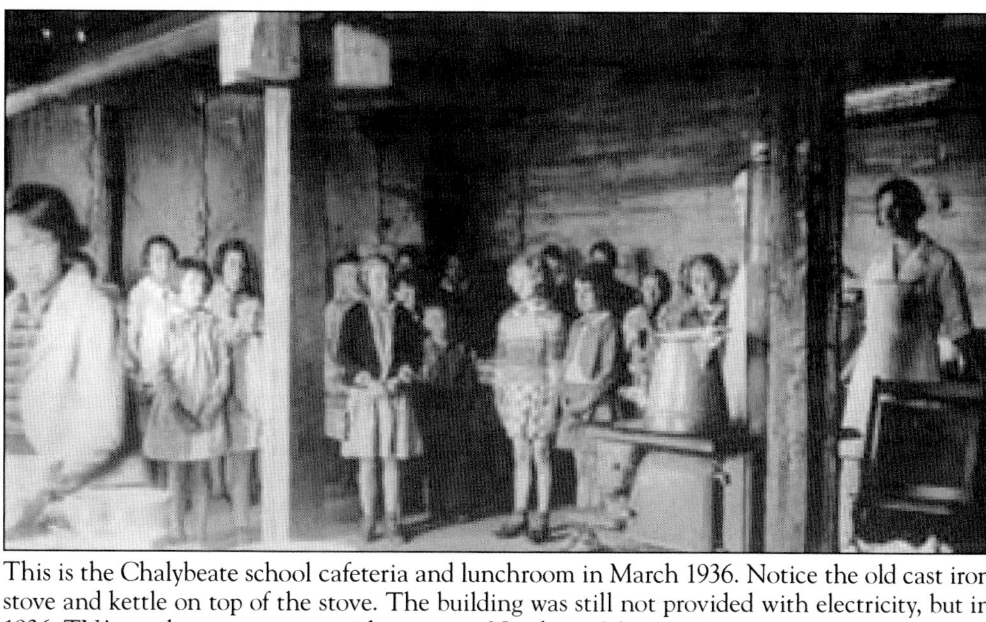

This is the Chalybeate school cafeteria and lunchroom in March 1936. Notice the old cast iron stove and kettle on top of the stove. The building was still not provided with electricity, but in 1936, TVA was beginning to provide power to Northeast Mississippi.

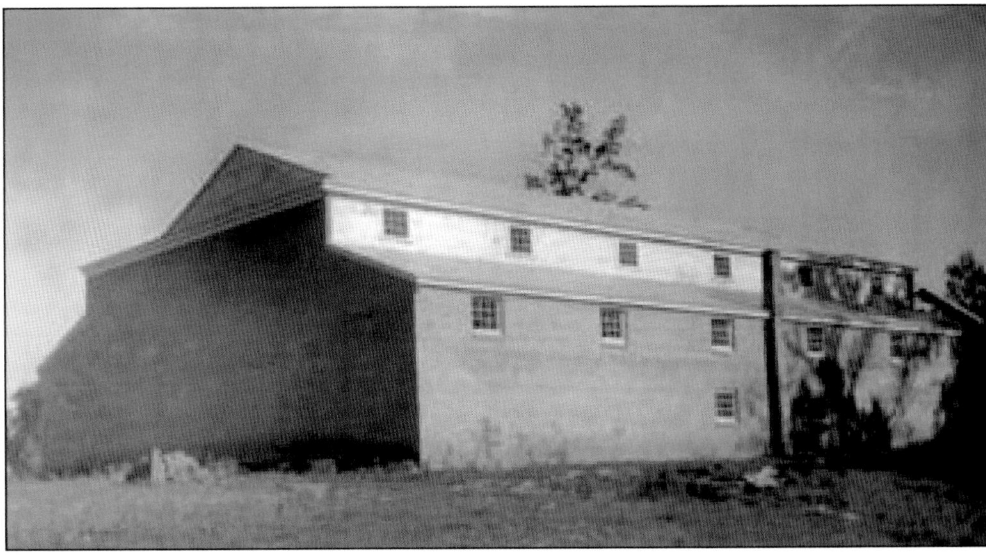

In the 1930s, the Chalybeate School building was constructed and is still being used as a kindergarten through eighth grade level school, with an auditorium and administrative offices. This school is a progressive quality school with great fundraising abilities.

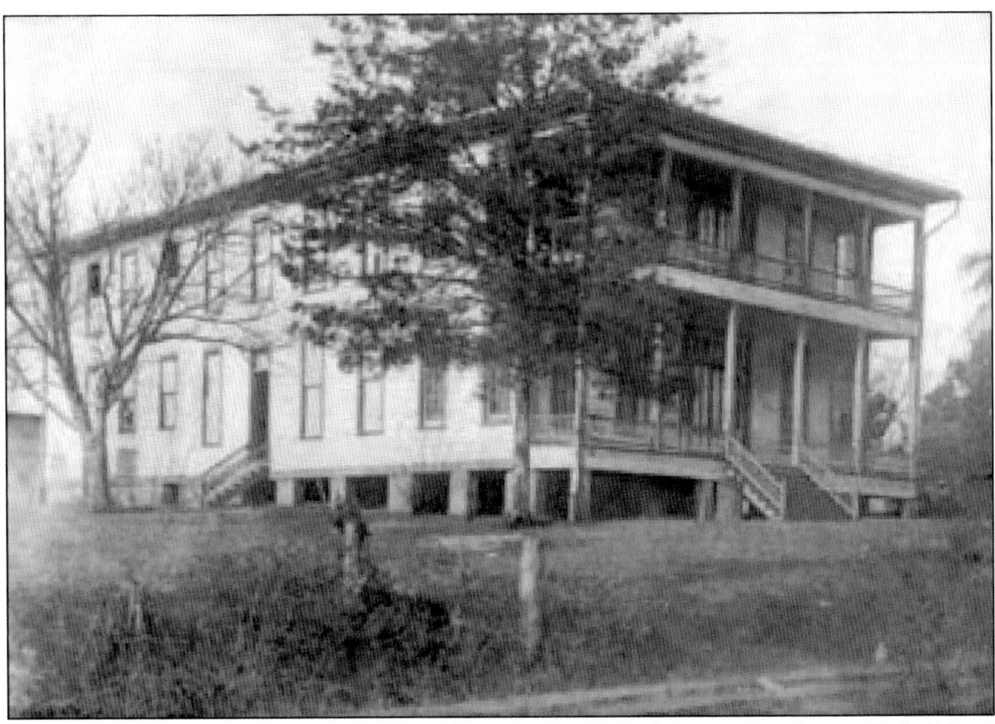

Known as the Ripley Male and Female College, this building also served as Ripley High School from 1883 to 1914. This photograph was taken in 1908, as the building was located in downtown Ripley, just one block from the courthouse square.

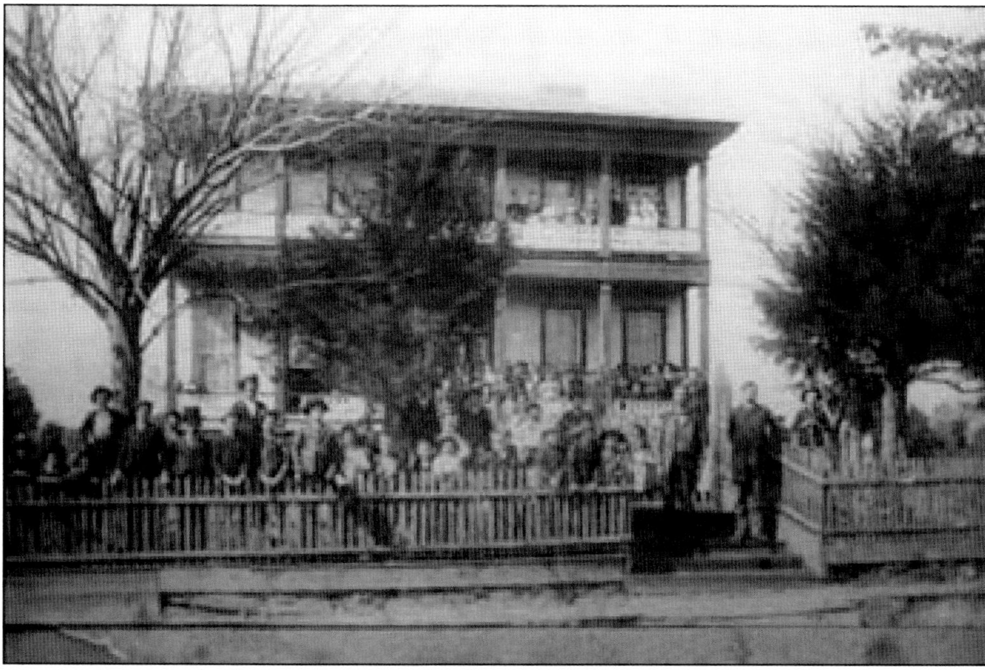

This building was built in 1883 to replace the second Stonewall College building, which had been destroyed by fire. In 1886, it became Ripley Male and Female College (Academy). It then became the school for the Ripley Separate School District 1905. This building served the town until the new building was built on South Main Street in 1914.

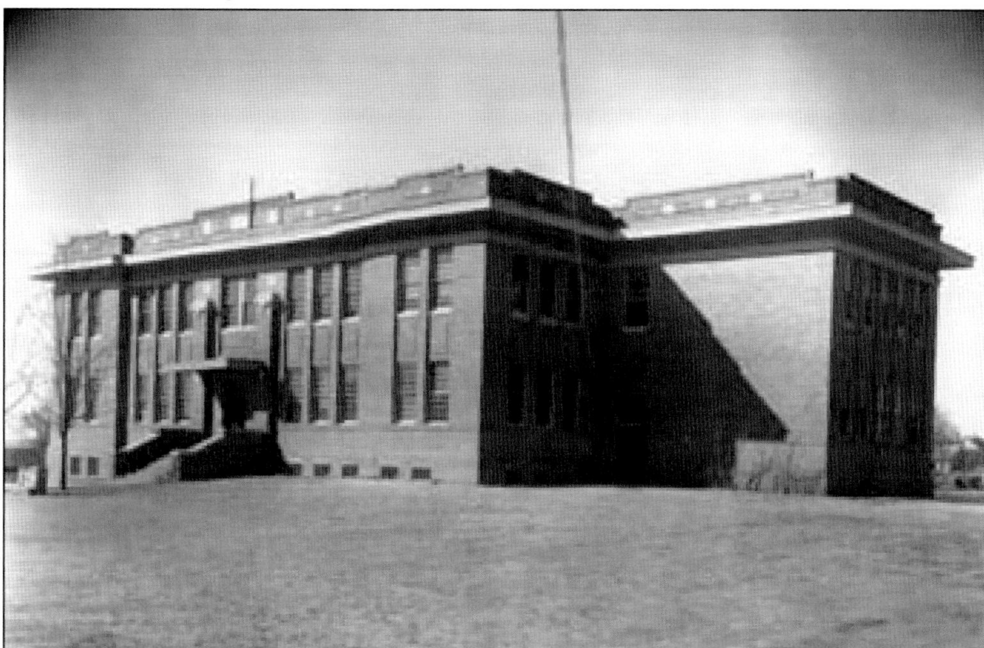

This 1950s photograph shows Ripley High School with many of its students. The building was facing east and this is the southern end of the building. The gym was located just to the south of this picture.

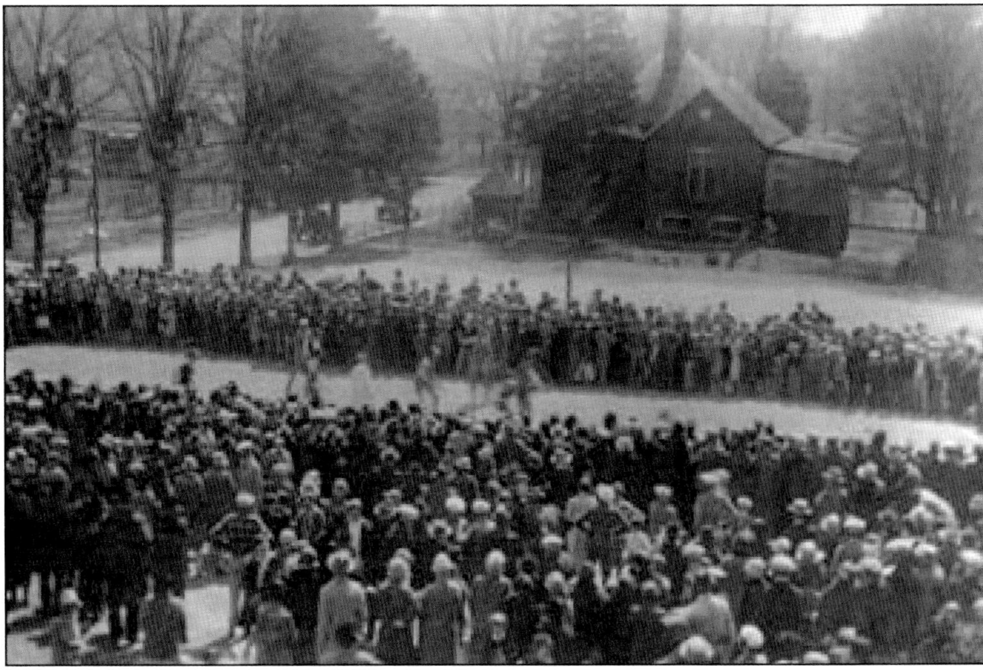

The 1925 Tippah County basketball tournament was held at Ripley High School on an outdoor court. The house at the top was built in 1885 and now belongs to Duane and Sherri Bullard. Notice the fans that congregated in the trees on the left and the very large crowd of people. Ripley was playing Buena Vista in the finals and it is believed that Faye Reid's father was the official in the ballgame wearing white.

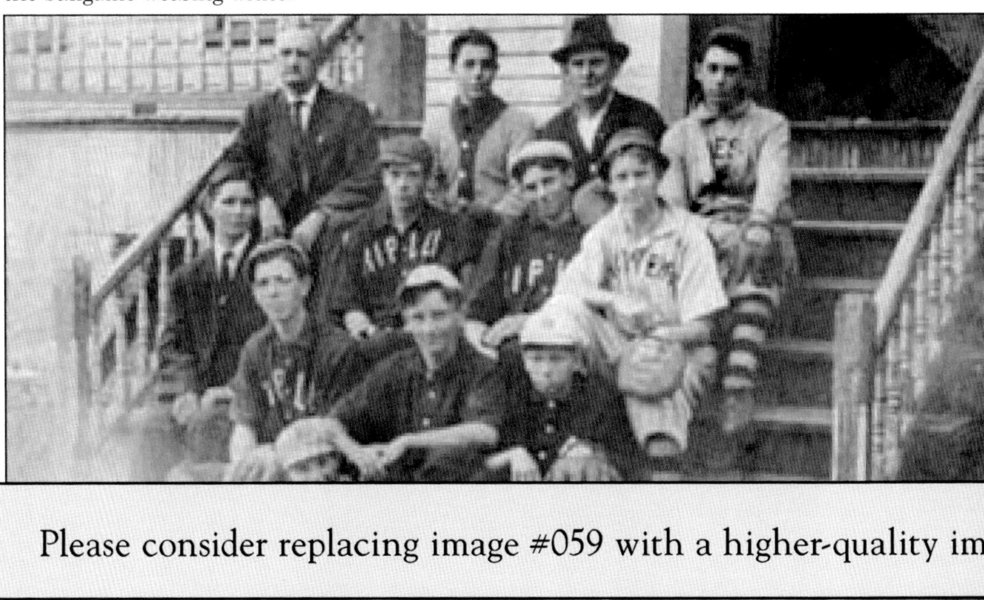

Pictured is the Ripley baseball team in the early 1900s. Pictured are, from left to right, (first row) Wayne Finger (mascot); (second row) unidentified, Doug Parks, Mack Nelms, and Bill Finger; (third row) Cayce Duncan, Lee Wallace, and Joe Burns; (fourth row) Professor Lynch, John Fant, Shelby Barnett, and Cliff Giles.

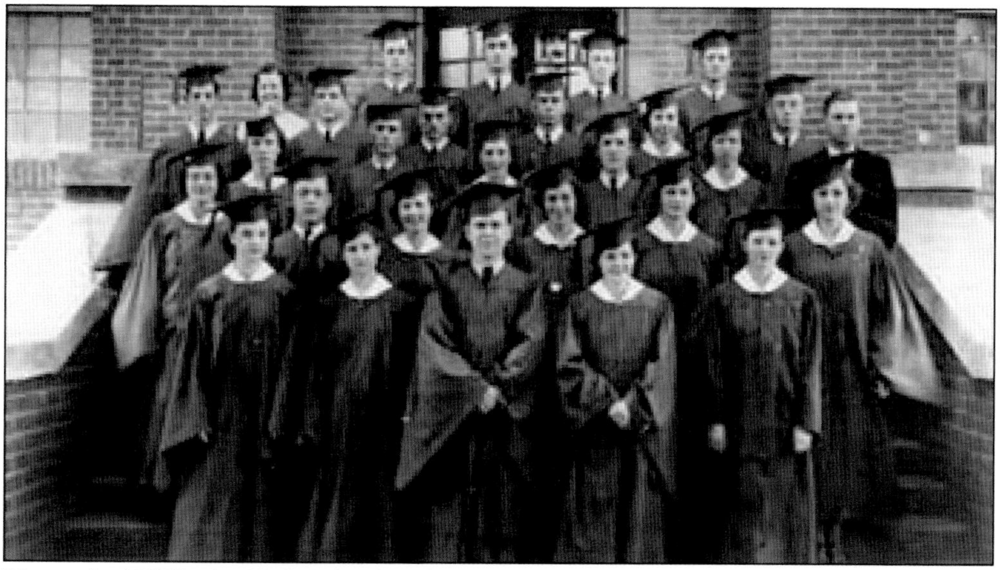

This is the 1937 Ripley High School graduating class. Pictured are, from left to right, (first row) Josephine Dickerson, Addie Mae Jamieson, Bill Gurney, Elizabeth Cox, and Mildred White; (second row) Verda Reed, Mansel Jamieson, Onie Frances Smith, Jamie Finger, Lillian Pickens, and Martha Alvis; (third row) Evangeline Dickerson, Wade Carter, Winifred Finger, James Wingo, Mattie Lee Elrod, and Supt. Travis McCharen; (fourth row) Portis Gandy, Emma Bostwick (sponsor), Edward Nabors, Elmer Yancey, Herman Reed, Virginia Linebarger, and Charles Murry; (fifth row) James K. Weatherly, Olin Mauldin, Collins Mitchell, and Clarence McCollum.

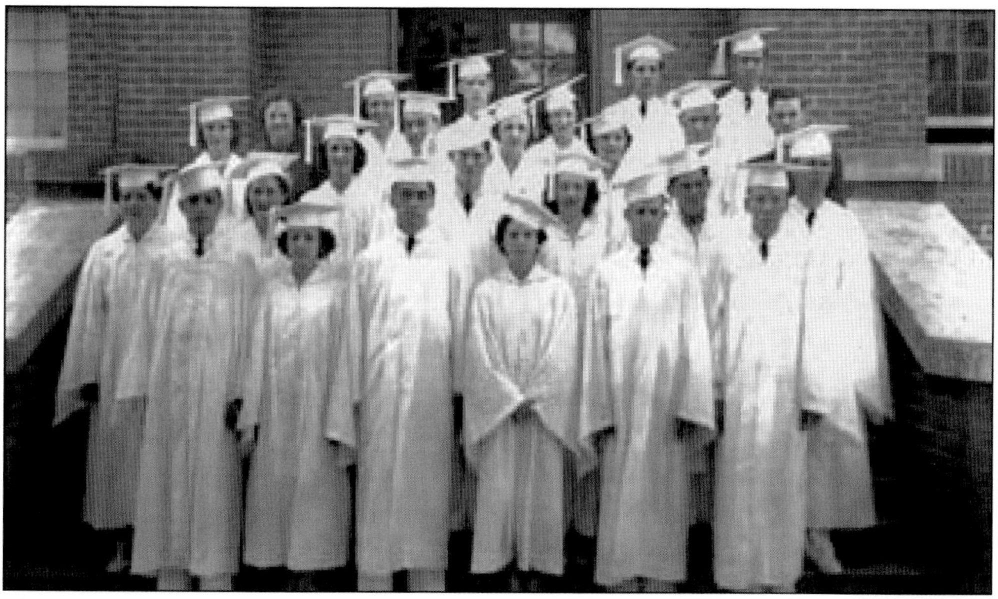

The 1938 Ripley High School graduating class is pictured here. Members of the class are Buck Mohundro, Ruth Barkley, Sperry Bartlett, Jane Gurney, Eugene Webb, Alton Meadows, Marietta Moffitt, Louise Hill, Ernestine Haney, Billy Smith, Bobbie Craig, Cliff Giles Jr., James Kelly, Sara Dees Peeler, Emma Bostwick, Shan Clayton, Ruth Rogers, Naomi Wicker, Mavis Thompson, Wesley McGar, Travis McCharen (principal), Allie Golden Conner, Hugh Moore Merritt, Bertie Childers, and W. M. Dickerson.

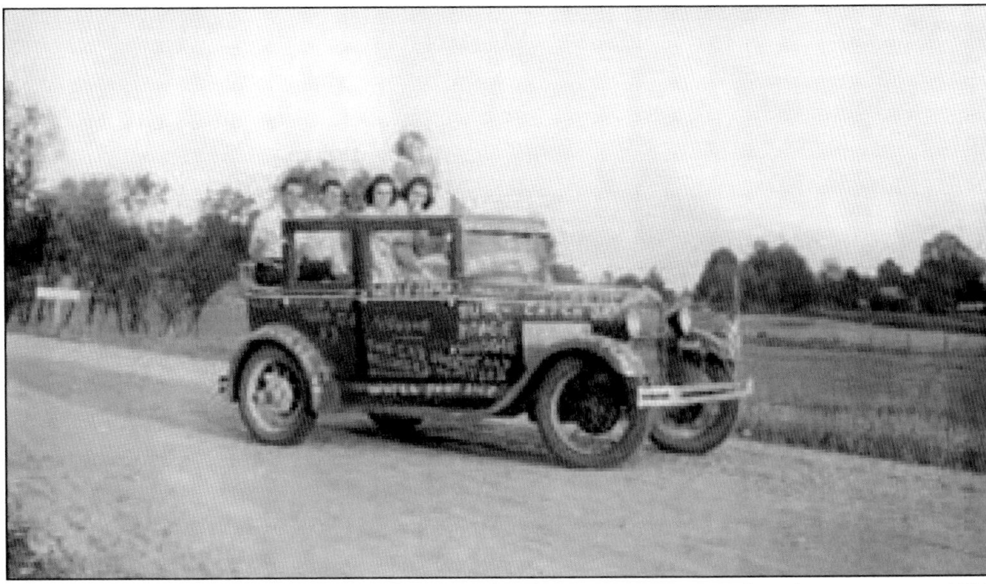

This is a late 1930s or early 1940s photograph of a teenage group of students in a pre-1920 automobile that was decorated with graffiti. It was patriotic enough to have a couple of flags adorning the vehicle.

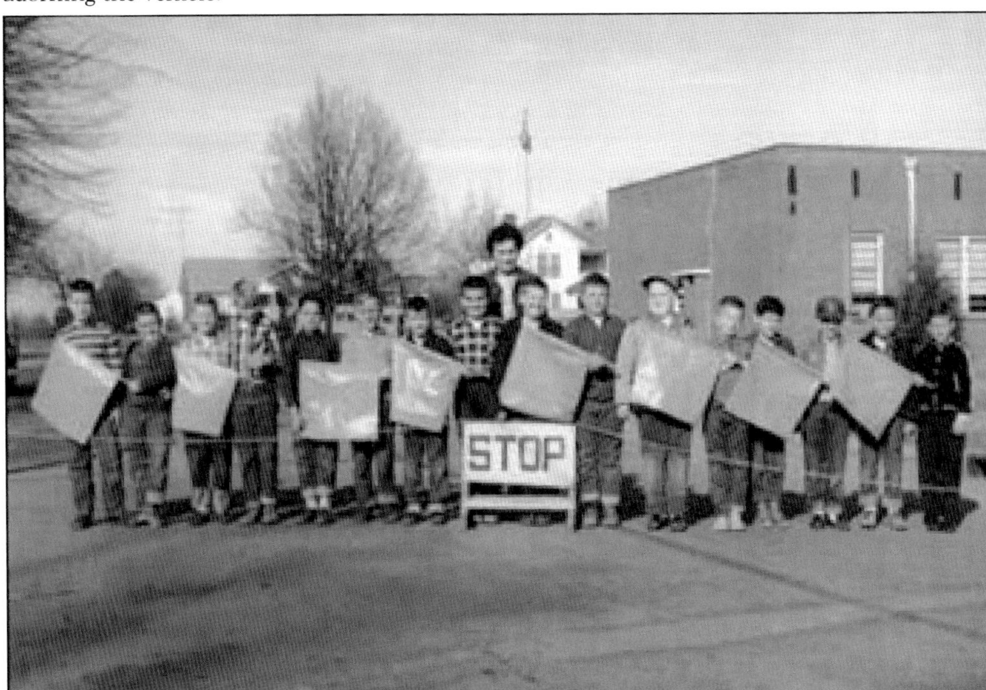

This early 1960s photograph shows flag patrol boys at the Ripley Elementary School. These youth helped get the school students off their buses and helped the kids cross the street safely. Those pictured are, from left to right, Jerry Wallace, Kyle Smith, Eddie Watson, Darrell Hurt, David Carter, Joe Estes, Doyle Caviness, Terry (Butch) Carter, Philip Nance, David Griffin, Dick Ballard, Maylon Sanford, Marshall Allen, Donnie Cousar, Steve Stubbs, and Greg Barkley. Eunice Nabors, also pictured, was the principal at the time.

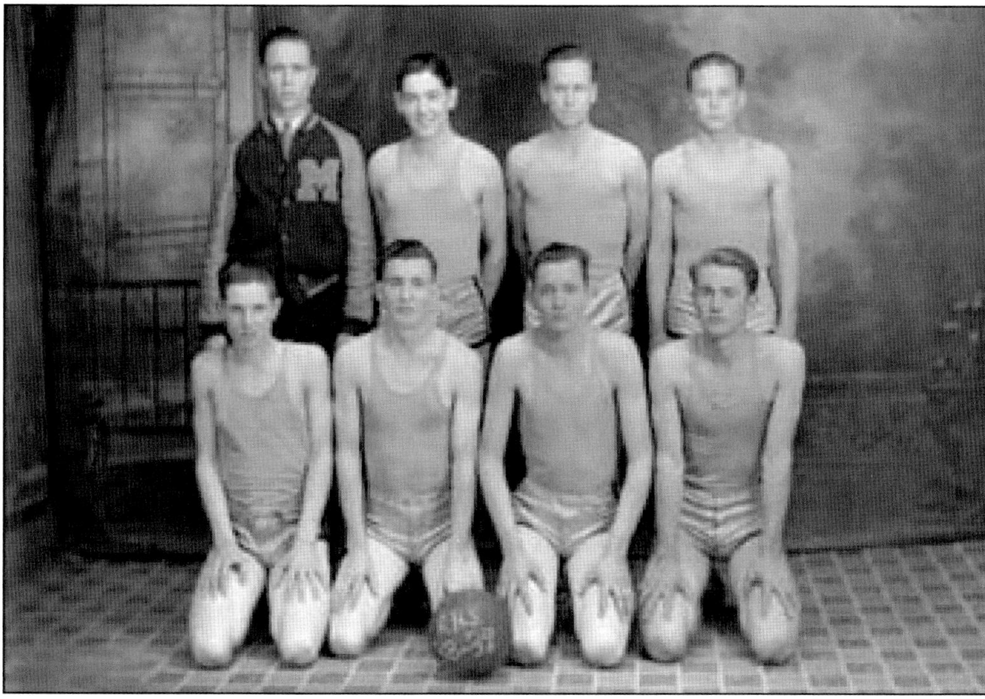

This photograph is of the 1938 to 1939 Ripley High School men's basketball team that includes "Nath" Pannell, Dave Bennett, and Faye Reid.

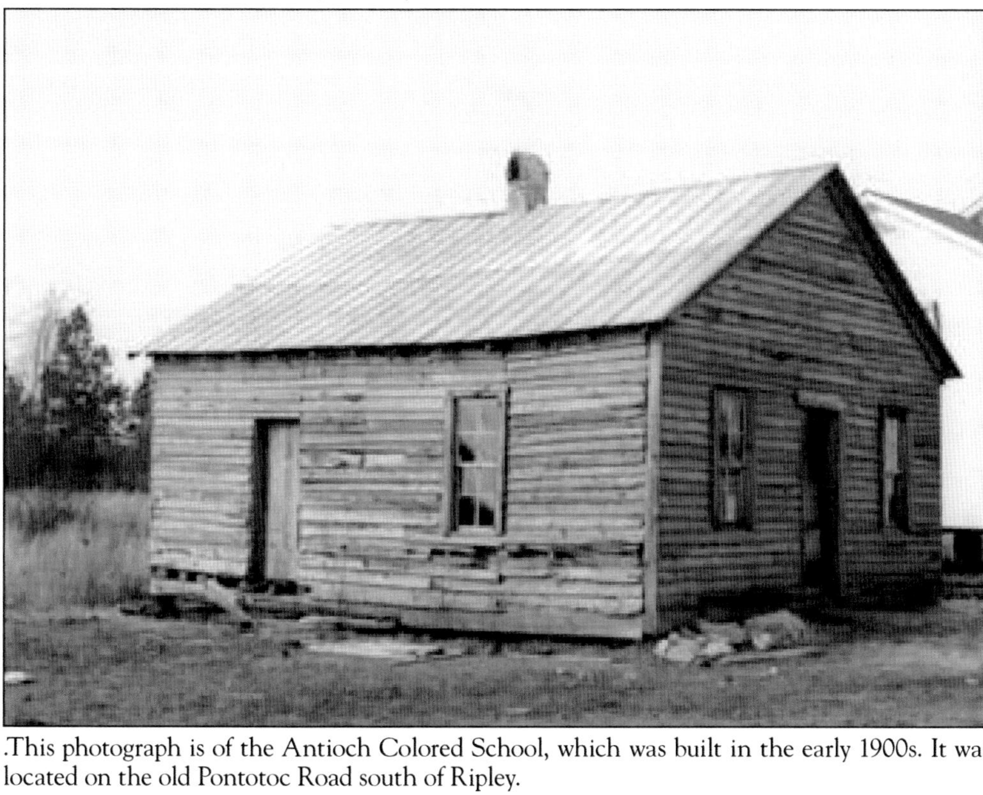

.This photograph is of the Antioch Colored School, which was built in the early 1900s. It was located on the old Pontotoc Road south of Ripley.

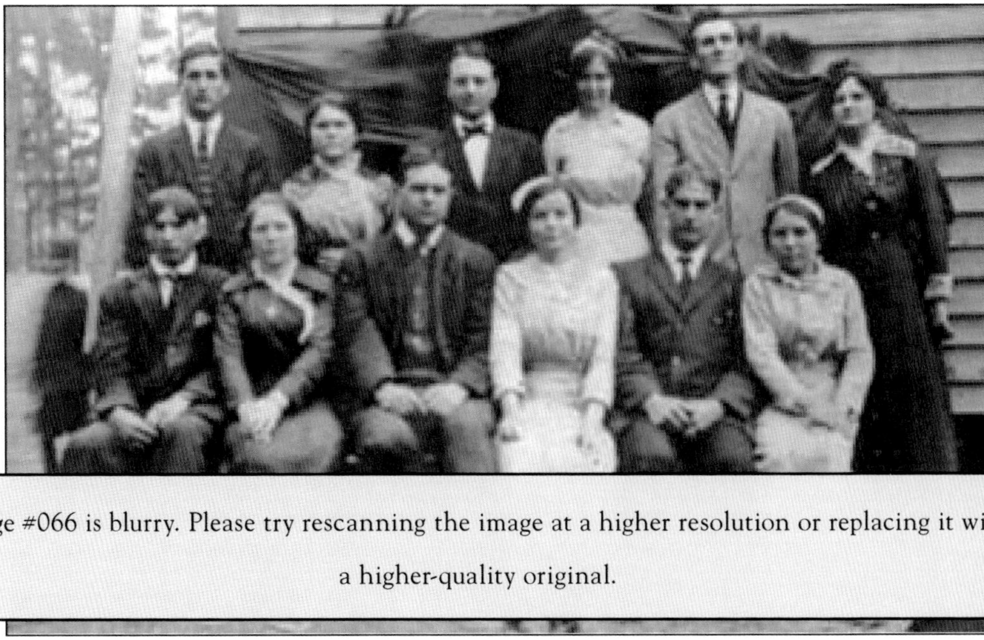

The Spout Springs School, located just off Highway 2 East, was started at the turn of the century and the building is still standing and used by Spout Springs TCDC. Those pictured are, left to right, (first row) Lee Robbins, unidentified, John Richardson, Johnny Childs, Howard Taylor, and Sue Bell Mauney Robbins; (second row) Sam Mauney, unidentified, Ollie Richardson, unidentified, Sasson Tiegher (teacher), and another teacher who is unidentified.

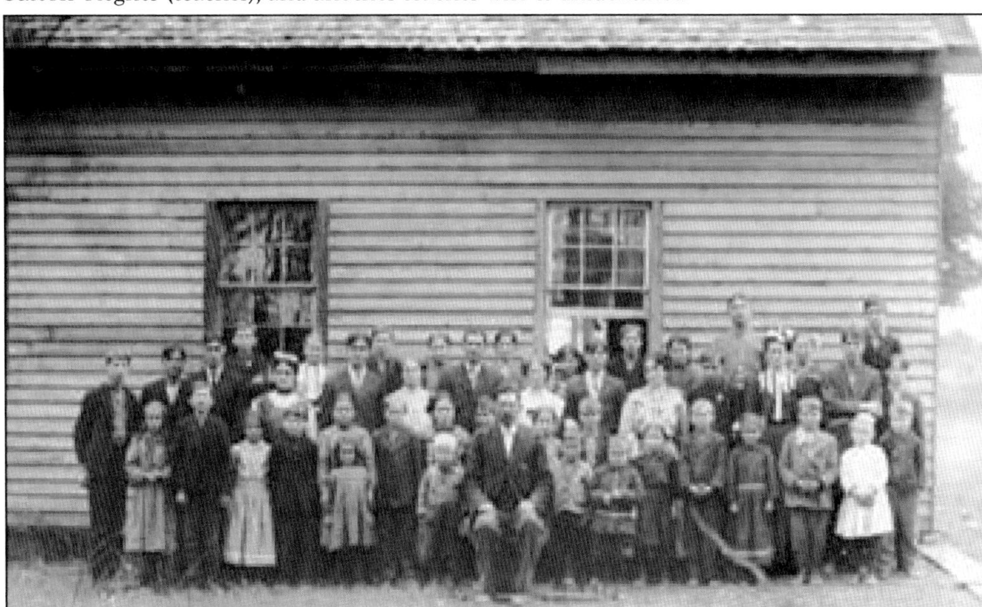

This early 1900 photograph of the Spout Springs School showed many more male students than most schools of that time frame and an unusually large percentage of older boys. The teacher, Joe Stevens, is seen out front and among those pictured are Onie Taylor Rogers, Byrd Taylor, and Minnie Taylor Phillips.

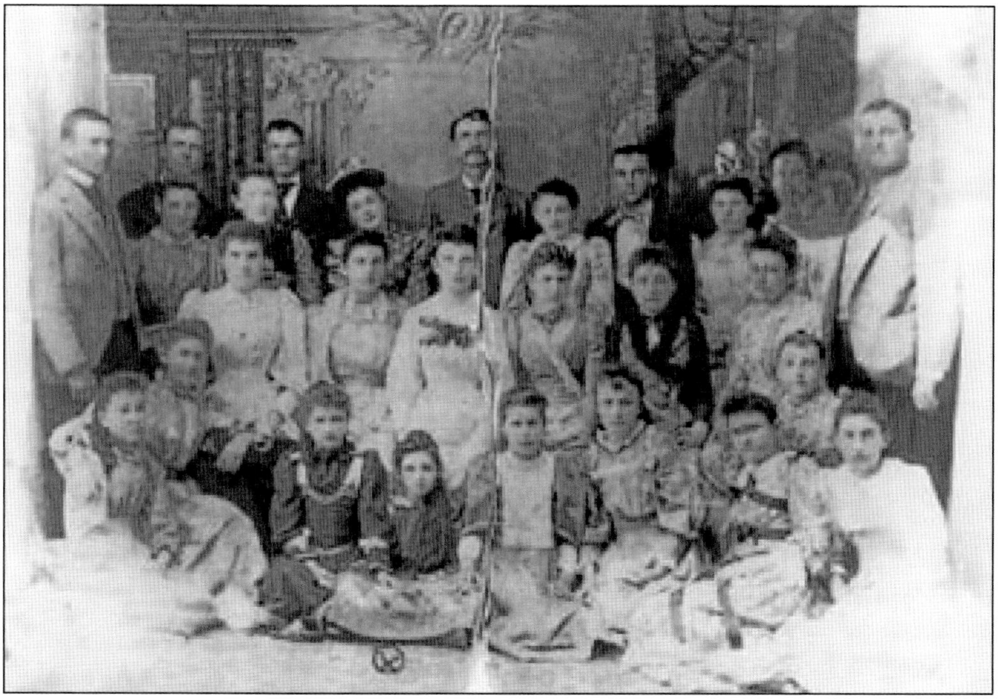

This is the Ripley Academy where the old high school was located on South Main Street. The academy had two German teachers; one of them is pictured on the back row in center with a mustache. The smallest girl on front row is Nancy McCord who married Ira L. Clayton, parents of Hugh N. Clayton. Nancy was born in 1882. This photograph was taken in the early 1890s.

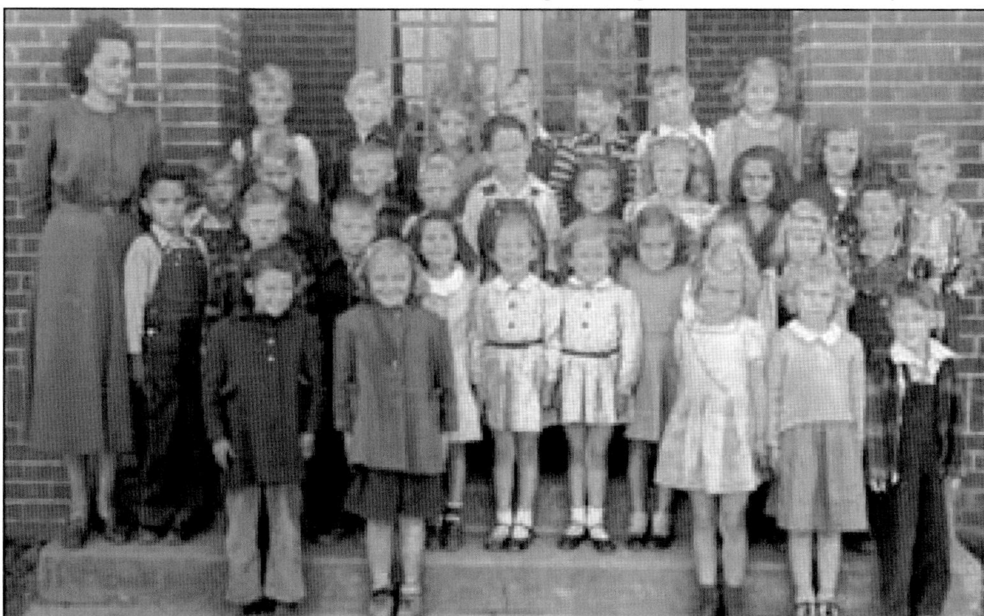

A Falkner Elementary School photograph from the 1930s shows the sons and daughters of families that made their living from the land by raising cattle and farming. The twins in the front center of the picture were especially happy this day.

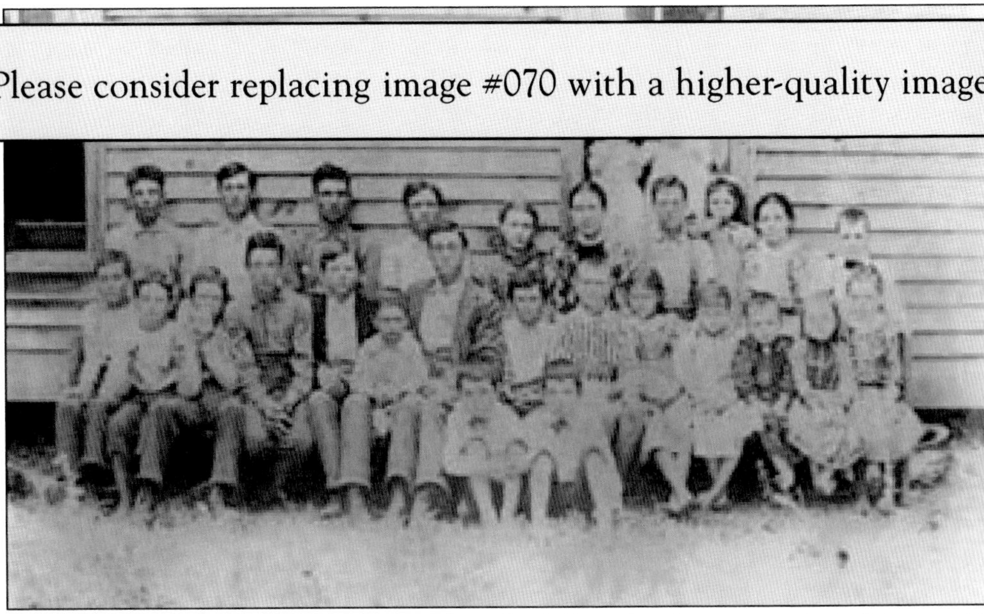

New Hope School was known as a one-teacher school. Seated in the center is Ira L. Clayton with a youngster leaning on his knee. Some of Ira Clayton's younger brothers and his sister were his pupils. He married Nancy McCord and they were the parents of Hugh N. Clayton, a noted person in Tippah and Union counties in future years. This picture was made in the late 1890s.

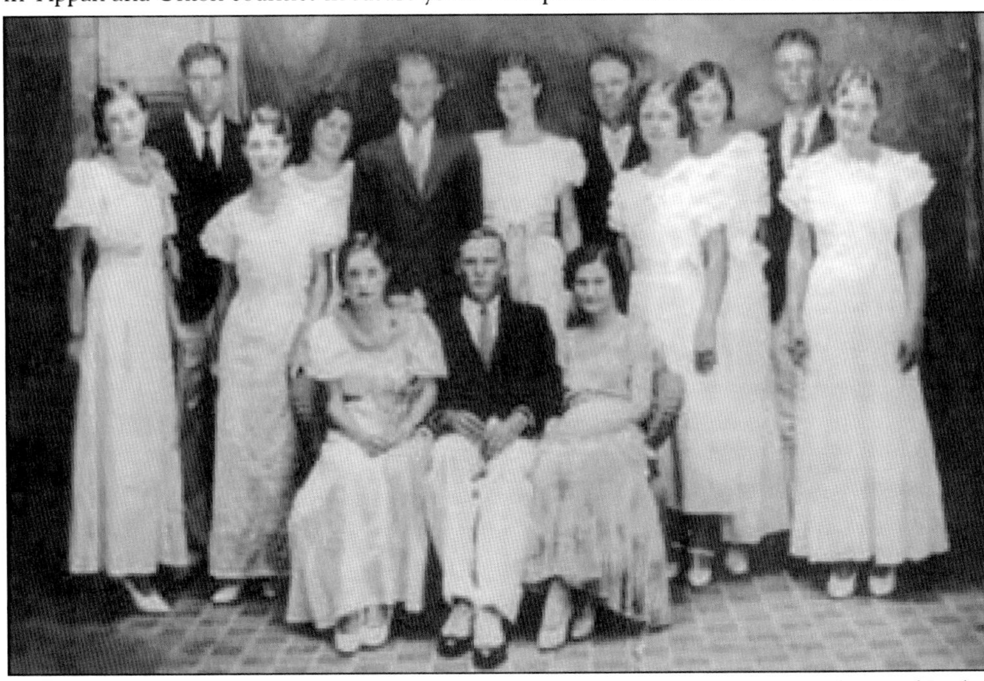

The graduating class of 1933 at the Peoples School is seen here, located just northeast of Ripley. Pictured are, from left to right, (seated) Sherman Mauney, P.A. Moffitt, and Velma Godwin (teacher and class sponsor); (standing) Ruby Mauney, Vance Braddock, Mildred Medford, Eunolia Paseur, John Allen Harrell, Ella Van Echols, Jeff Hurt, Mary Vie Boyette, Pauline Wilbanks, Vardaman Mauney, and Lee Opal Carmichael.

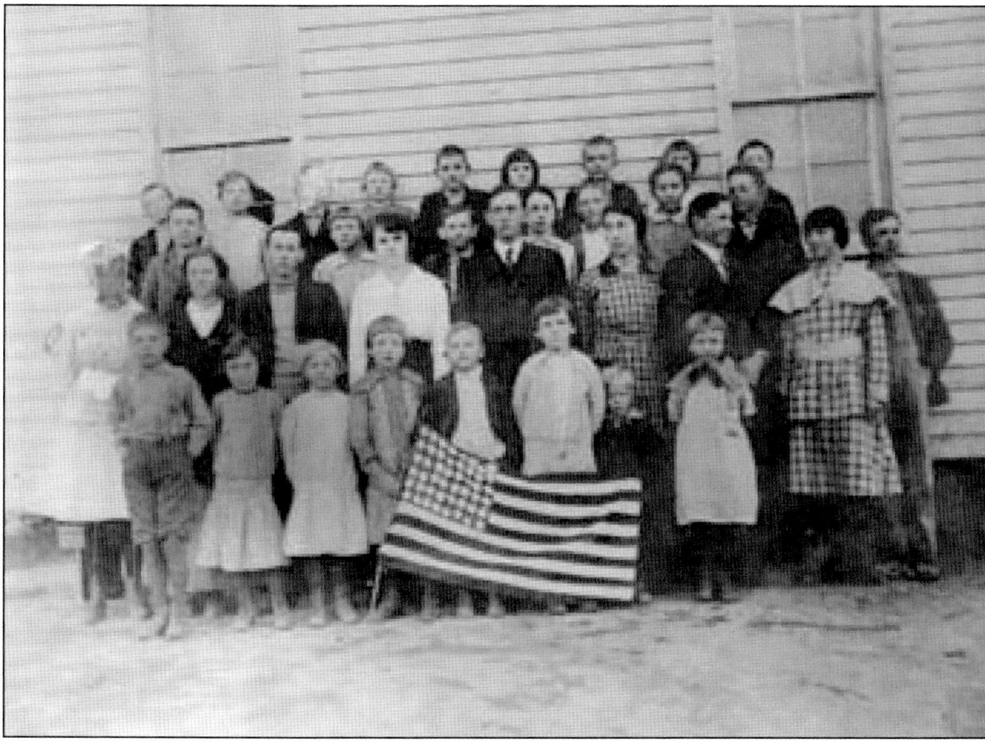

This photograph is of the Ball Hill School during the 1920s. The school was small and getting to and from school was difficult. The flag shows 48 stars, which we know it was after 1912 when Arizona was added as the 48th State.

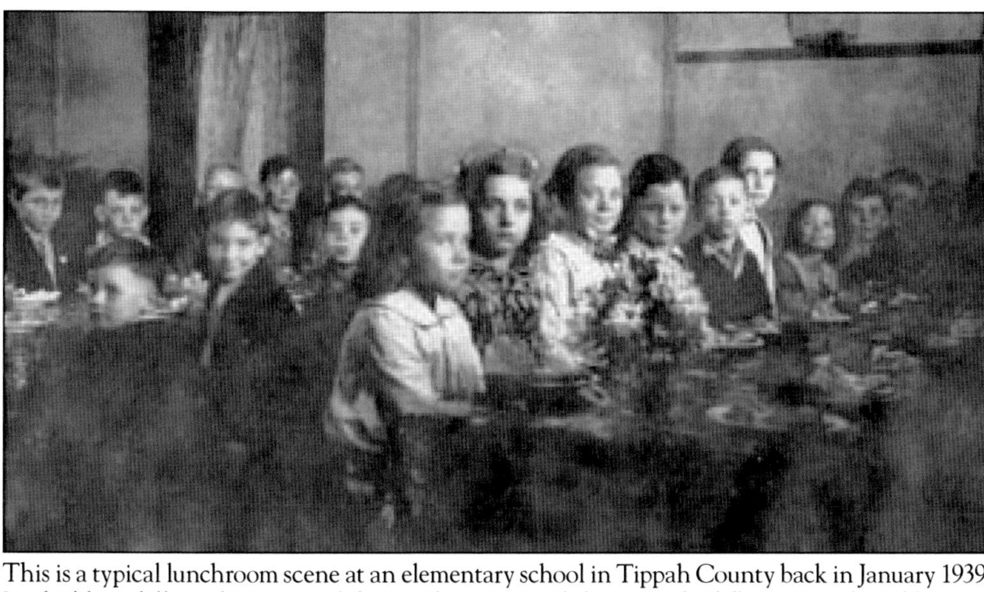

This is a typical lunchroom scene at an elementary school in Tippah County back in January 1939. Looks like a full meal was served during that time and they even had flowers on the table.

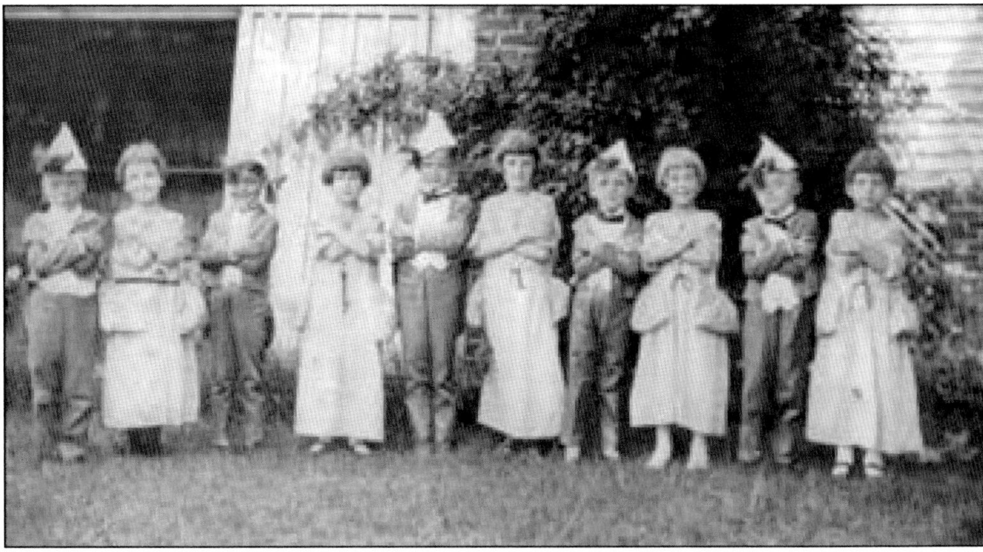

Ripley Elementary School's class dressed up for an occasion at school. Those pictured in the 1922 photograph are, from left to right, Junior Finger, Marie Davis, Lorenzo Adams, Polly Daniel, J.L. Henson, Bertha Finger, Dewitt Braddock, Eudora Murry, Gordon Clayton, and Constance Eaves.

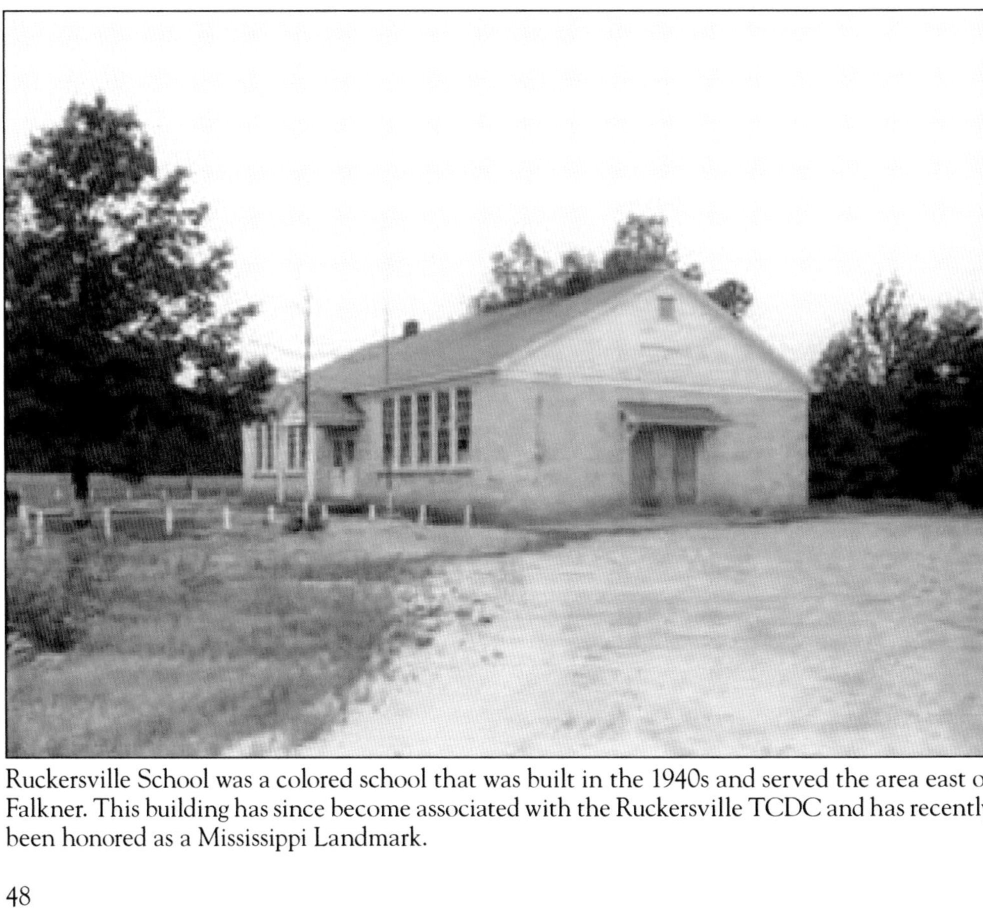

Ruckersville School was a colored school that was built in the 1940s and served the area east of Falkner. This building has since become associated with the Ruckersville TCDC and has recently been honored as a Mississippi Landmark.

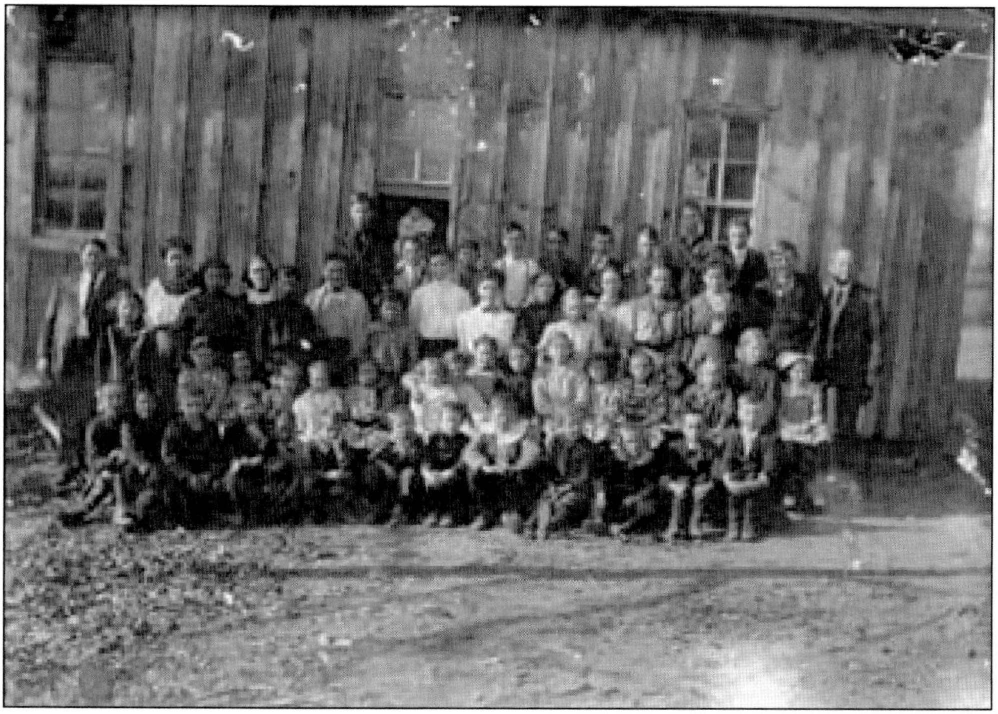

This is New Prospect School, which was located near where Leland Grisham lived. Oscar Jones is standing at the far left and Professor Jobe, visiting the superintendent, was standing at the far right. Others in the picture include Velma McClusky, Wardie or Irene McClusky, and Ione Mitchell.

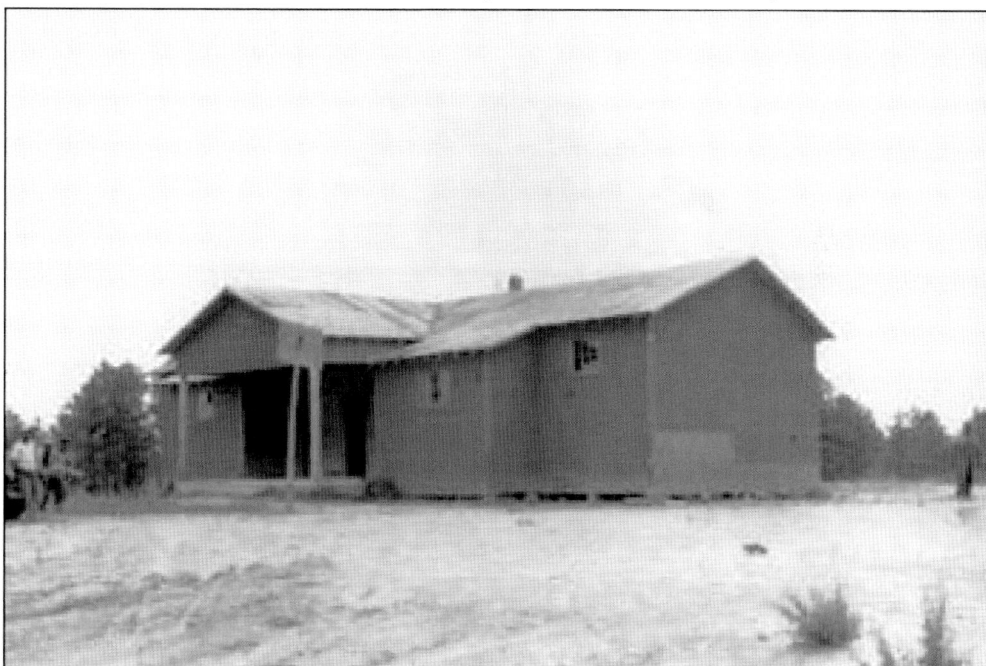

The White Oak Colored School was located on Murry Spur Road, about one mile east of Highway 15 North in Ripley. This photograph was taken in the 1940s before the schools were desegregated.

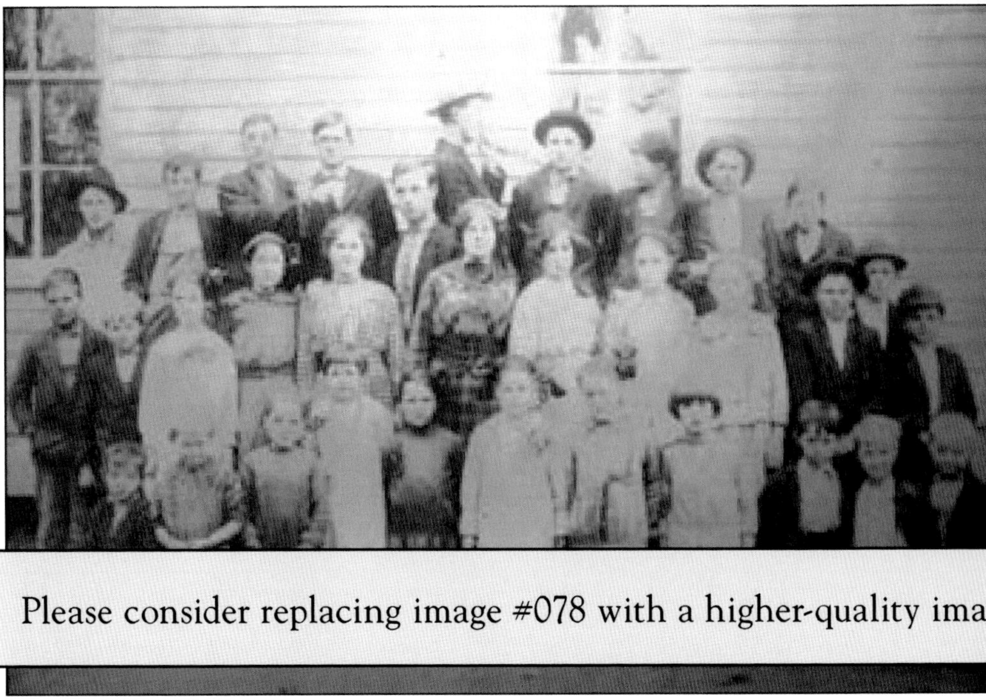

This is the school known as Wicker, which was located northwest of Ripley near Wicker Mountain. This 1920s photograph shows kids of all ages getting together to make a memory we see almost 90 years ago.

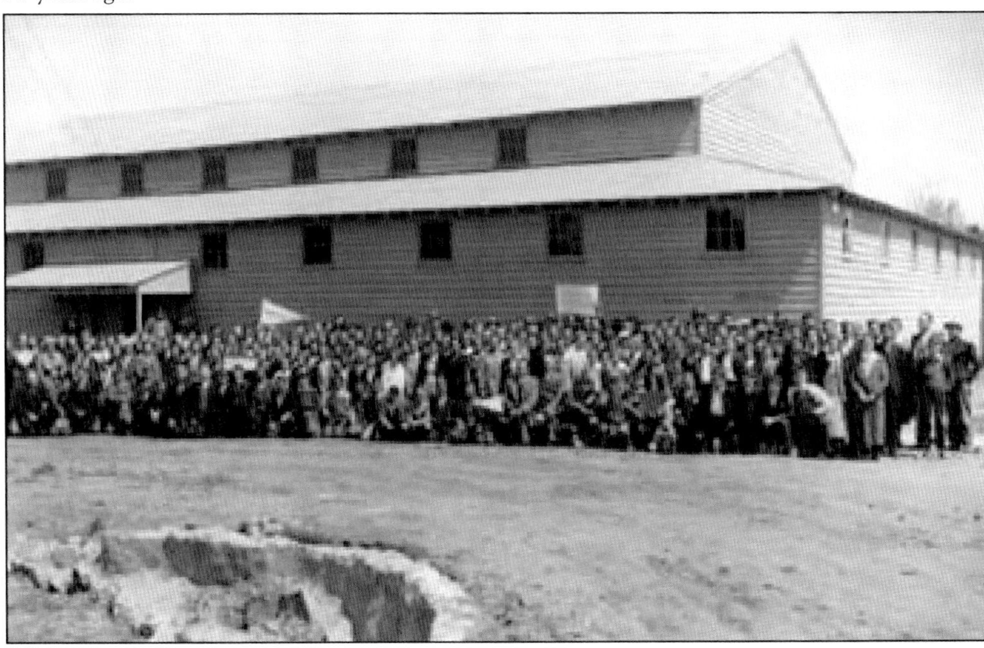

This Ripley gymnasium, built in the late 1920s, is shown in this 1930 photograph of the 4-H Club Rally with students from throughout the county. The gym was located at what is now the southeast corner of Highway 4 and City Avenue. It was replaced by the shirt factory and later the Ripley Fire Station.

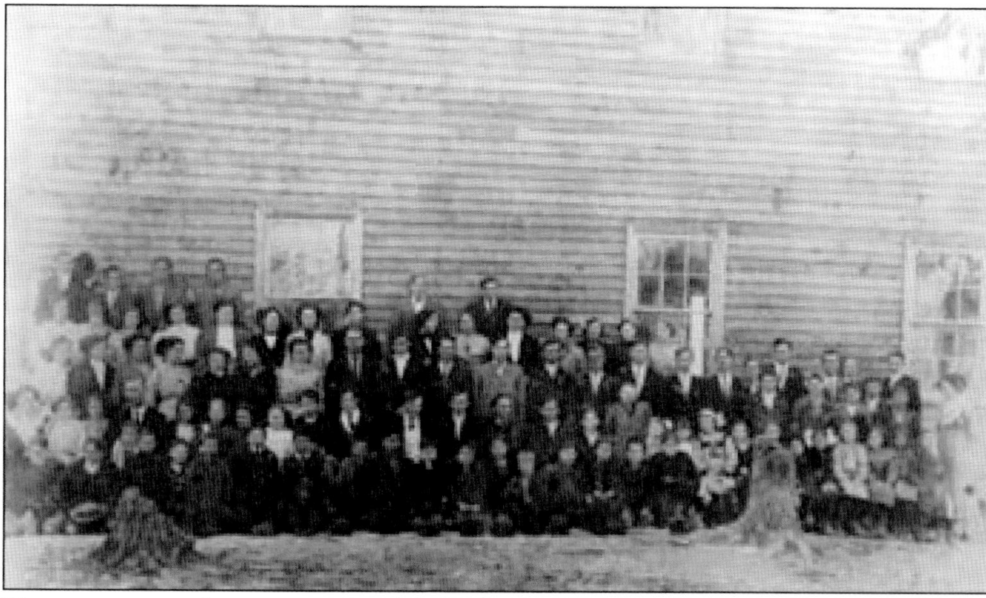

This two-story wooden structure served the Walnut area from 1905 to 1923. Walnut was the largest community in northern Tippah County after the highway and railroad bypassed Chalybeate. This was a pretty large school where the kids were dressed up very nicely.

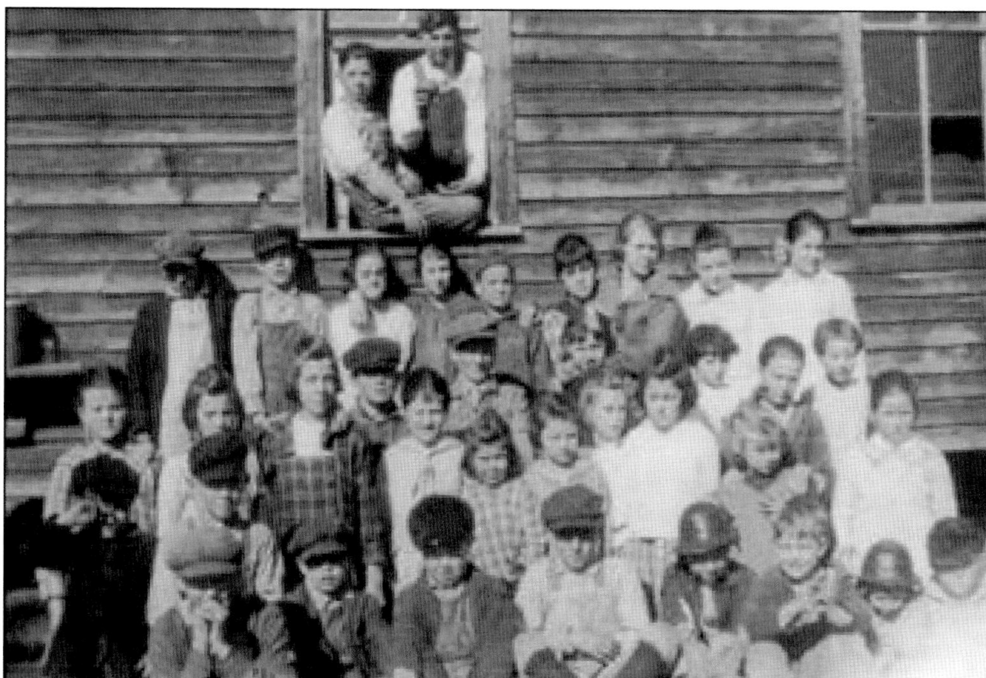

This was a typical county school in the mid-1920s, with boys wearing newsboy hats and overalls. The school was built with weathered lumber and did not have any paint on it.

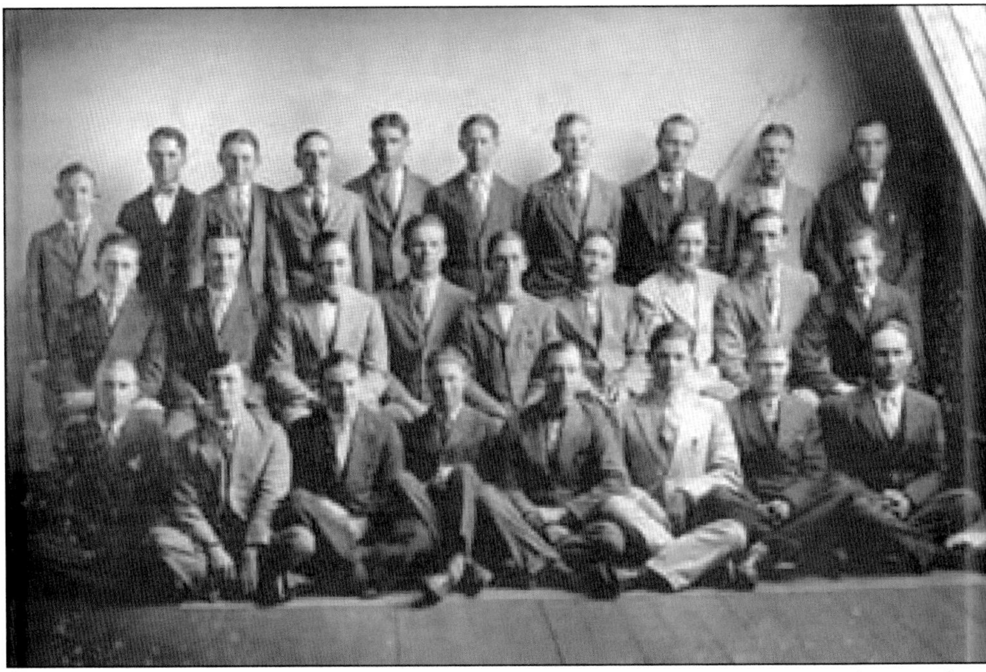

Pictured here are students at Mississippi Heights Academy in the early 1900s. These students came from different states and many communities to room and board and get a great gentleman's education. The school, located in Blue Mountain across from Blue Mountain College, served until 1941.

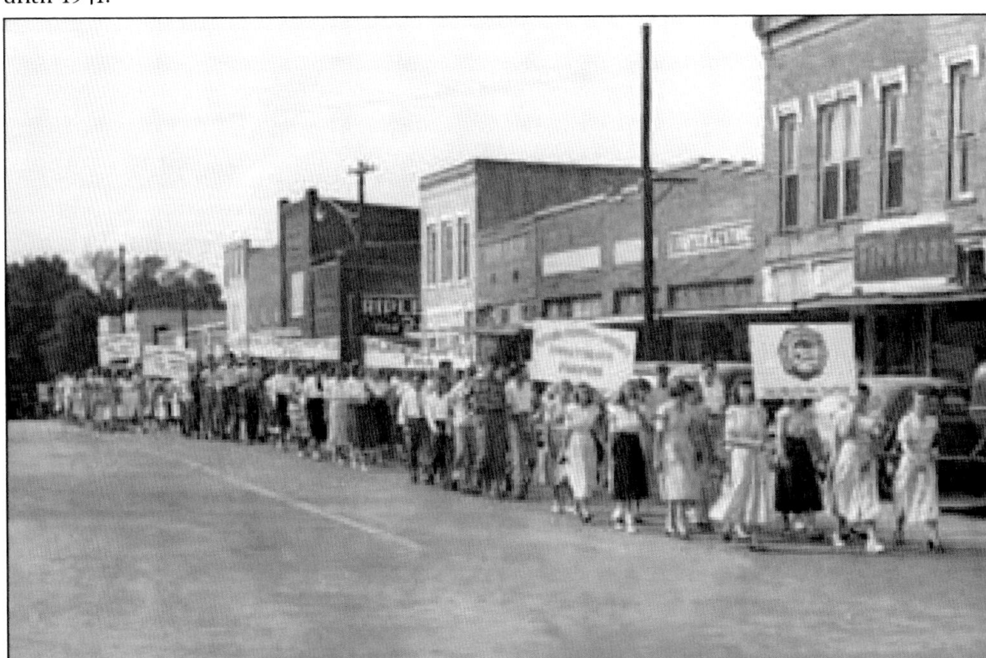

A Future Homemakers of America (FHA) and Future Farmers of America (FFA) countywide parade is seen going through the west side of Ripley Square during the 1950s. The building on the left was the old Ripley Hotel and the last building on the left is Elliott's Firestone dealership.

Six

CHURCHES

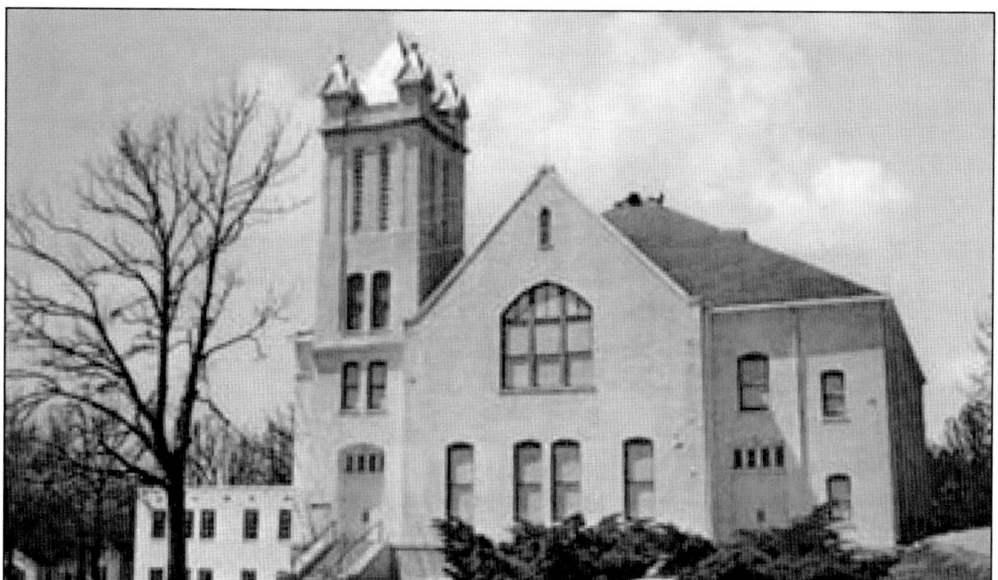

Lowrey Memorial Baptist Church was started by Gen. Mark Perrin Lowrey in the 1870s, and is located next door to Blue Mountain College. The church is beautiful and contains bell chimes and a pipe organ that can be heard throughout the campus.

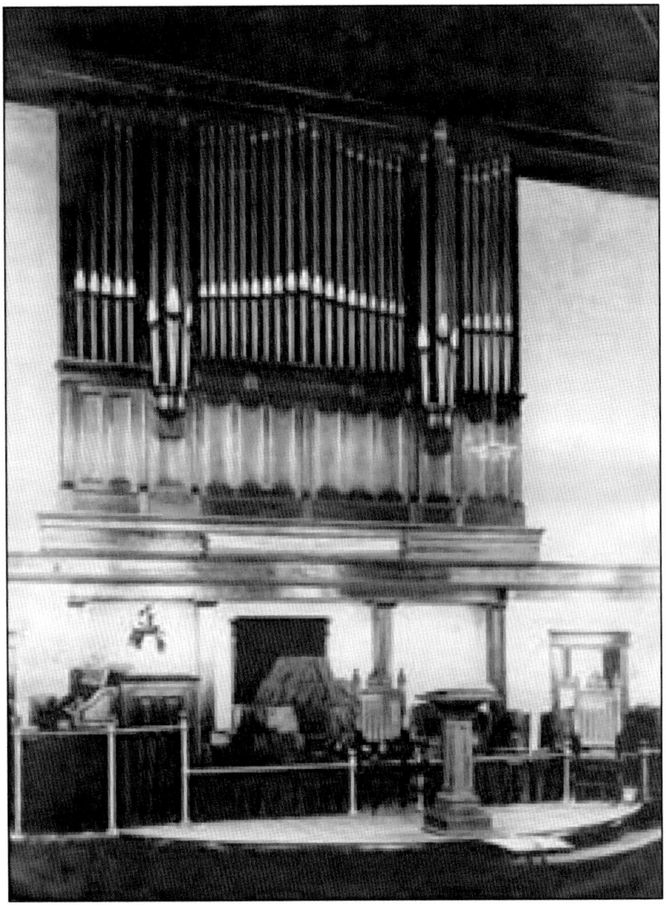

The beautiful pipe organ has been a part of Lowrey Memorial Baptist Church for more than 130 years and will continue to serve Blue Mountain for many more.

First Baptist Church in Ripley held their baptismal services in a concrete pool located just outside of the church. This ceremony took place around 1905 and shows Lottie Street being baptized.

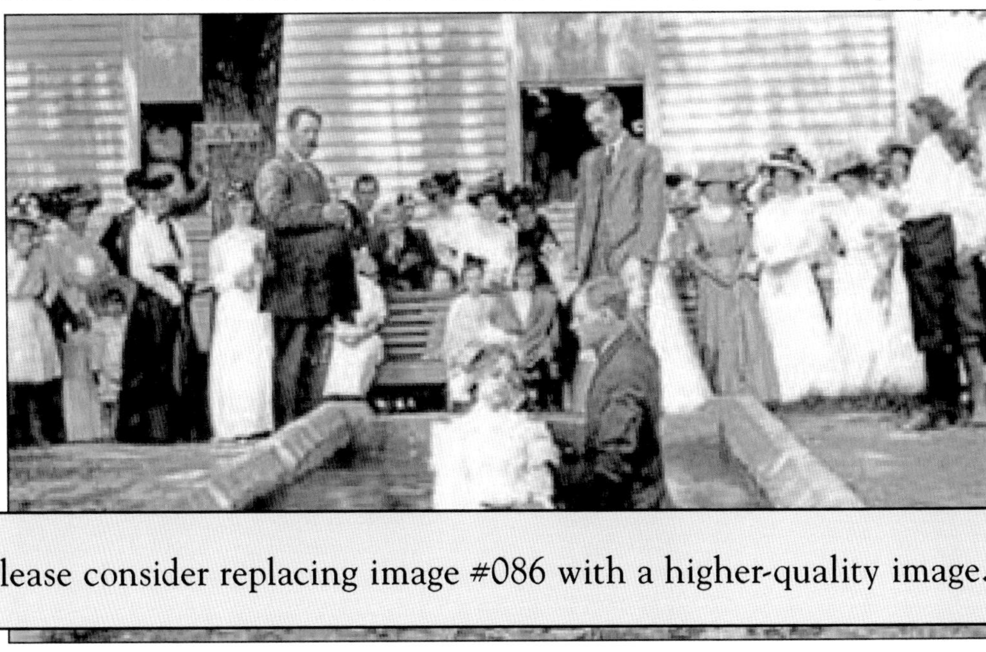

In 1884, First Baptist Church in Ripley, Mississippi, was built. A few years later in 1915, it burned. This building faced west and stood at the northeast corner of Mulberry and Main Street. The home of Col. W.C. Falkner was on the block west of the church. Willie Falkner Carter had a stained glass window installed in the church in memory of her father inscribed with "He that giveth to the poor, lendeth to the Lord." At some time before the church burned, the window was removed and it was installed in the Carter home.

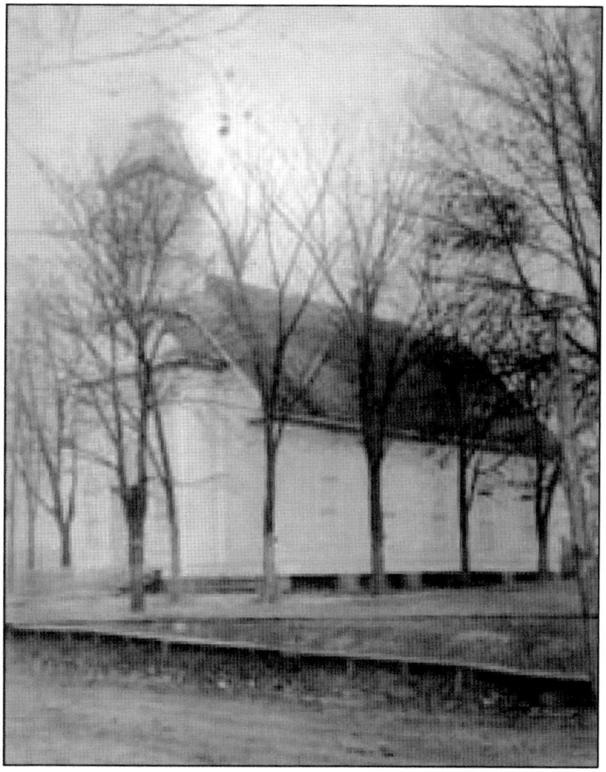

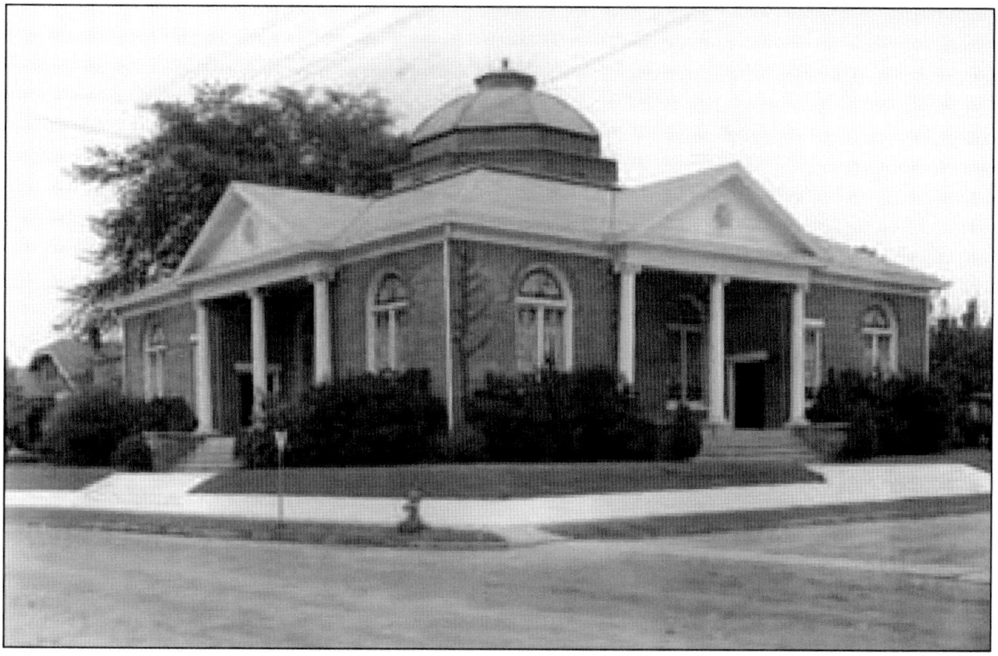

The First Baptist Church building was located on the northeast corner of North Main Street and Mulberry Street in Ripley. It was built in 1916 and was torn down in 1956 to move into the new church building located on Pine Street, just one block northeast of this structure. This photograph was taken in 1938.

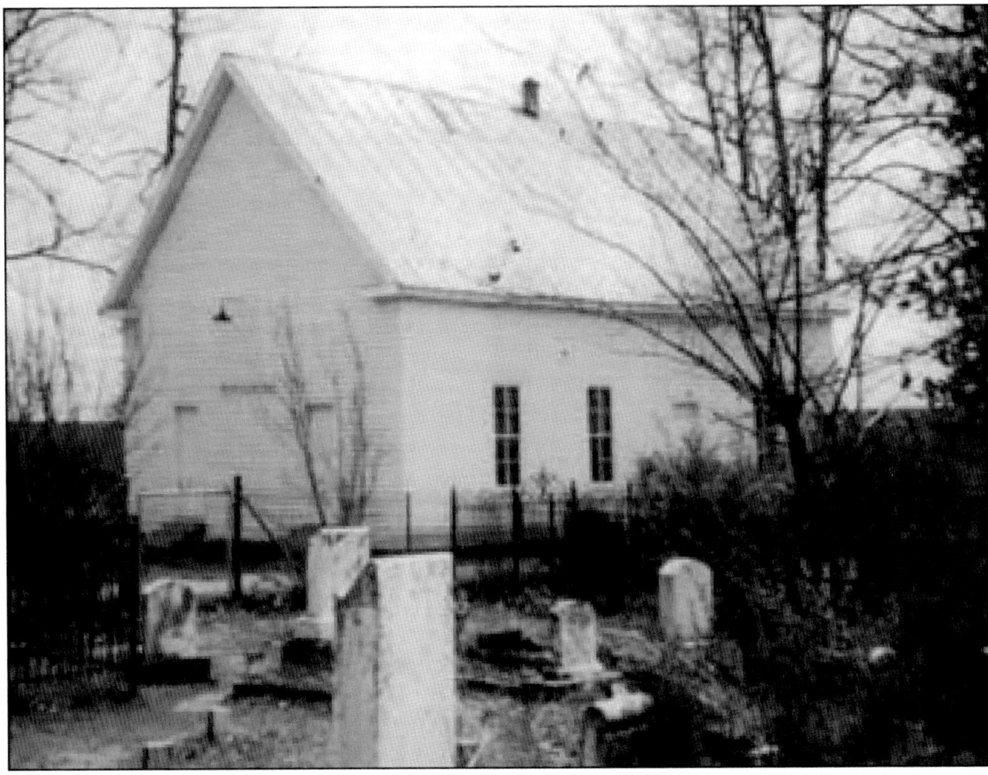

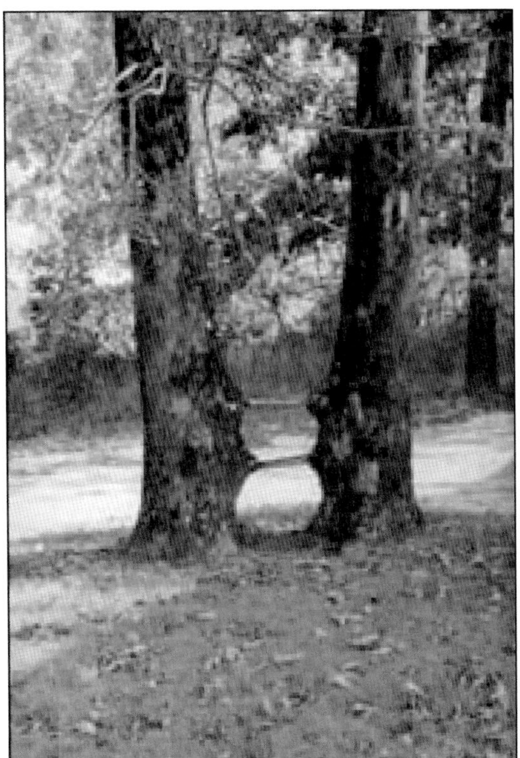

Wier's Chapel Methodist Church, located on Highway 370 (Dumas Road), is known as the oldest standing church building in Tippah County.

This tree structure is known as an upping block and is located at Wier's Chapel Methodist Church located on Highway 370, southeast of Ripley. The Grose 1811 Dictionary also calls it a leaping stock or jossing block, which are steps used for mounting a horse. He sits like a toad on a jossing block, said of one who sits ungracefully on horseback.

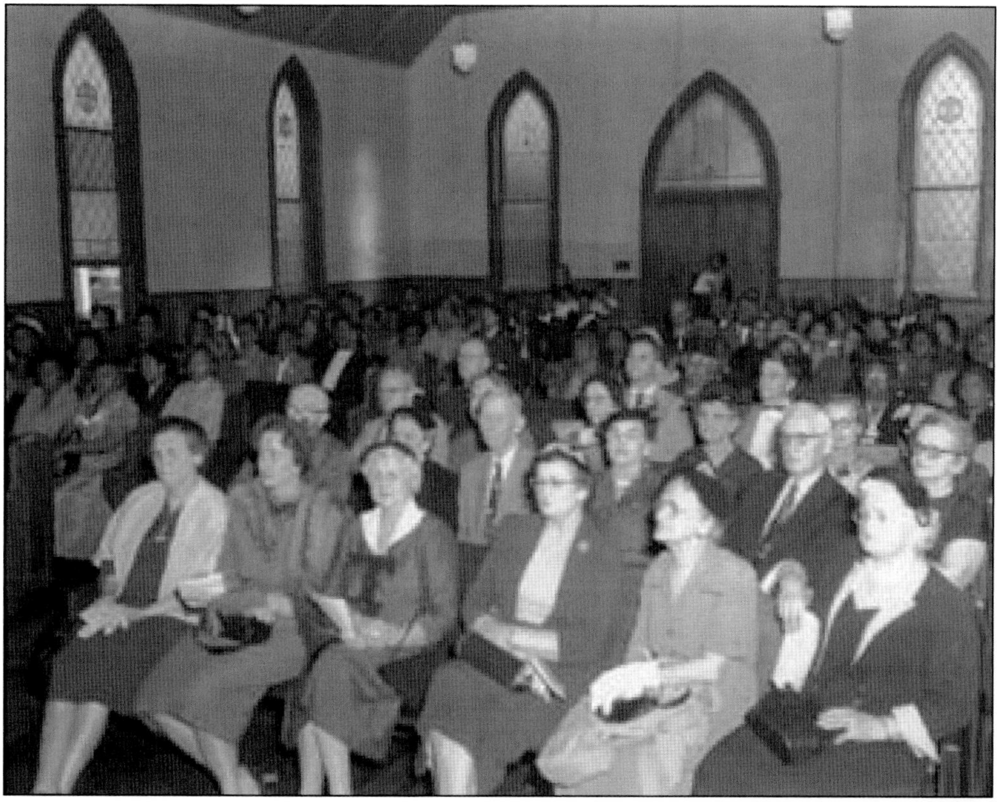

St. Paul's Methodist Church hosted a great multiracial dedication for renovations that were completed in 1950. Pictured here are, from left to right, (first row) Mrs. Palmer Smith, Mrs. John Hudson "Dot" Finger, Mrs. Fred B. Smith, unidentified, Mrs. W.W. Davidson, and Lena Ray; (second row) Lee Cox, Clara Cox, Tom Counseille, Mrs. Tom Counseille, Edd Johnson, and Anna Johnson; (third row) Ellis Finger, Mrs. Ellis Finger, Mary Miller Murry, Anna Murry, Irene Pitner, unidentified; (fourth row) Noverta Witt, M. O. Hailey, and unidentified.

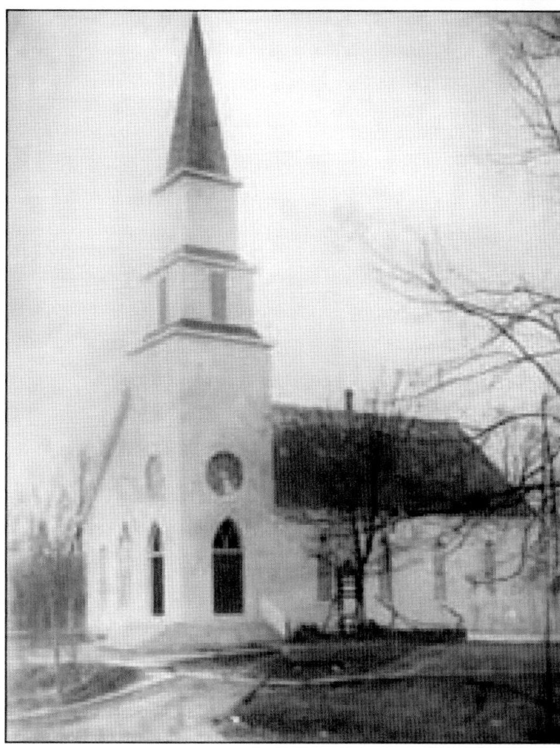

First Methodist Church was built in 1887 on the corner of South Main Street and Water Street in Ripley, with the doors facing north and east. The building was removed in 1925 to make way for a new brick church.

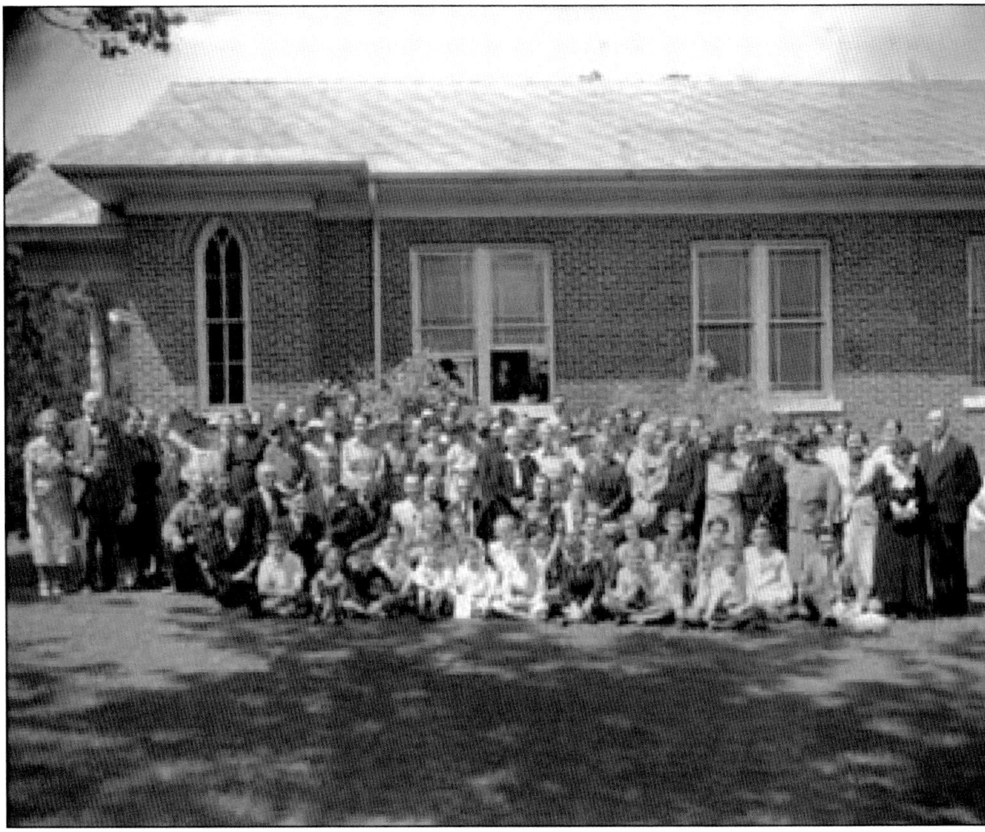

This is Ripley Presbyterian Church as it appeared in the late 1930s with members and their families. The church is located at the southeast corner of Jackson Street and Cooper Street.

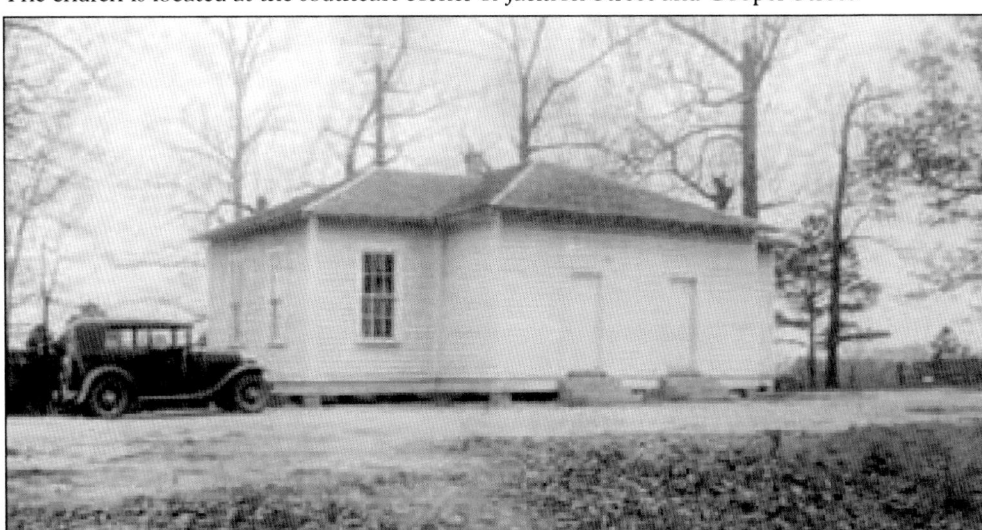

The new Prospect Presbyterian Church on Highway 370 South was organized in 1874 in Dumas and was later moved to the present location north of Dumas, where a cemetery was also established. Today, a modern brick building stands on the site of the old church.

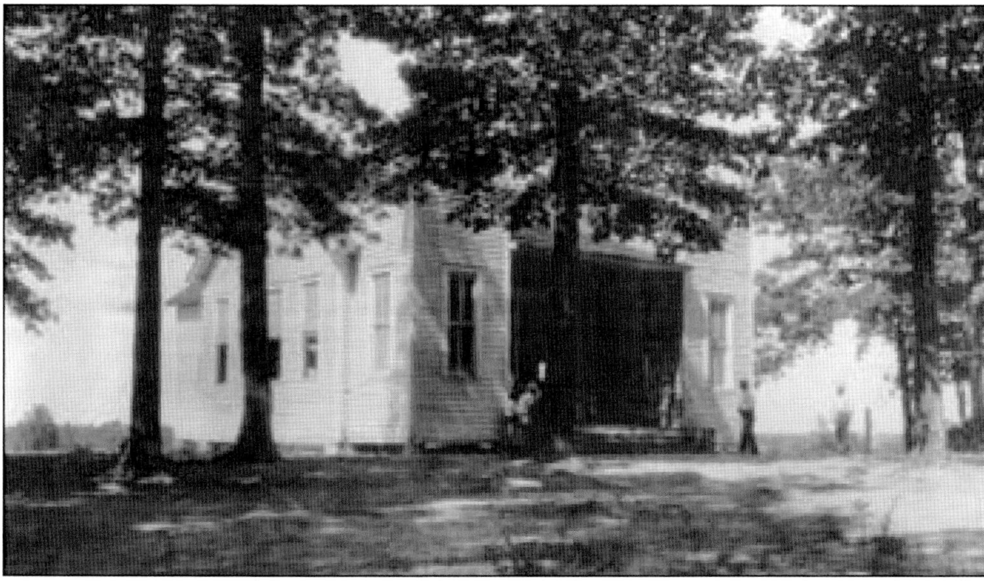

Westminster Presbyterian Church off of Highway 4 East was organized in 1920. The building was dedicated on Thanksgiving Day in 1924. Mary McCarley had suggested that the church be named Westminster. This photograph shows how it looked in 1945 with twin towers and a large walk-in porch. Today, a brick church building stands on the site.

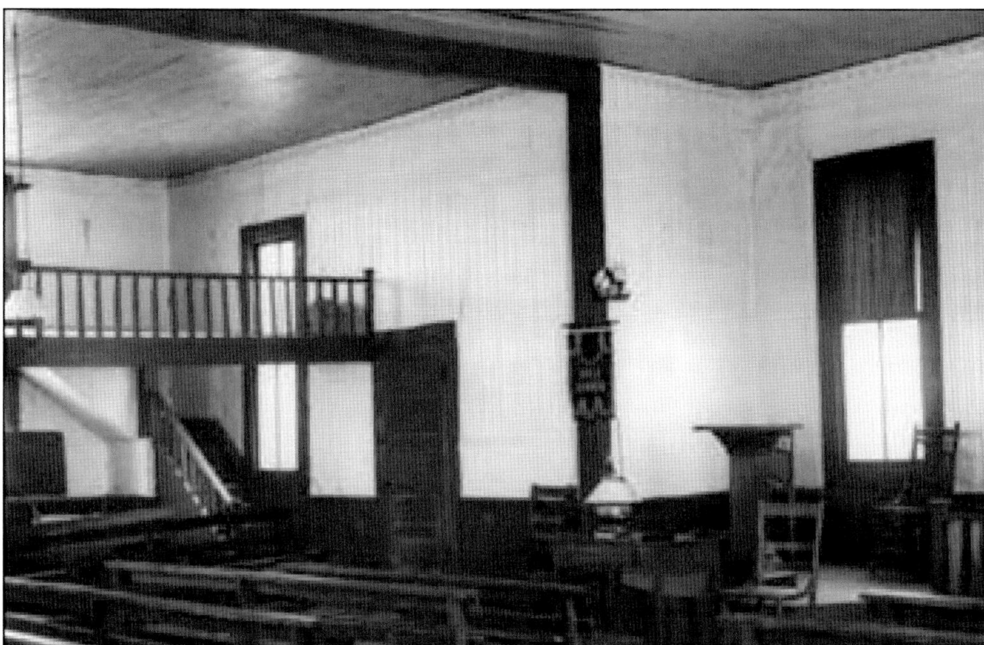

Westminster Presbyterian Church as it looked in 1945. The inside of the church had a small pulpit located in front with a stairway giving access to the upstairs. Pews were placed in a semicircle around the pulpit.

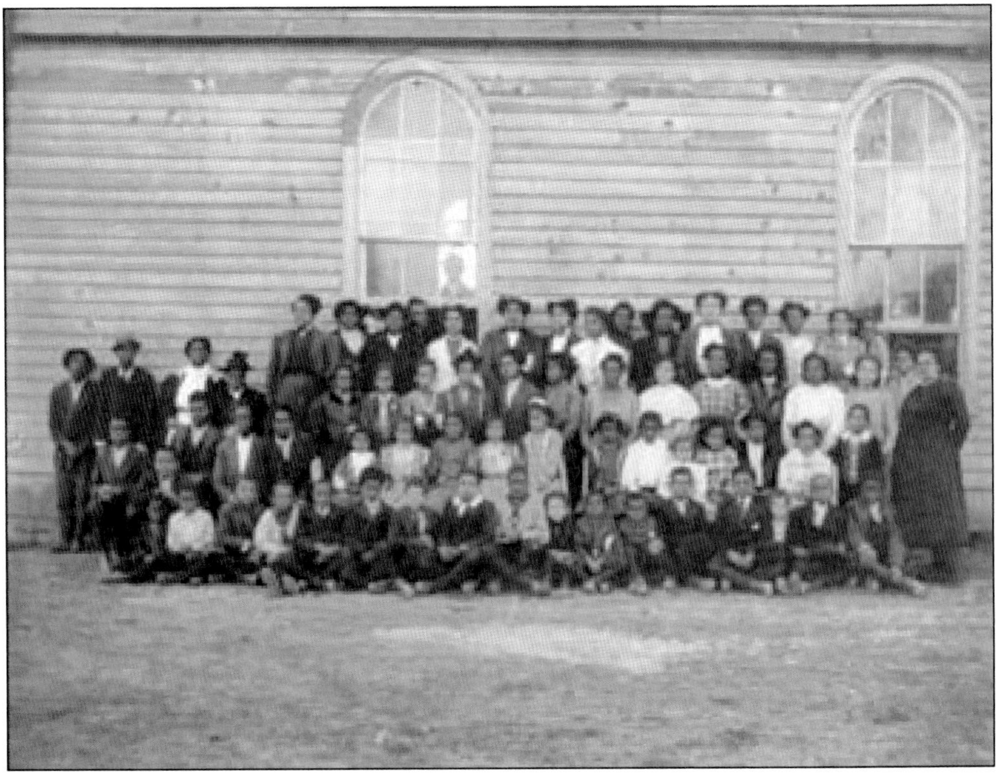

In this c. 1900 photograph is Ripley Second Baptist Church. This was the largest African American church at that time in Ripley that had its own school program. Around 60 students attended this school and it was not funded by the state until later in the century.

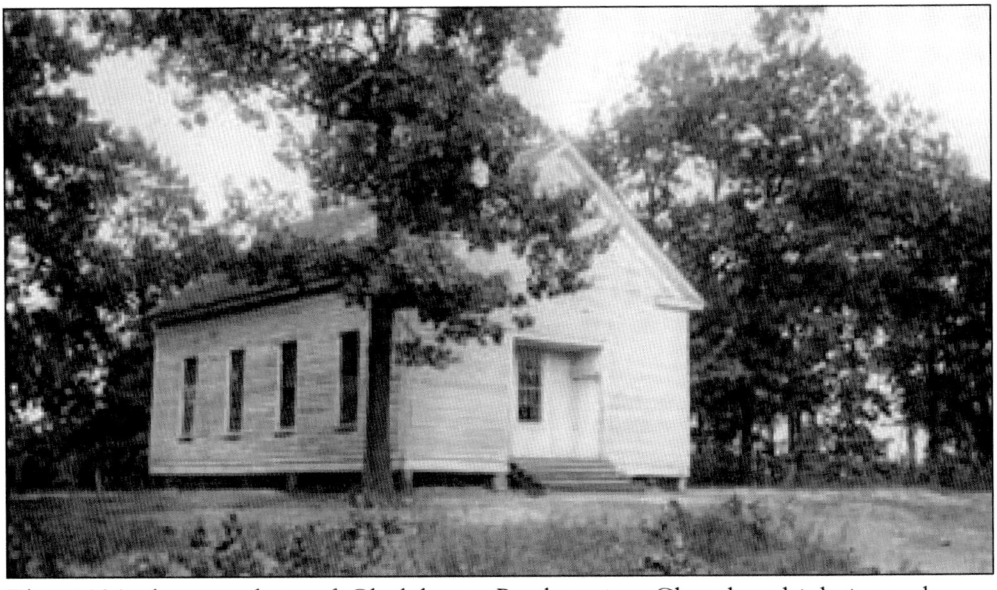

This 1936 photograph is of Chalybeate Presbyterian Church, which is no longer standing today.

Seven

Tippah Treasures

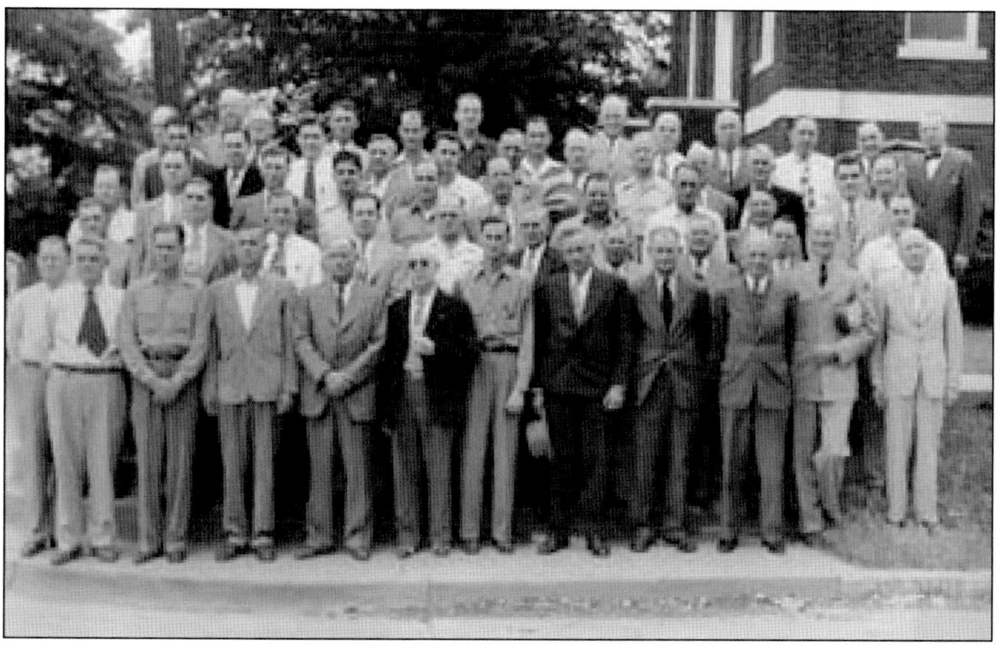

Ripley Rotary Club in the early 1940s with names for almost everyone known. Pictured here are, from left to right, (first row) Ernest Weatherly, Fred Meritt, Luther Barkley, Ab Guyton, David E. Guyton, Lawrence Miller, John Street, Homer Gunn, Lawrence T. Lowrey, unidentified, James Brown, and William Pitner; (second row) Lamont Richardson, Lynwood Dees, Cecil Furtick, unidentified, Charlie Morton, John Miller, Mr. Bennett, Sam Moore, unidentified, and Pete Brown; (third row) Tom Braddock, James Shumaker, Wallace Holliday, Bobby Smith, Price Johnson, Mr. Phillips, Oscar Shannon, Charlie Miskelly, Jimmy Finger, and Cecil Ramer; (fourth row) Vance Braddock, Allen Wright, Bob Hutto, Guy Ferrell, Dr. Tommy Sweat, Sidney Boyd, Palmer Smith, Bob Smith, E.P. Johnson, Willie Gossett, and Rev. Charlie Smith; (fifth row) Jim Hudspeth, Malcolm Gillis, Dr. R.W. Street, Lawrence Callicutt, Bob Fortier, Easley Ballard, Dr. W.E. Johnson, Fred B. Smith, Rev. George Gay, J.E. Buchannan, William H. Anderson, Wilfred C. Tyler, and Erst Long.

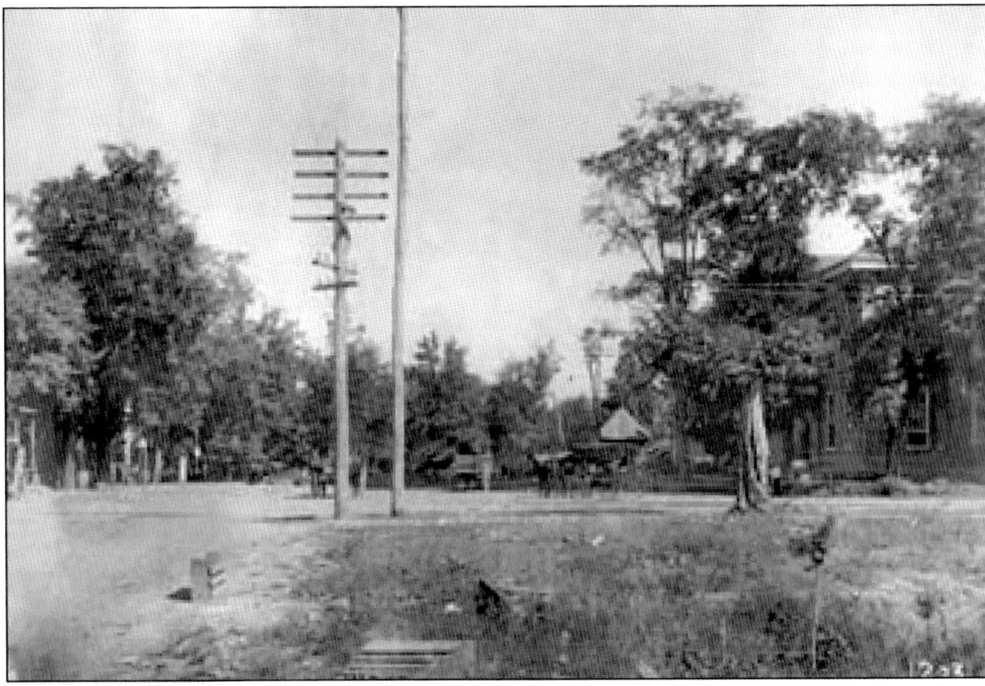

This picture comes from the 1870s and shows a western view of the Tippah County Courthouse looking north. No buildings were on the northwest corner of the square or on the southwest corner of the square. Since the county did not have electricity, the poles were carrying telegraph lines for communication. Colonel Falkner's office, R.J. Thurmond's office, and the bank were located on the western side of the square. The courthouse was rebuilt in 1870 after a fire during the Civil War, and many of the stores that had also suffered fires had not been rebuilt at this time.

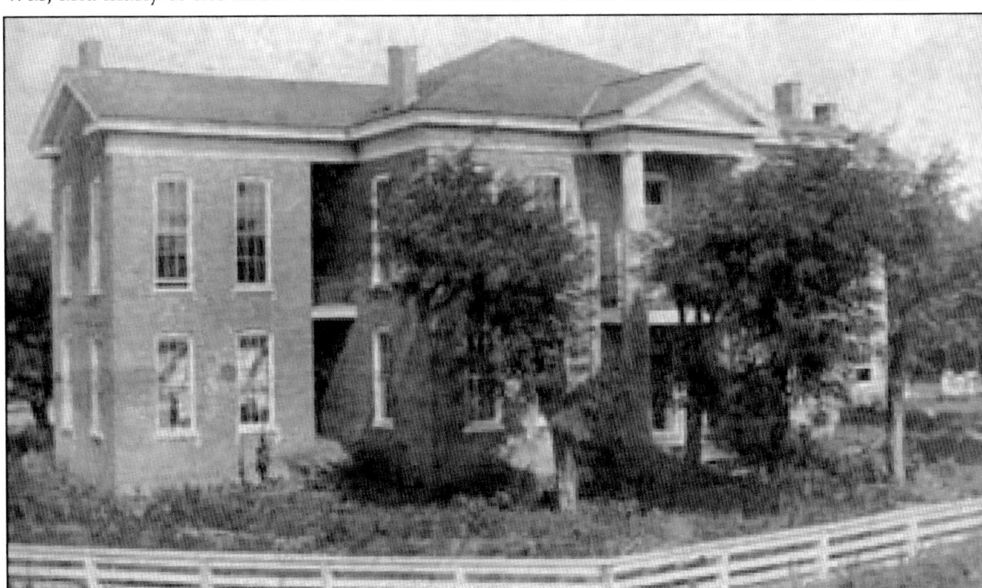

This is the Tippah County Courthouse, which was rebuilt in 1870 after being burned during the Civil War. This 1906 photograph shows how the courtyard grew during the summer months. A metal fence replaced the wooden fence in later years.

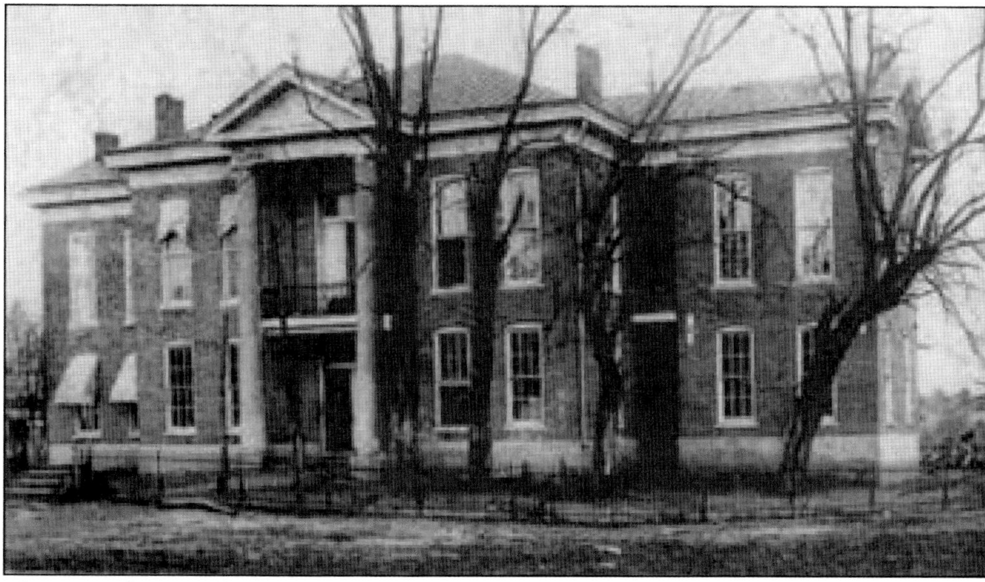

This 1920 photograph of the Tippah County Courthouse was made during the winter months with doors and windows still left open to let the heat out. Notice the stile in the fence to keep large animals from entering the courtyard.

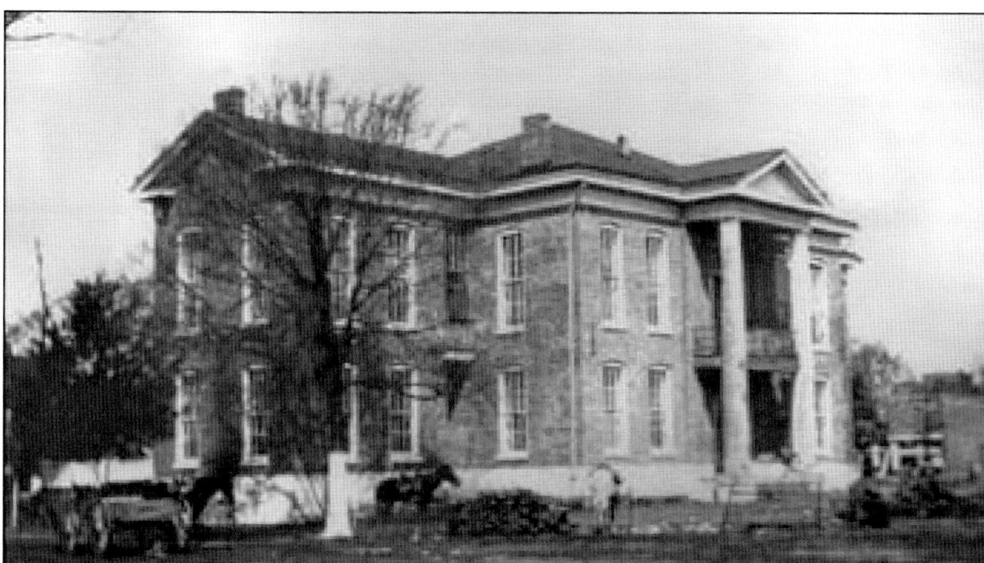

Seen here is an eastside view of the Tippah County Courthouse, which stood from 1870 to 1928. This early 1900 photograph shows horses tied up in the courtyard, wood stacked for use in the fireplaces, and wagons parked on the south side of the courthouse.

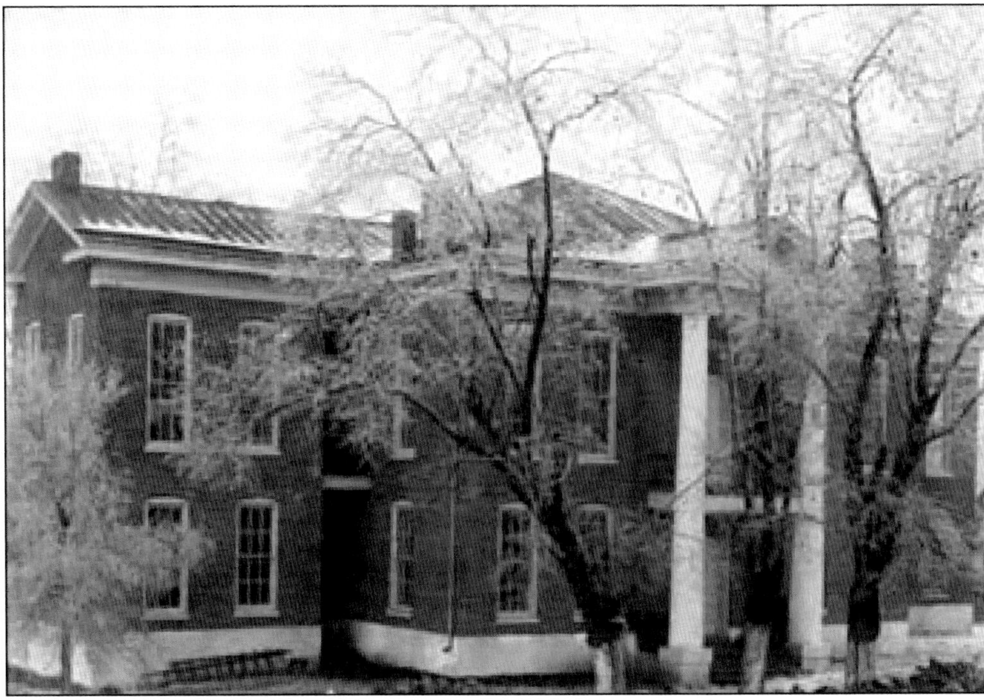

Tippah County has had four courthouses and this one was built in 1870 after the second courthouse was destroyed by fire during the Civil War. This building stood until 1928, when it was redesigned into the courthouse that is still in use as of 2011.

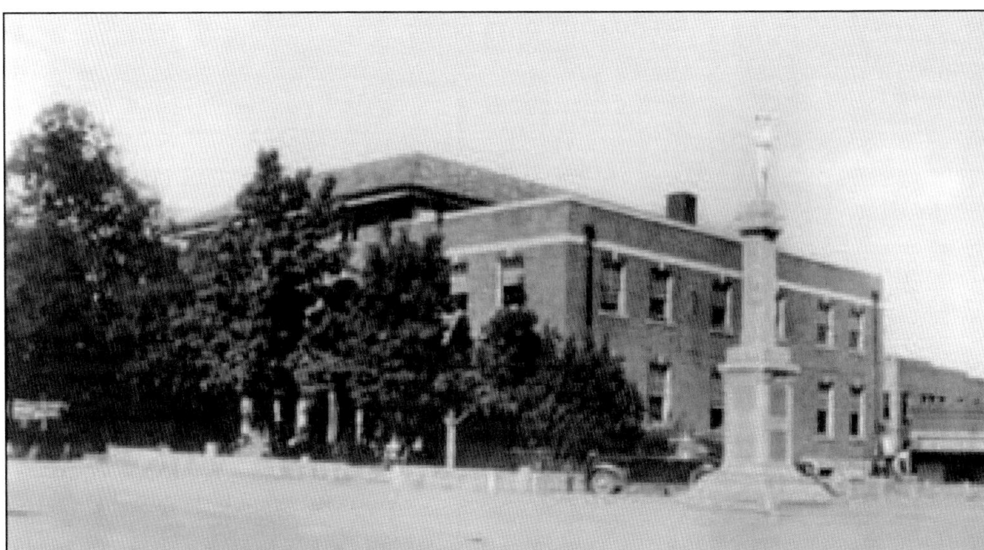

This late 1930s view of the southwest corner of the Tippah County Courthouse shows a summer day with the windows open for ventilation and many shade trees. The Confederate Memorial in the street was later moved to the east side of the courthouse after a Gay Truck Lines truck knocked it down in the 1970s.

The seven Tippah County Confederate veteran survivors of Capt. A.C. Rucker's Company B, 34th Mississippi, are pictured in this 1907 photograph. Pictured are, from left to right, (first row) Capt. A.C. Rucker; (second row) Hon. Thomas Spight, Capt. H.A. Stubbs, and T.A. Hunt; (third row) M.S. Phyfer, J.J. Kinney, and Eld. Jos. Pearce.

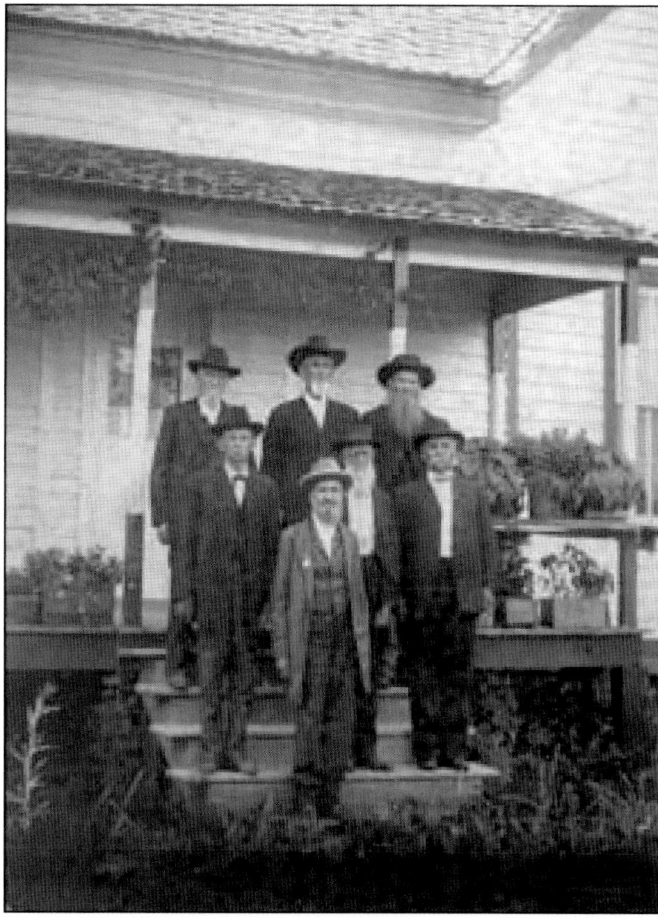

Pictured here are Tippah County Confederate veterans in the late 1890s, with Rev. W.E. Berry standing in center of photograph with a long white beard. Reverend Berry was the husband of Mother Berry at Blue Mountain College and the son-in-law of Gen. Mark Perrin Lowrey, founder of Blue Mountain College.

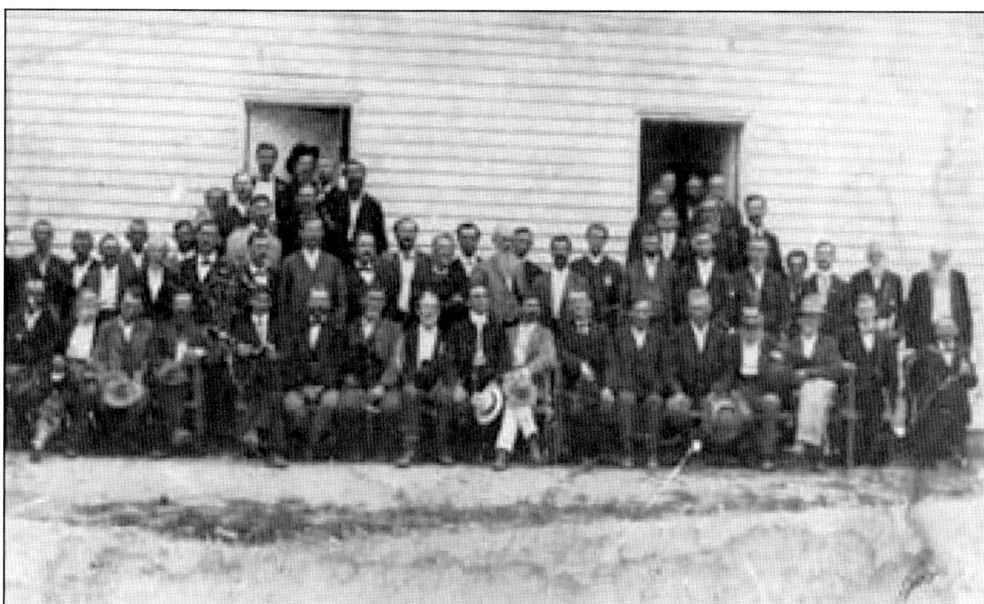

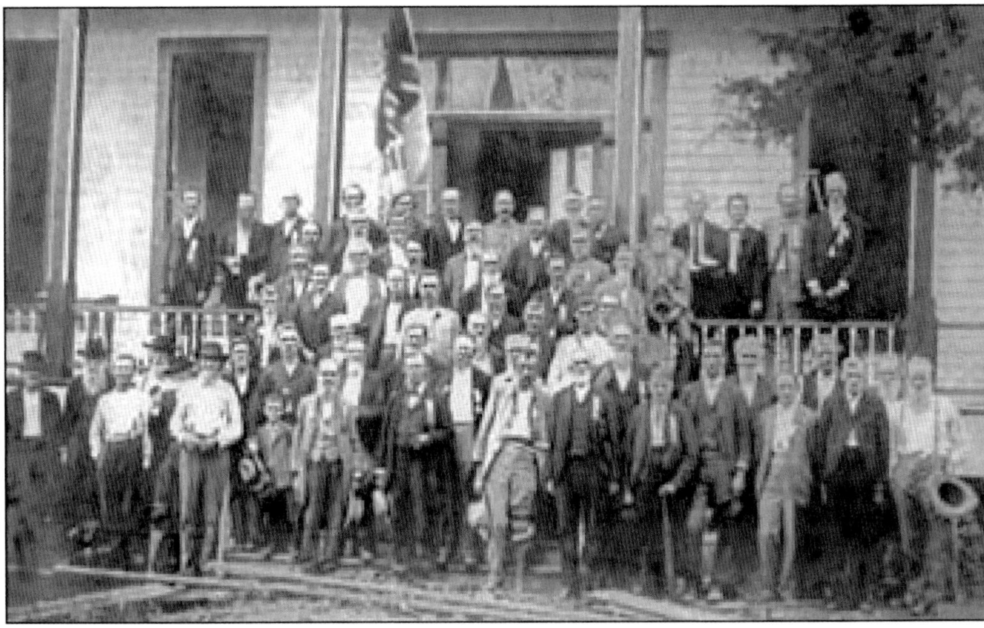

Pictured is the Confederate veterans reunion, which was held at the Ripley School on South Main in 1904. Those shown above are E.B. Aldridge, J.M. Childers, John Perkins, Capt. J.M. Rutherford, Capt. H.A. Stubbs, Capt. James Jeffries, J.W. Street Sr., J.E. Hovis, D.J. Hill, W.M. Chism, B.F. McAlister, M.J. Bennett, J.M. Murphy, Miles Paseur, John Young, Jim Murry, T.J. Coombs, W.H. Shelton, J.N. Ross, W.C. Johnson, H.T. Jones, W.B. Wommack, S.O. Love, Ty Morton, J.W. McKelvey, O.A. Porter, Newt Neely, Capt. Spight, Capt. A.C. Rucker, R.E. Gresham, Toney Mercer, J.R. Brown, D.T. Bartlett, David R. Childers, J.R. Barber, J.D. Richardson, J.A. Davis, W.W. Anderson, Sam Miskelly, J.H. Head, J.M. Renfrow, E.S. Barber, John Garner, Ira South, J.U. Widker, T.M. Jennings, Finas Hodges, Pink Pundin, M. Reed, W.S. Hawkins, Ty Keith, John Parish, W.D. Robbins, J.H. Nance, and three others whose names are unknown.

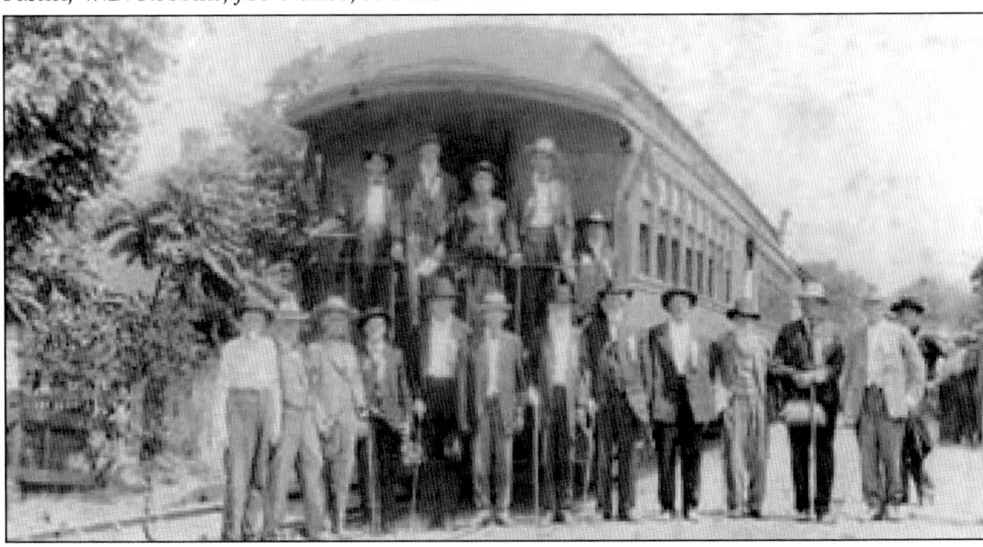

Pictured are a group of Confederate veterans in a pre-1905 photograph from the back of a train located near the Ripley depot. Those identified include Capt. Thomas Spight, seen sixth from the right, bottom row, and W.E. Berry, seen seventh from the right, bottom row.

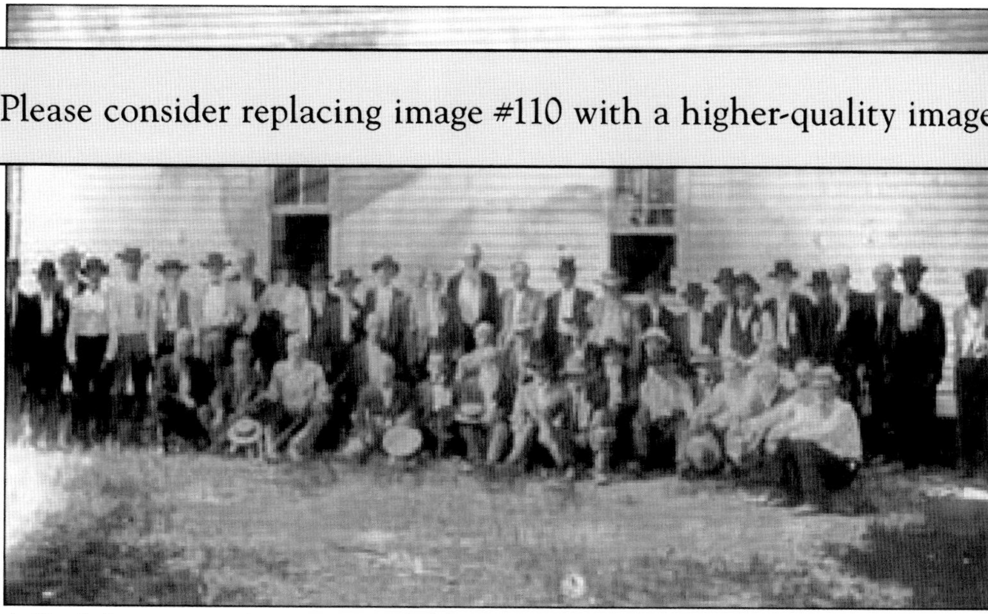

A Confederate veteran's reunion was held in 1898. Pictured are W.E. Berry (front row center with long white beard), Capt. Thomas Spight (front row sixth from right side), Robert Lewis Yancey (tallest gentleman with black hat to the right of center in middle row), and Tucker Spight (standing second from right side).

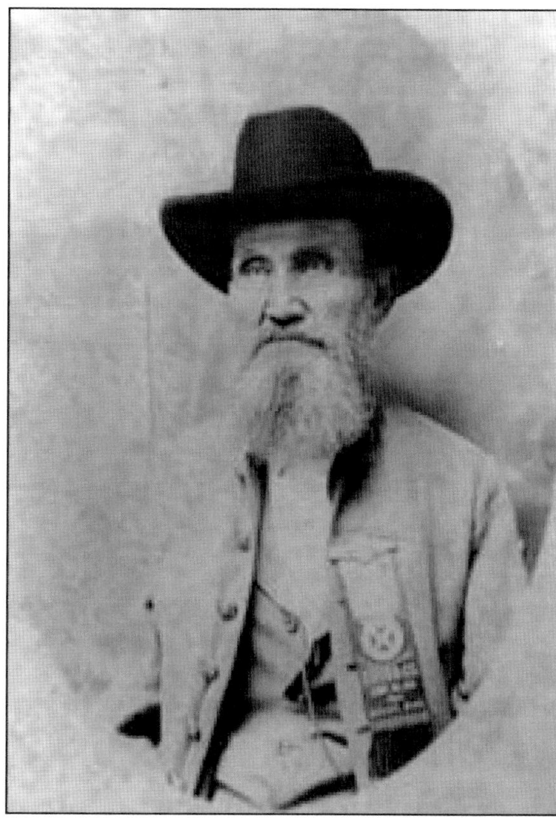

Capt. Abbott C. Rucker was the oldest white man in Tippah County when he died on February 6, 1919. He was buried at the Rucker graveyard four miles northeast of Ripley. He was buried with full Masonic honors. Captain Rucker had celebrated his 97th birthday on December 16, 1918 after having served his Tippah County in several public offices. He was a leader in the Presbyterian Church and Ripley Masonic Lodge, and was a member of the Lodge for nearly 71 years. He was a Captain in the Confederate Army and devoutly loved the gray.

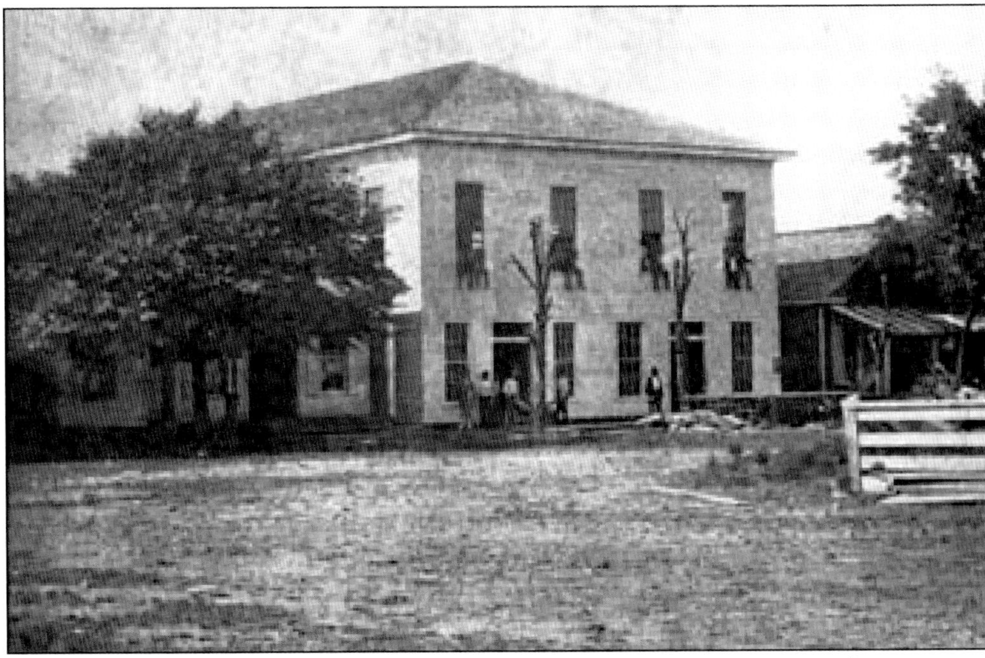

The Ripley Town Hall was located on the south side of the square during the late 1800s to early 1900s. This side of the square had a fire that destroyed the buildings, but new buildings were rebuilt in 1906. During his landlord years, W.W. Robinson owned the town hall building.

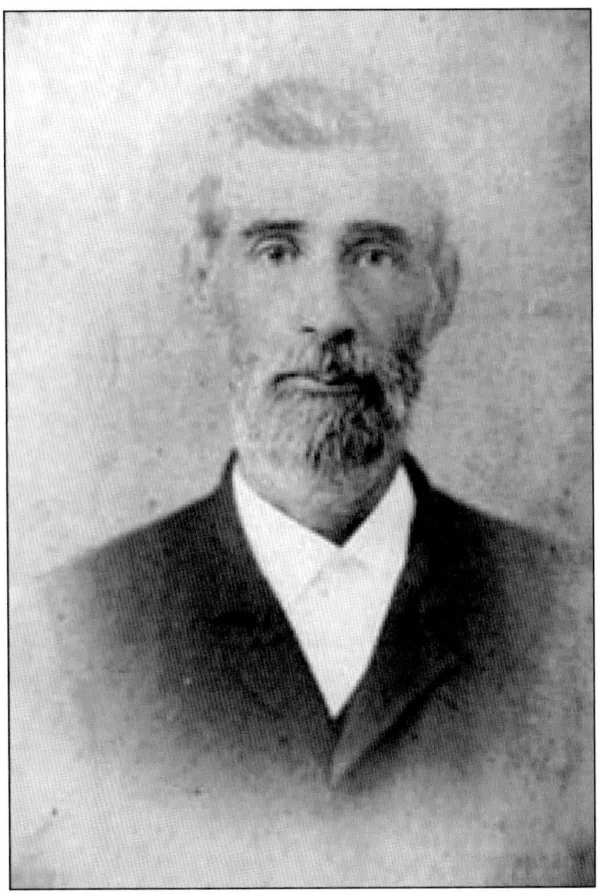

W.W. Robinson was one of Tippah County's leading citizens that began his legacy as a schoolteacher in the 1860s, a retail merchant in the 1870s, a deputy clerk in the 1880s, and a landlord in the 1900s. He even owned the Ripley City Hall that burned in the early 1900s.

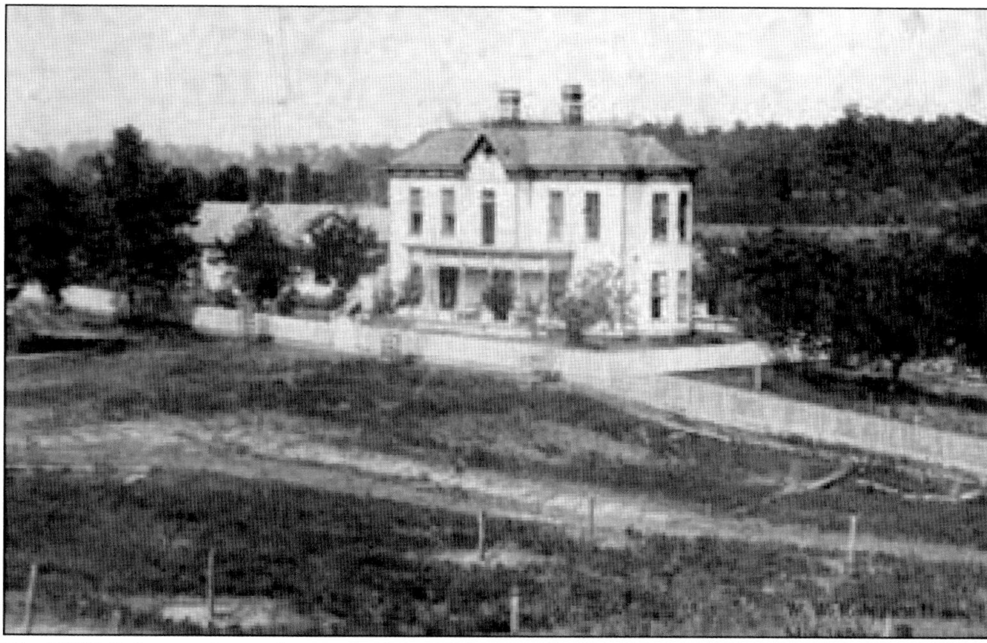

The W.W. Robinson home during the late 1800s was a fine house with a beautiful fence surrounding it. Mr. Robinson was a schoolteacher in the 1860s, a merchant in the 1870s, a deputy clerk in the 1880s, and a landlord in the 1900s.

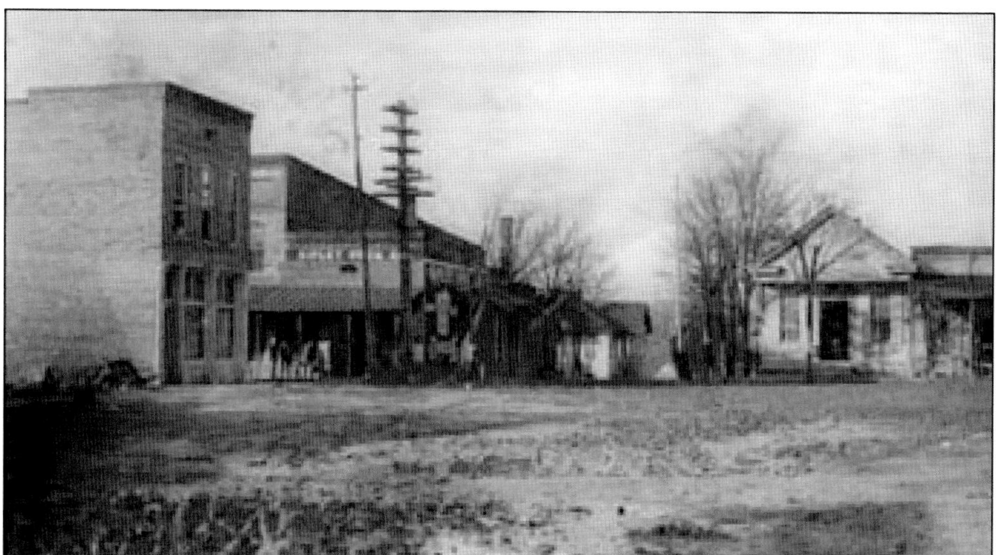

This early 1900s photograph of the southwest corner of the square in Ripley shows the Ripley Drug Company in the center. The building on the left was the Bank of Ripley. The small building on the right is the site where the First National Bank and later the Peoples Bank were located. Notice the dirt and mud on the square and also notice the telephone pole with all the telephone lines on it. The first telephone company, owned by the Pitner family, was located upstairs above the Bank of Ripley. Annie Pitner was the switchboard operator.

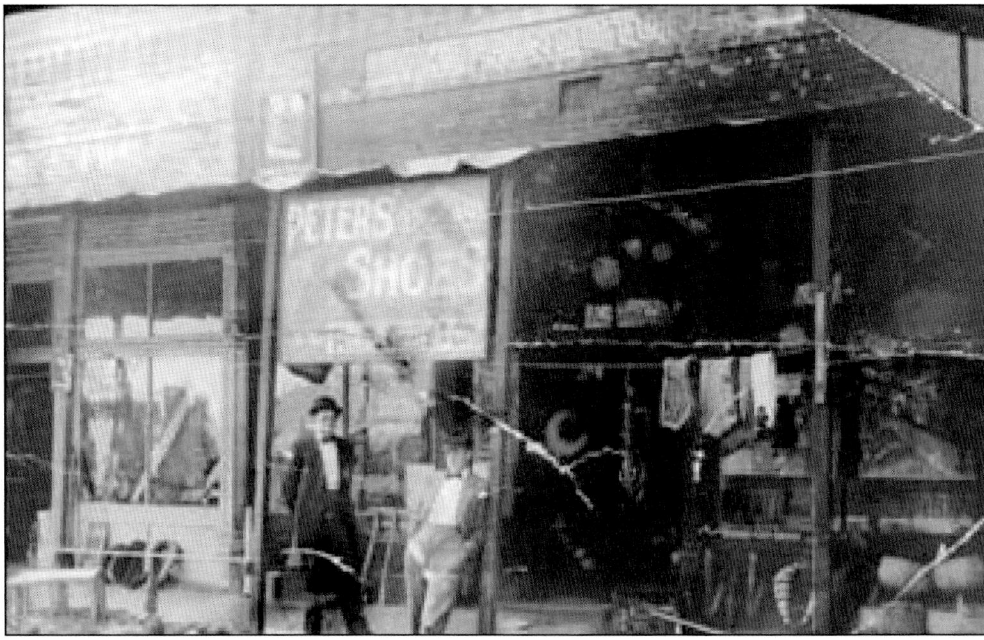

The old Red Front Store located on the south side of the square was owned and operated by Laurence Clayton and Ira L. Clayton and was known as the A.N. Clayton Store in 1912. Store signs show Duke's mixture of smoking tobacco and Peter's Shoes with diamond soles.

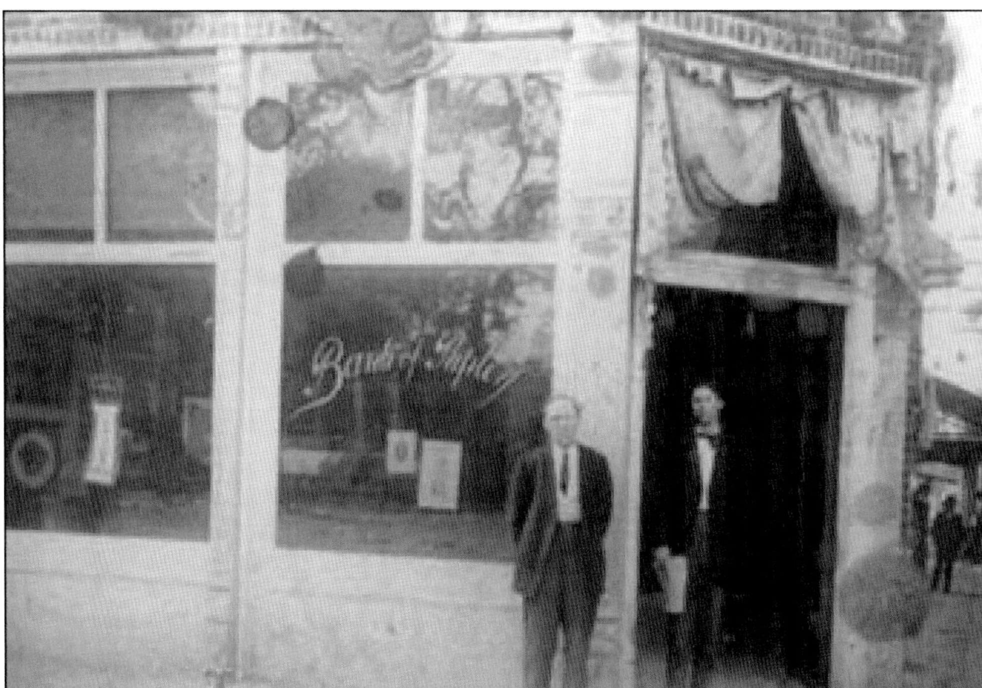

The early 1900s photograph shows the Bank of Ripley at its location at the southwest corner of the courthouse square.

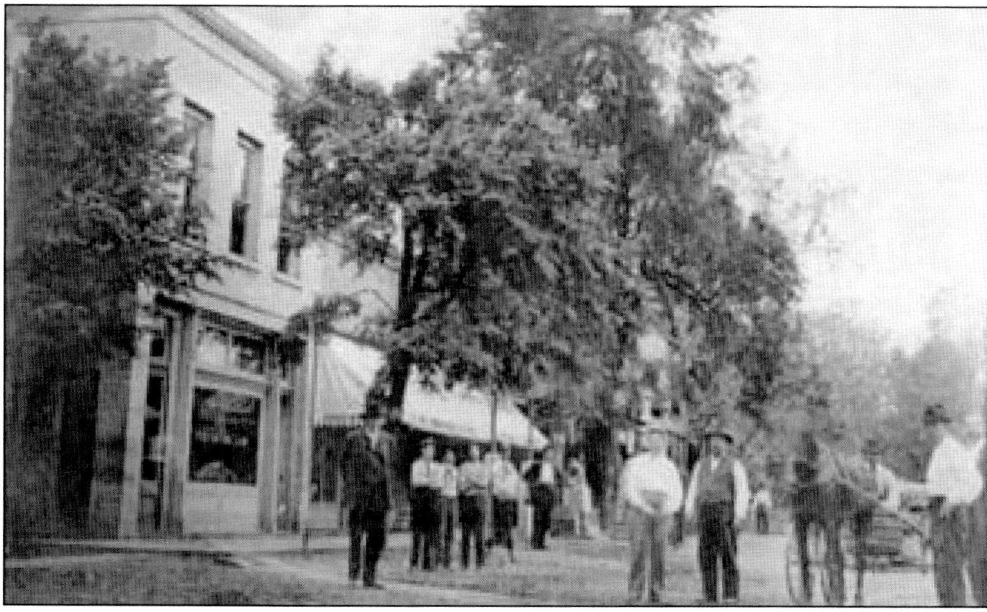

This is the west side of the Ripley Square, c. 1909. The building on the left is First National Bank. The building later became the Peoples Bank with the office of Fred B. Smith upstairs, the founder of Peoples Bank in 1925. Next-door is C.W. Phyfer and Company Drug Store, which later became Nelms Drug Store, and then Tate's Drug Store. The streets of Ripley remained unpaved until the mid-1930s.

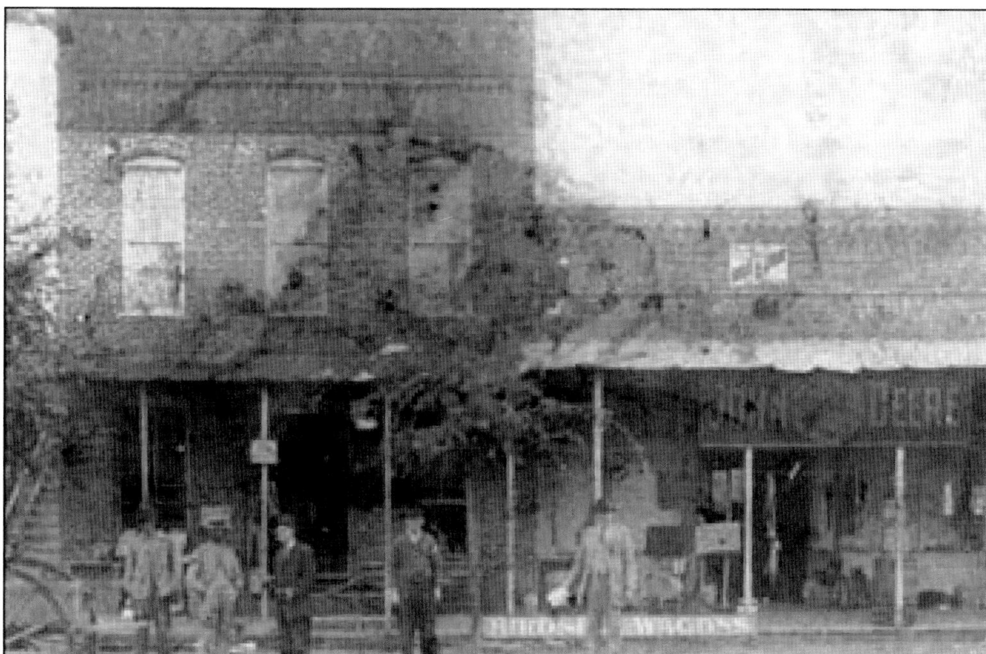

Known as the A.G. Barnett Store, this view is of the south side of the square and the eastern corner. The stairway on the left later gave way to an indoor stairway on the right hand side of the building. This had to be the first John Deere sign in the county at the entrance to the store where wagons and farm equipment were sold.

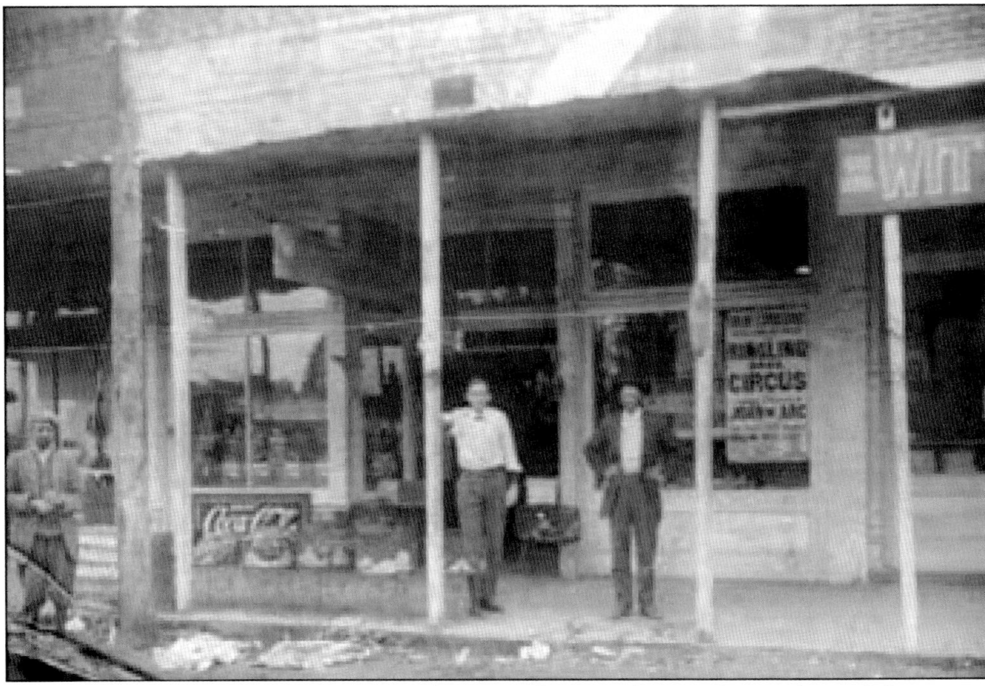

The Robert McCord Grocery as seen in this 1910 photograph was taken in front of the grocery that was located on the south side of the square. The Coca-Cola sign and the Ringling Bros. Circus advertisements were positive signs of posterity in Tippah County.

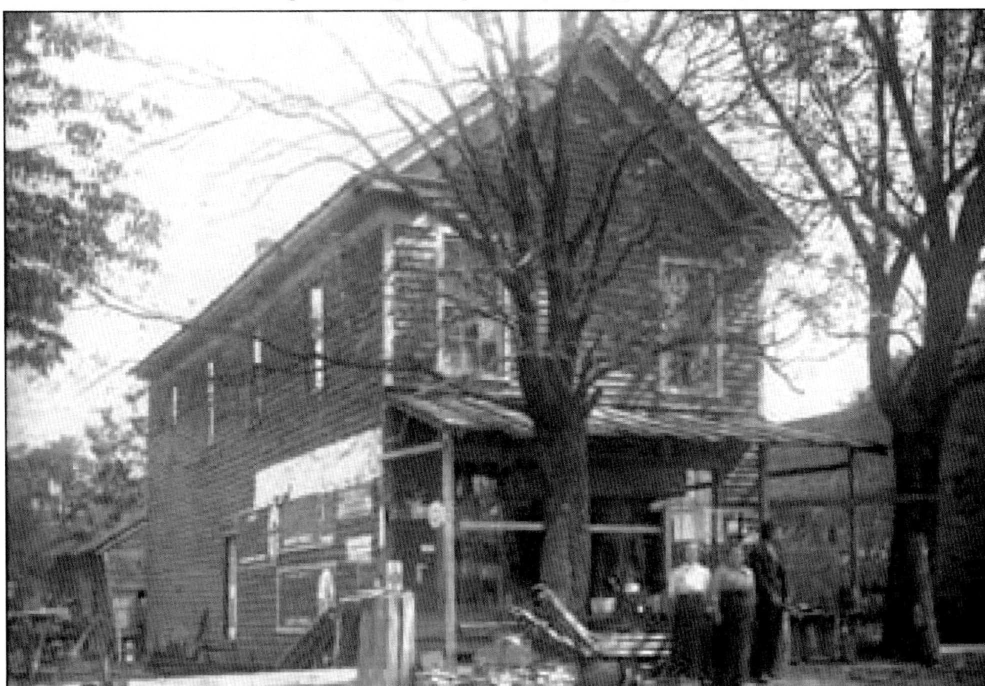

This is the Joe Moran Store that was located somewhere on the north side of the square in Ripley. This picture was taken in the 1890s and shows farm equipment for sale.

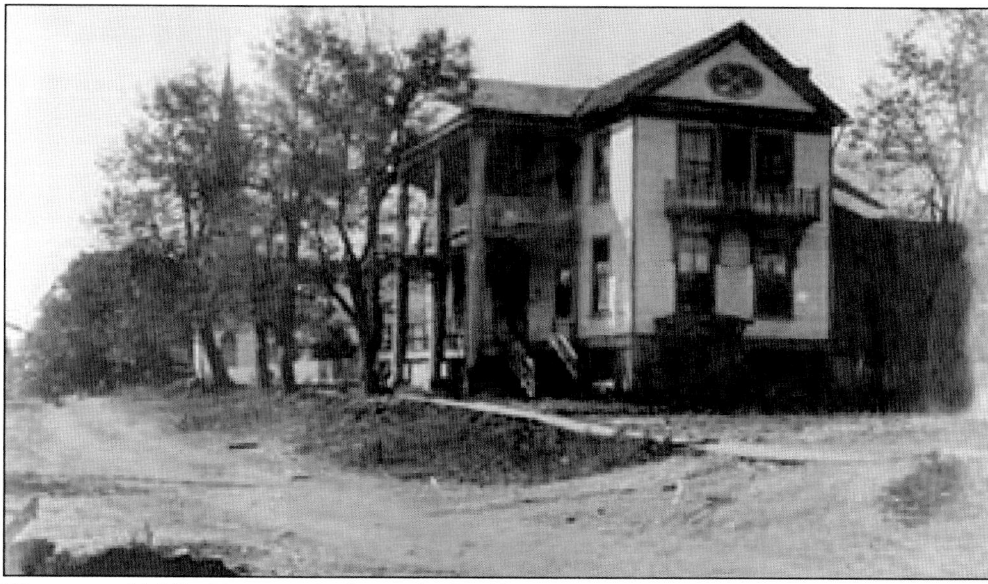

The original Miller Tavern, which was built of logs, was one of the first structures in Ripley in the late 1830s. It was built the founder of Ripley Methodist Church, C.P. Miller. In 1844, the large Greek Revival part of the building was added facing Main Street. The tavern was located just south of Walnut Street on the west side of Main. Miller's Tavern later became known as the Brown House and then McDonald's Hotel and remained until it was torn down to make way for the Ripley Hotel that was built in 1926.

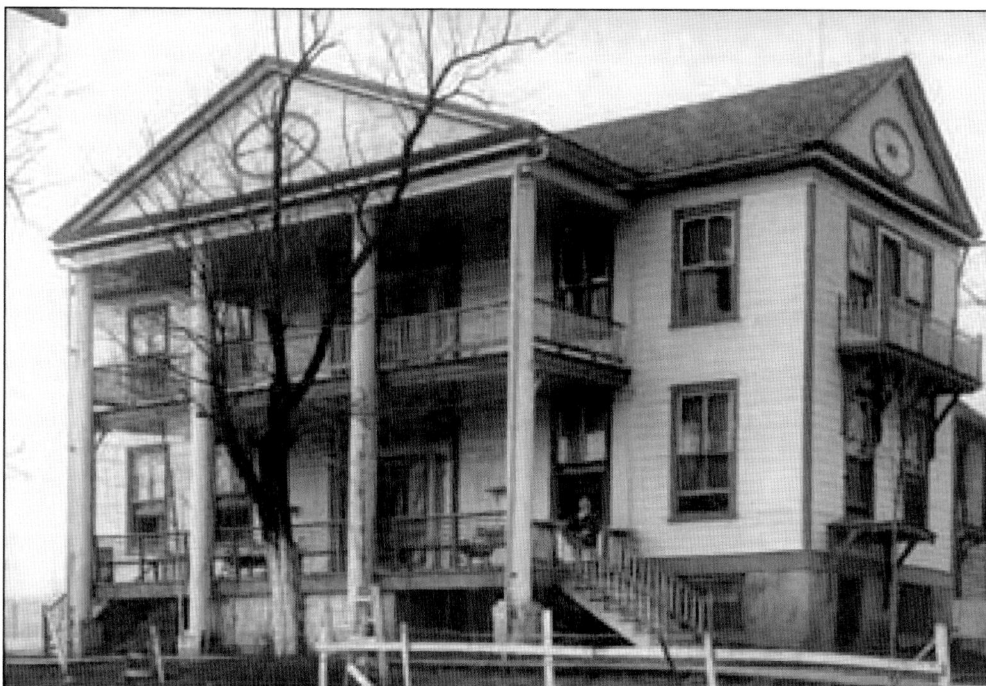

This began as C.P. Miller's Tavern and later became the Brown House and McDonald Hotel that was located on South Main Street in Ripley. This building was torn down in order to build the Ripley Hotel in 1926.

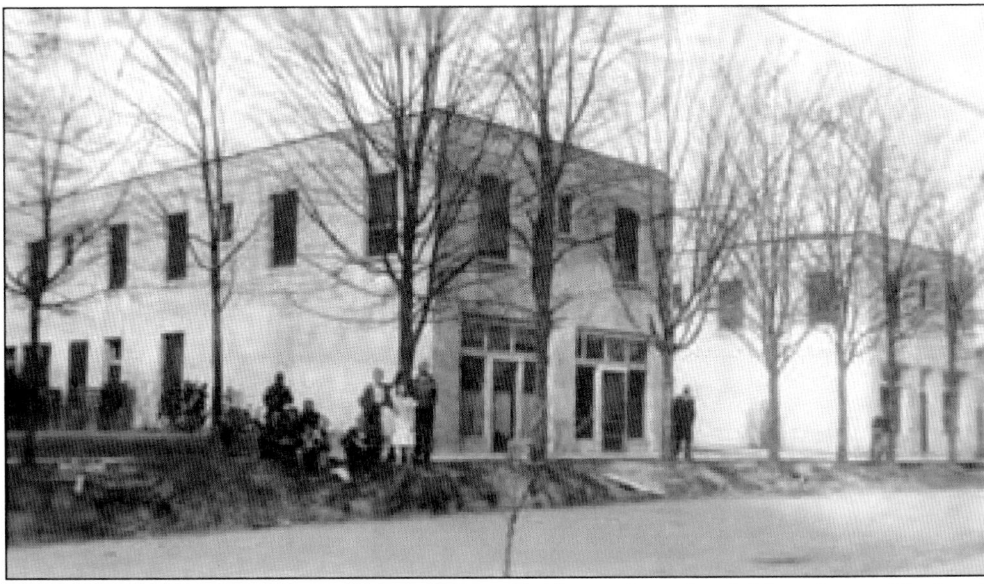

The Ripley Hotel is shown in this photograph and looks north on South Main Street. The hotel, built in 1926, was very much a part of Ripley with a banquet room and a restaurant located inside. Just one block from the square and less than a block from the railroad depot, the hotel was in a comfortable location for business.

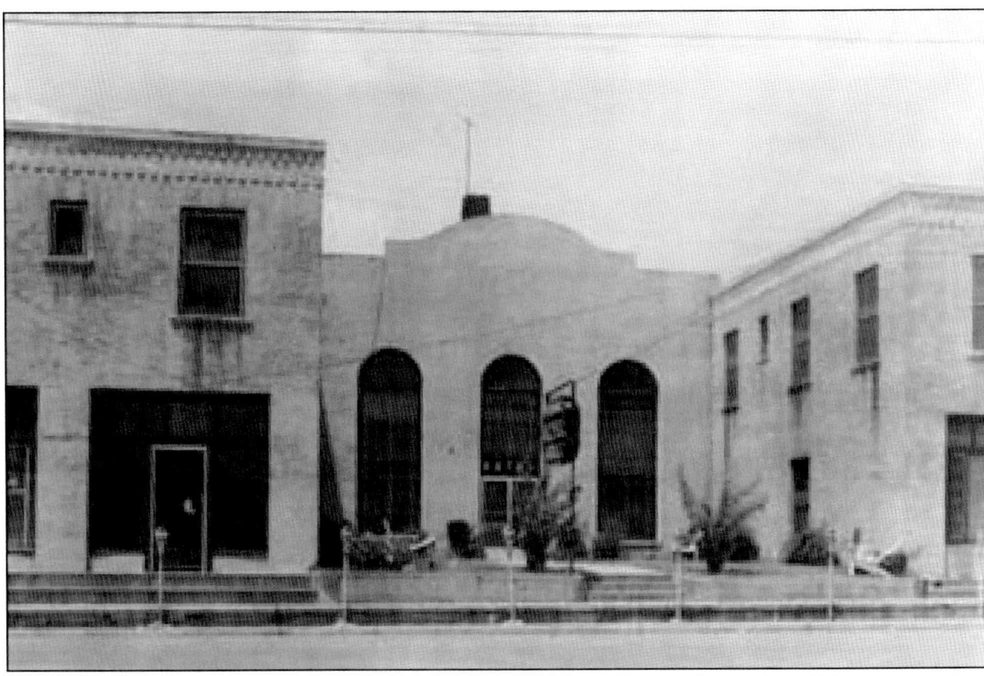

In 1926, Troy Craig built the Ripley Hotel on South Main Street. Rev. C.P. Miller built Ripley's first lodging house, the Tavern, on the same site in 1836. The original Tavern was built of logs. A much larger addition was constructed in 1844 and stood until 1926. It stood on South Main Street, north of the First United Methodist Church.

The Ripley Hotel had good help and a vegetable garden located next to it. Those pictured in the garden are Jim Pate, Andrew Wells, and Sudie Nelms.

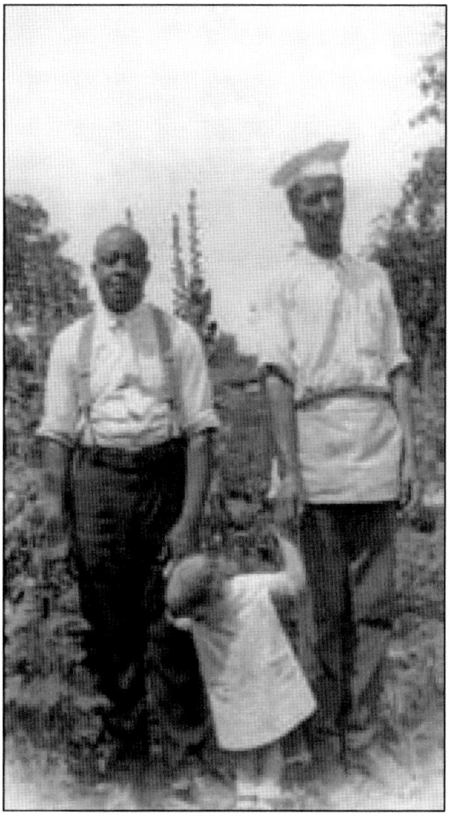

Roberson Hotel was a nice hotel that was built along the west side of the railroad on the south side of Jefferson Street. The hotel was just across the railroad from the depot and provided a great place to stay for overnight guests traveling by rail, especially traveling salesmen who would display their items for sale at the hotel.

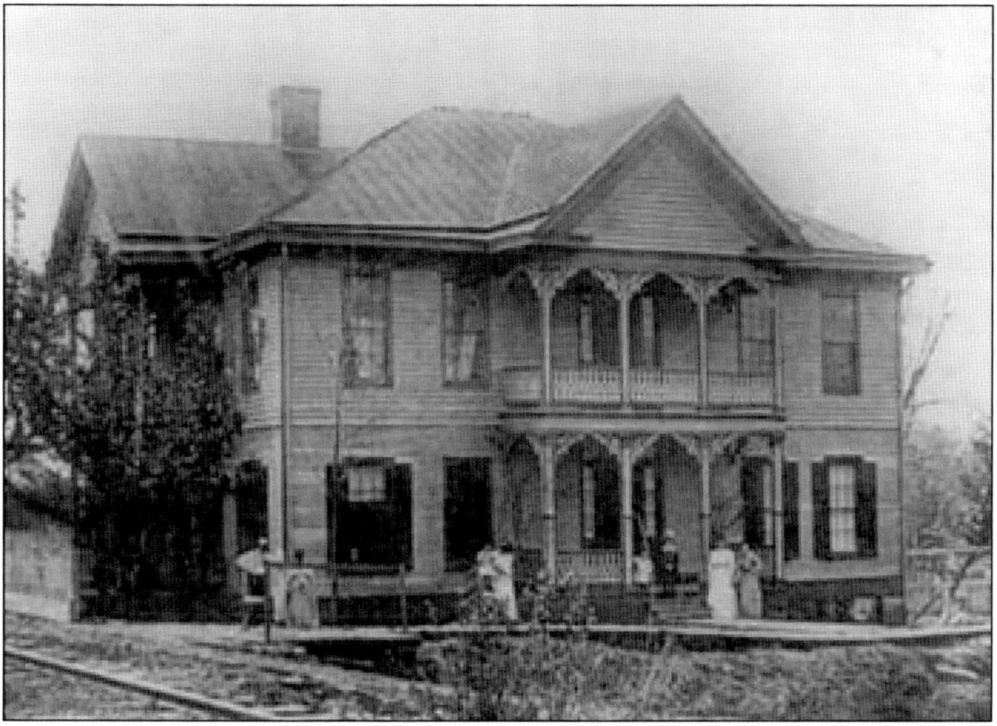

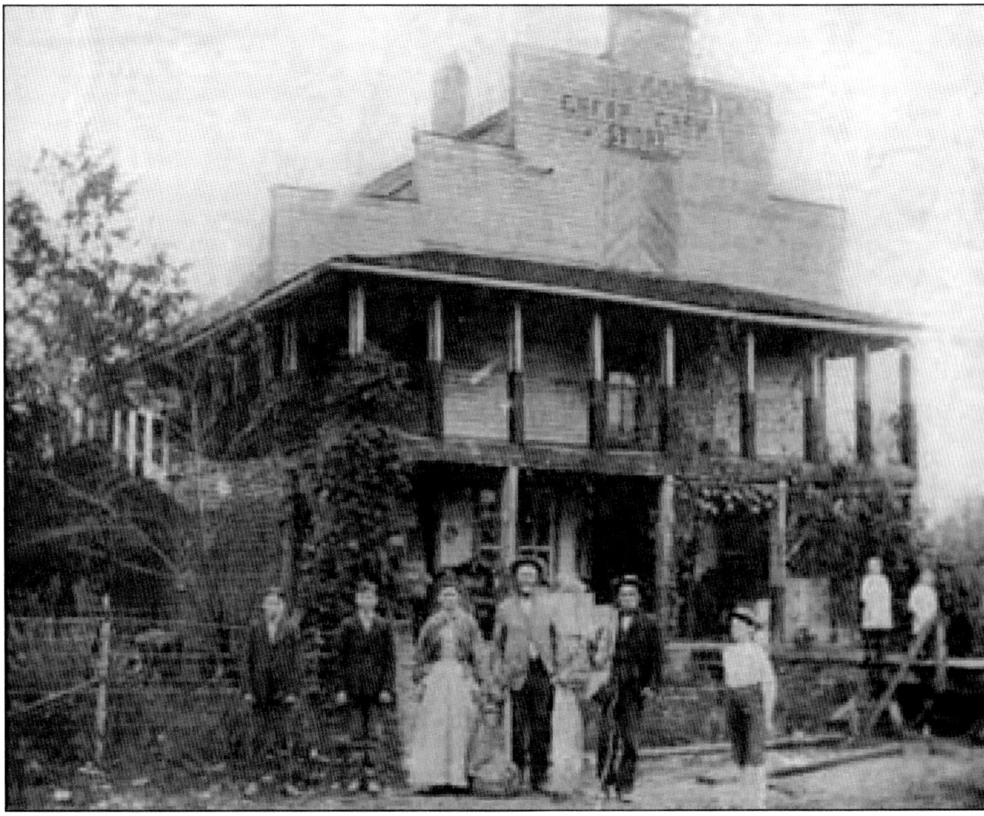

The Berry Connor Store and Hotel was located in Falkner and served that area for many years. Known as the Cheap, Cash Store, Connor's was a large three-story building with farm animals corralled behind the fence. A step up to a walkway designated the path of entrance into the store.

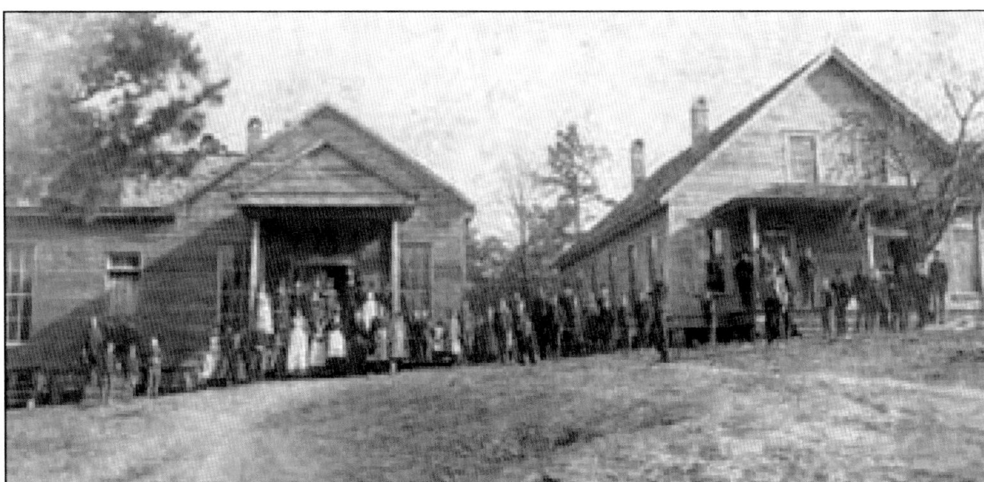

Fingers Store located just west of Falkner off of Highway 370, about one mile from the Benton County line, was a local business and store that was the center of activity in the area. This photograph was taken in the early 1900s and shows a game of baseball being played with a pitcher and a batter being seen at the left front corner of the building on the right.

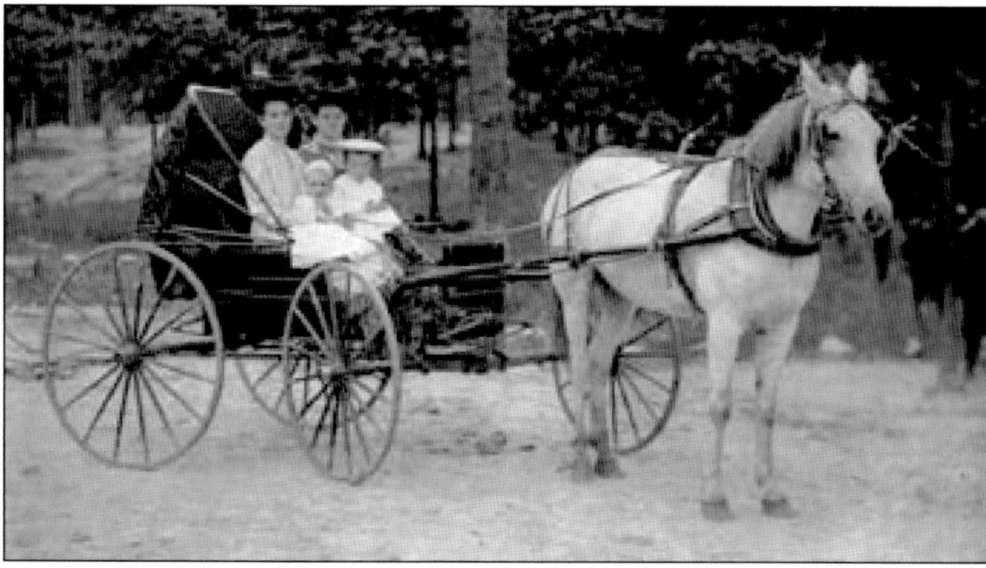

This 1904 photograph shows a horse and carriage being driven by Zora Bennett Harrison, (Helen Ray's mother). The young boy, Cecil Harrison, baby Leone Harrison, and Aunt Bloomer Garrett are also pictured.

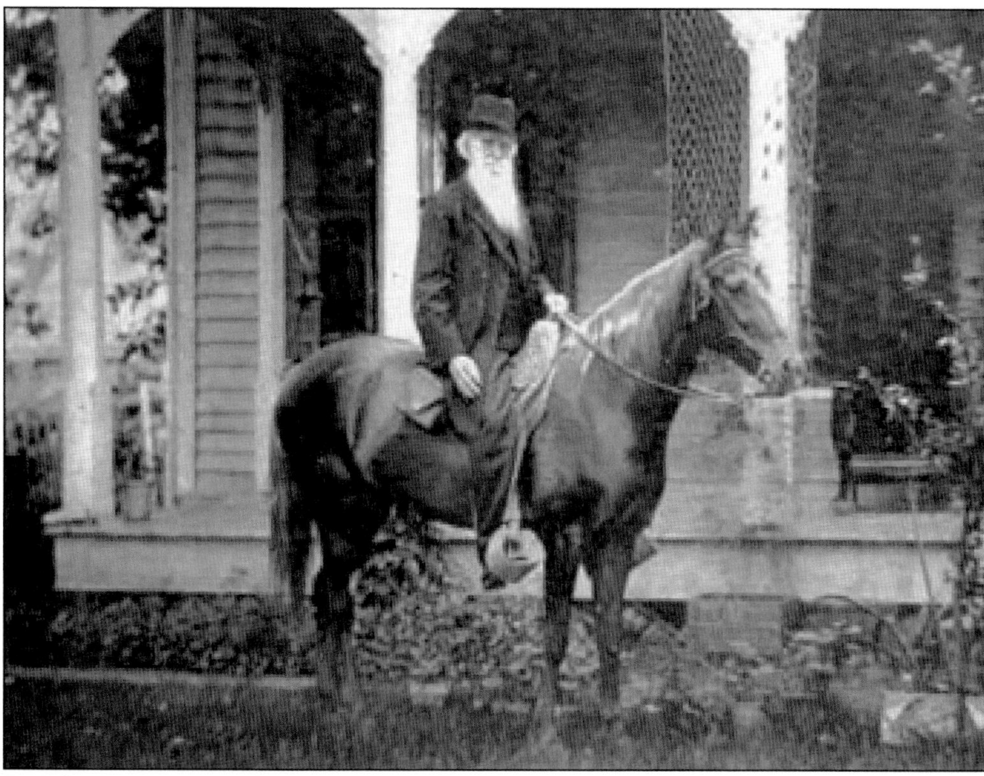

Dr. John Y. Murry was a leading doctor located in Tippah County who was the less controversial great-grandfather of William Faulkner. As the founder of one of the most prominent families in Ripley, the physician served one term in the Mississippi House of Representatives and was once the leading Mason in the State.

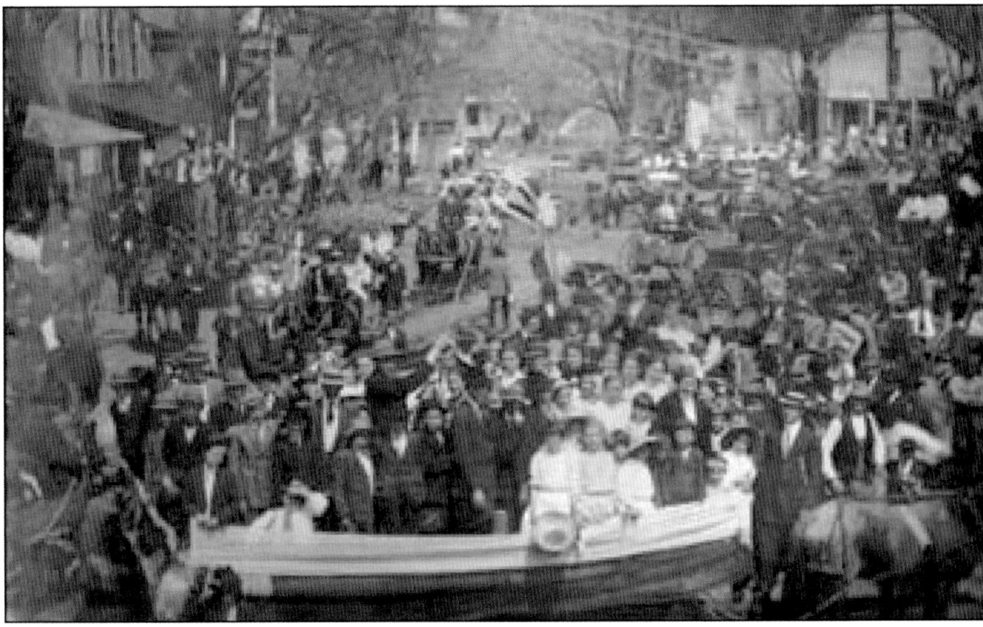

Field Day was a festival that Tippah County honored during the early 1900s. This was Ripley growing and maturing. Looking north on Main Street, hundreds of people were parading in their wagons decorated with flowers and banners.

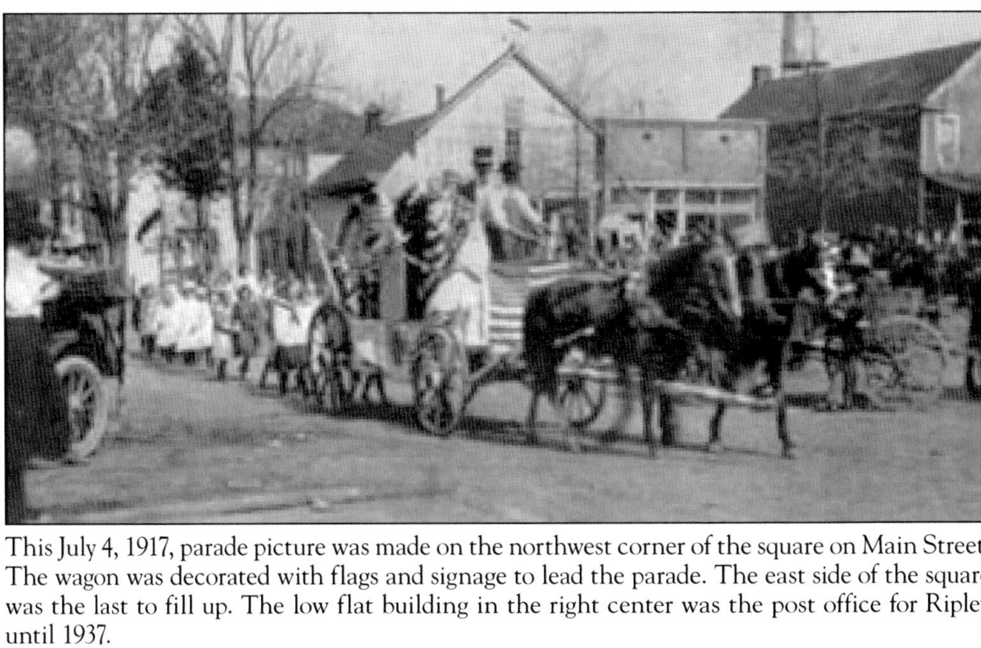

This July 4, 1917, parade picture was made on the northwest corner of the square on Main Street. The wagon was decorated with flags and signage to lead the parade. The east side of the square was the last to fill up. The low flat building in the right center was the post office for Ripley until 1937.

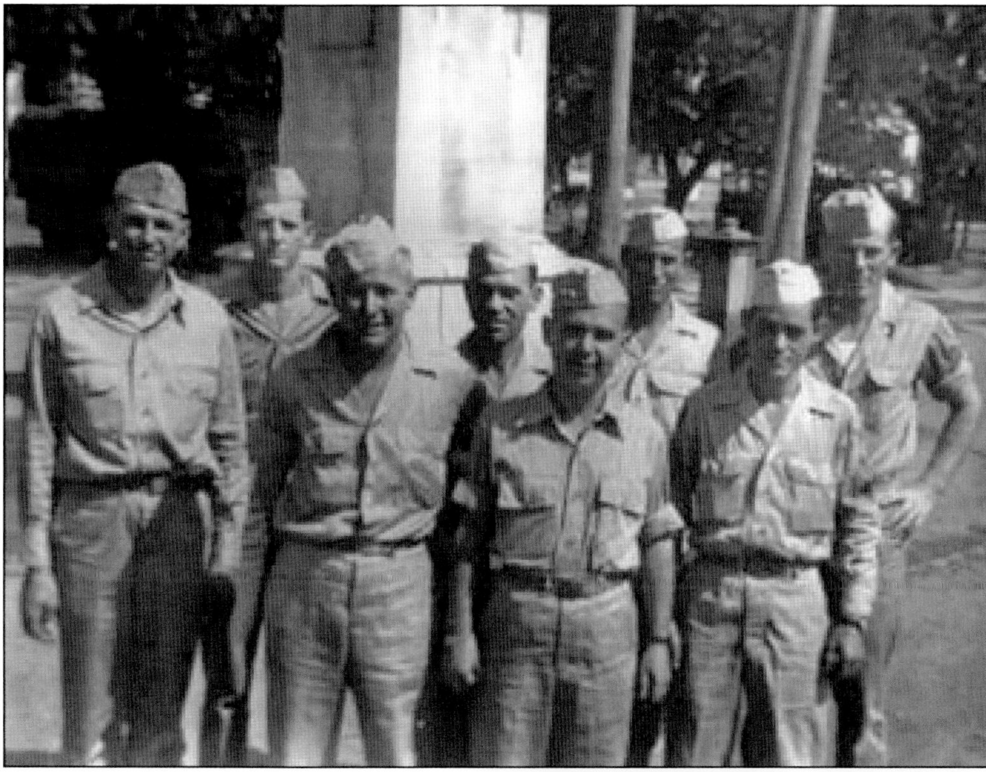

This group of Tippah County veterans got together for this picture while stationed in India during the WWII timeframe. Those pictured are, from left to right, Howard Martin, J.M. Smith, Frank Humphrey, Strawberry Stanford, Bill Gurney, Wayne Moffitt, Dr. David Ellis, and Bud Farrow.

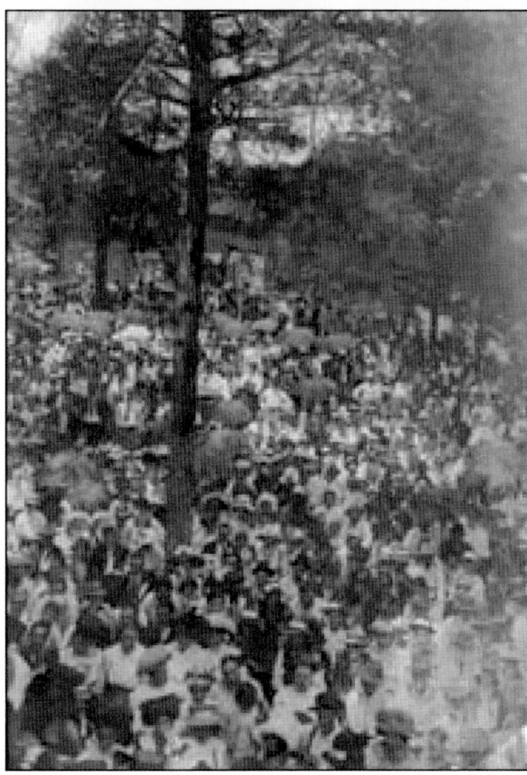

Known as Vardaman Day in Ripley in 1911, the vast crowd congregated in the yard of the J.A. Gurney's home, now the site of McBride Funeral Home. James K. Vardaman was a Mississippi House of Representative, a governor, and a US Senator. W.C. Gurney was present at this rally and sold $14 worth of lemonade that day. He said this was the first time in his 16 years that he had more than 25¢ cash at any one time.

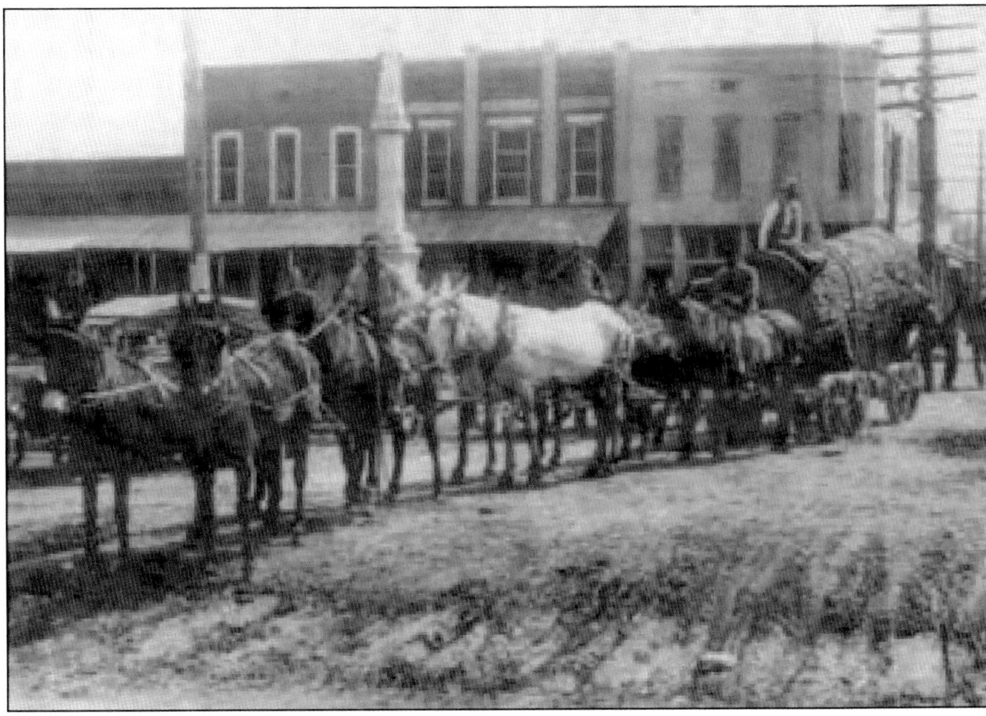

An early 1900s photograph of a large poplar tree said to be the largest at the time from Tippah County. The photograph shows an eight mule team pulling a large eight wheel wagon that was loaded down with an almost eight feet in diameter log. This is the first of three different loads of poplar sold by Richard Clark of Clarysville. This was being shipped to Hoosier Veneer Company in Ladogo, Indiana. The cut was almost 14 feet long and eight feet in diameter with more than 1,544 feet of lumber and weighed almost seven tons. The second load was six feet in diameter hauled by eight steers, and four mules brought the third load. Market price was at least $200 and after making furniture with, it sold for several thousand dollars.

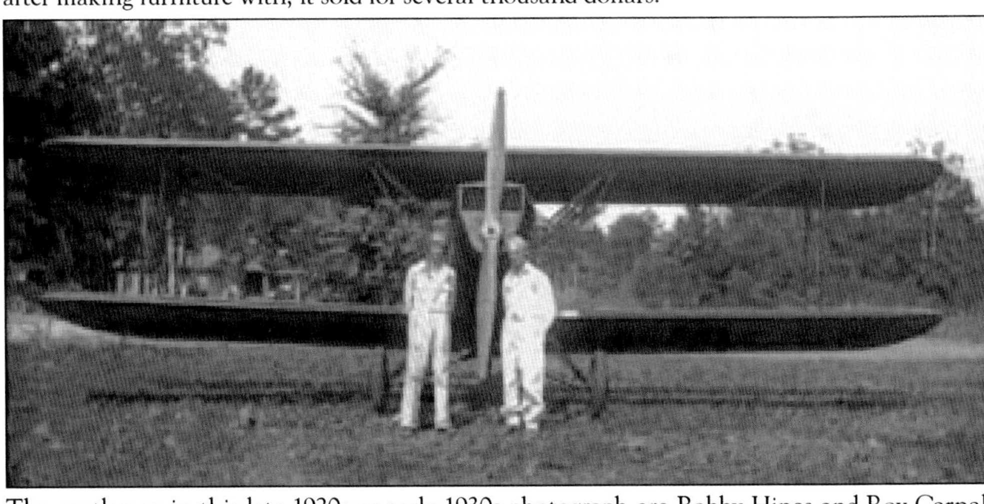

The gentlemen in this late 1920s or early 1930s photograph are Bobby Hines and Roy Carnal. The biplane made several landings and takeoffs in Tippah County before any airport was built. Bobby Hines and his brother Tommy Hines were killed on July 13, 1930, when their plane crashed while trying to clear some trees at the end of the landing strip.

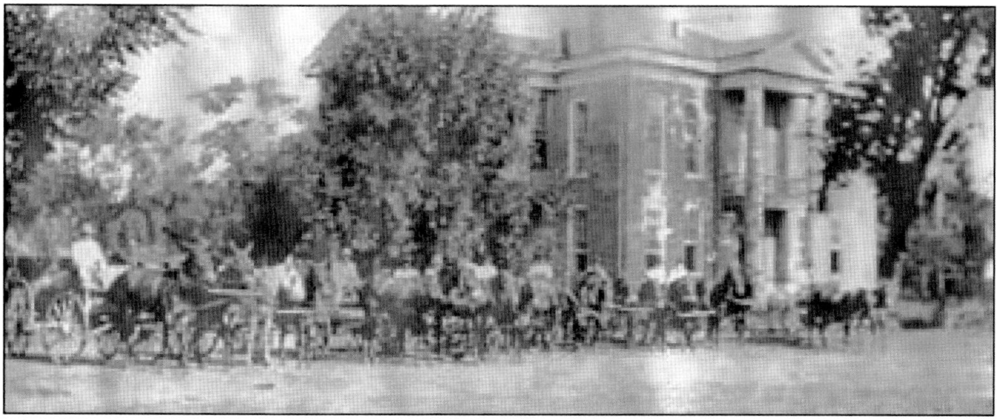

This 1918 photograph shows a northwest side view of the courthouse with a row of wagons that had just unloaded their wheat crop.

Please consider replacing image #138 with a higher-quality image.

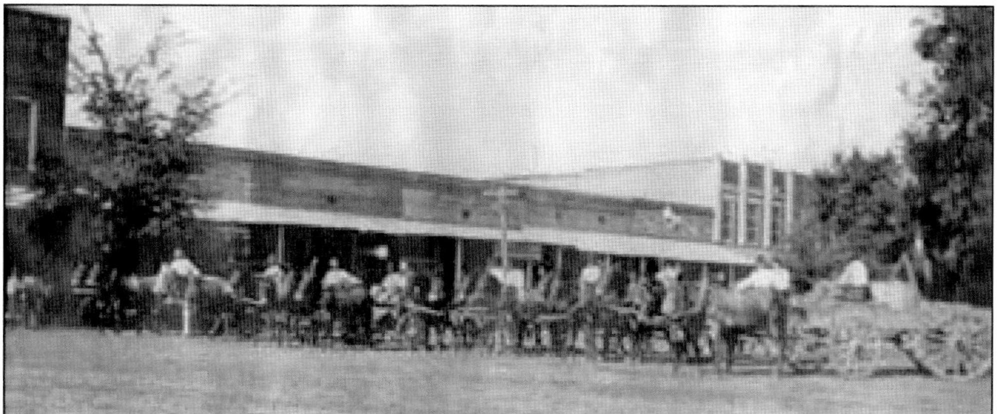

This is the same photograph taken from the opposite corner of the square or the Southeast corner. The same mules and wagons were driven to the opposite side of the square for another picture showing the businesses in the background. These buildings were built in the 1906 timeframe.

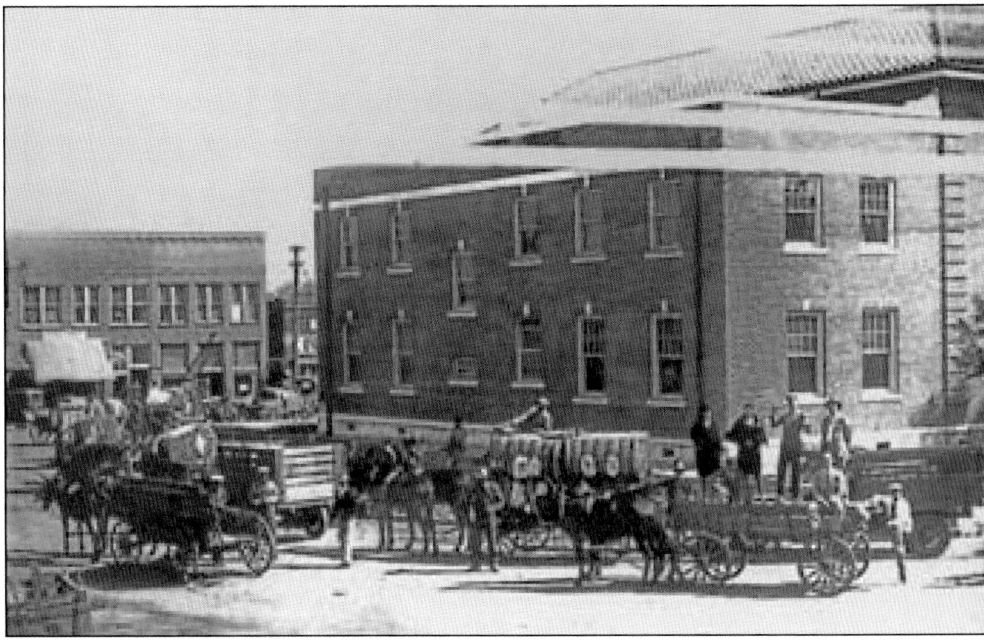

Cotton wagons circled the courthouse in the early 1930s after bringing their week's work to the county seat. Streets were still unpaved and the traffic was going clockwise rather than counter clockwise as in today's traffic.

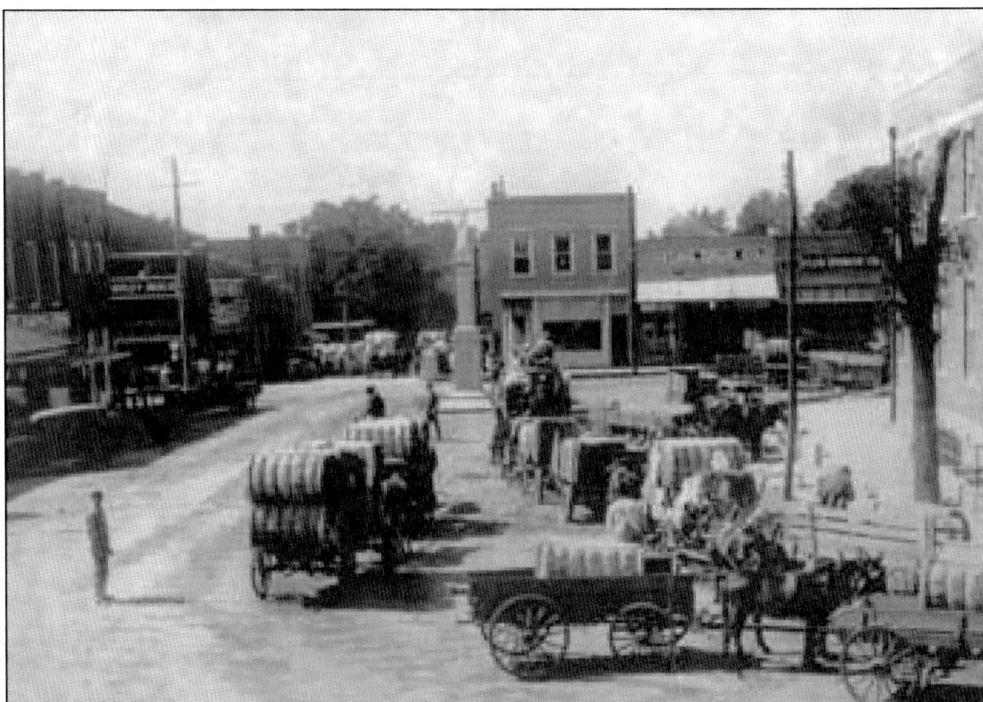

This 1920 photograph of the south side of the square shows cotton wagons and mules all around the square. The Confederate Monument was placed in the center of the roadway, but was later damaged by a truck in 1970 and moved to the east side of the courthouse.

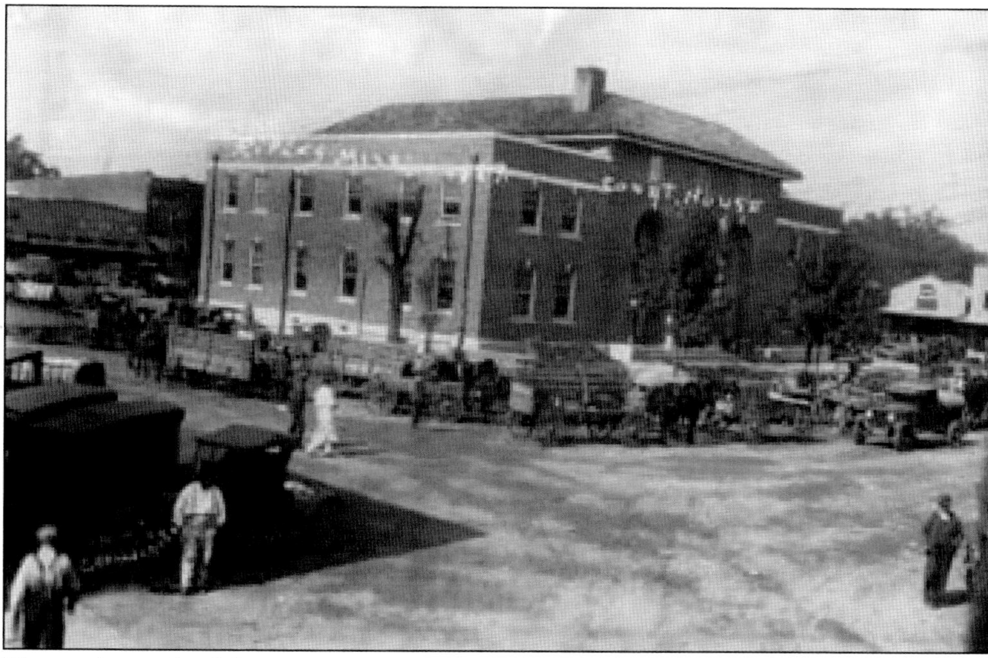

The northern side of the courthouse was lined with cotton wagons and mules that had already been loaded off of their cargo. The old cars and trucks show the time period of 1929. The courthouse had just been enlarged and renovated in 1928 and was the center of activity.

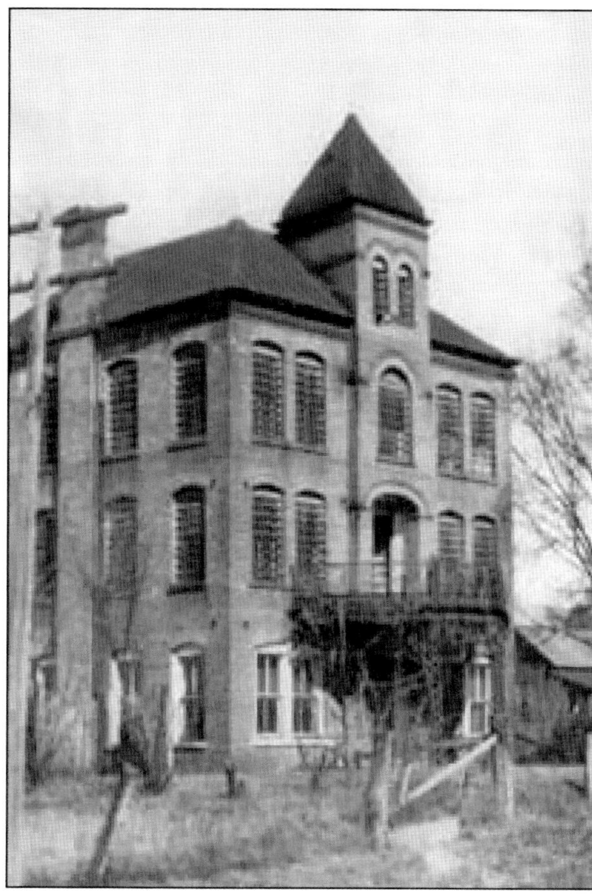

This is the old Tippah County Jail as it stood in 1920 near the railroad tracks in Ripley. This building was torn down in order to build the new jail in 1938. The ground floor housed the jailer and his family and the prisoners were on the other two floors. This building had many structural flaws that developed over time.

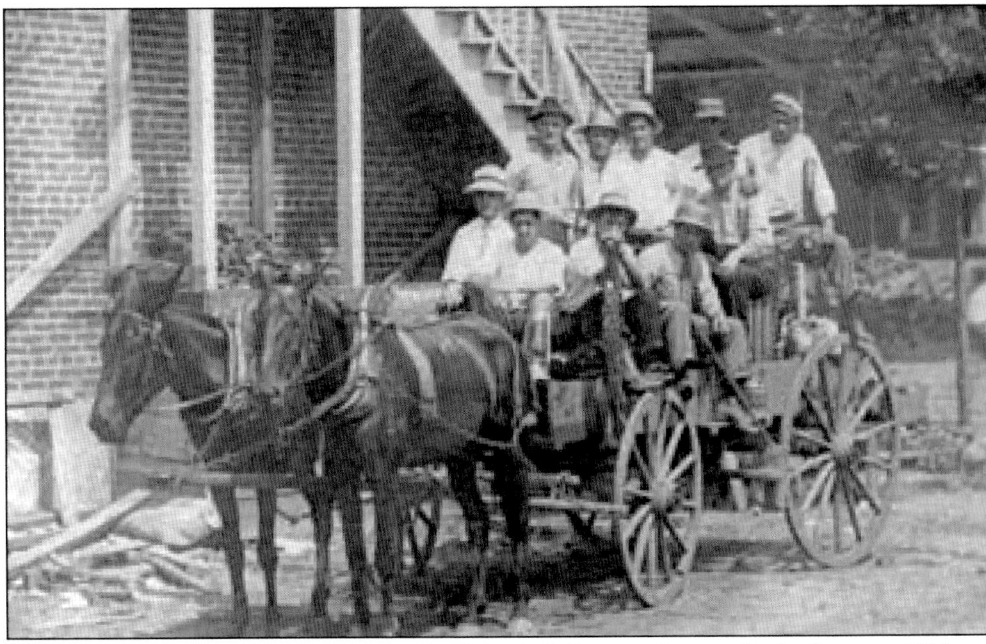

This photograph was taken on the east side of the A.G. Barnett Store in Ripley between 1910 and 1915. This photograph looking northwest from southeast side of the square features Lee Alvis, Bob McCarley, Roger Smith, Cliff Giles, S.M. Barnett, Roy Barnett, Clyde Pitner, Tom Murry, Tom Cox, and Leonard Smith.

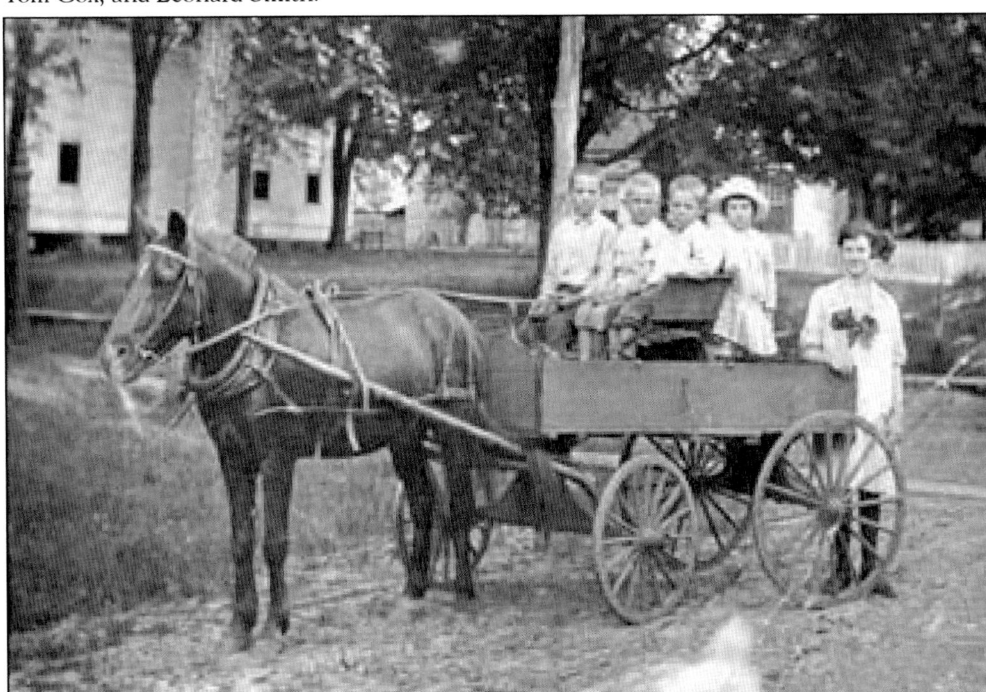

Pictured near downtown Ripley around 1914 are Robert Hines, Vance Murry, Lee Hines, Ada Hines, and Sarah Hines. T.C. Hines made the wagon in the photograph and the building on the left is the old First Baptist Church.

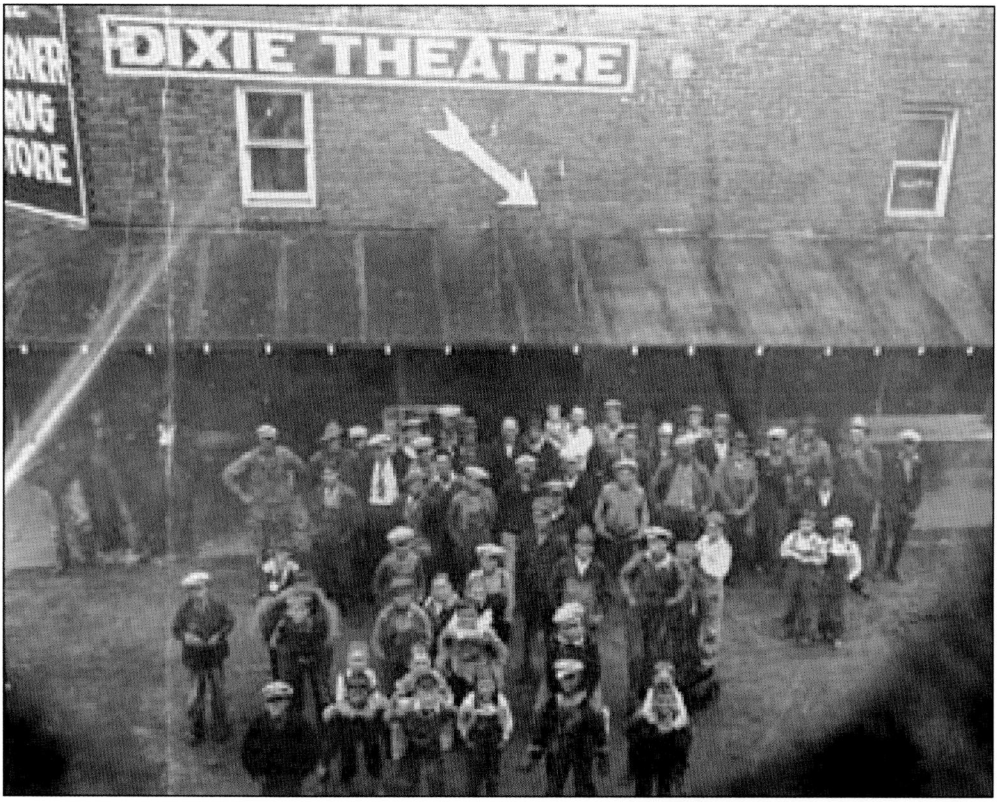

This Dixie Theater picture was taken from the rooftop of a building on the south side of the courthouse square in the late 1920s. Notice the tam hats that the young men were wearing. The time is probably a Saturday afternoon.

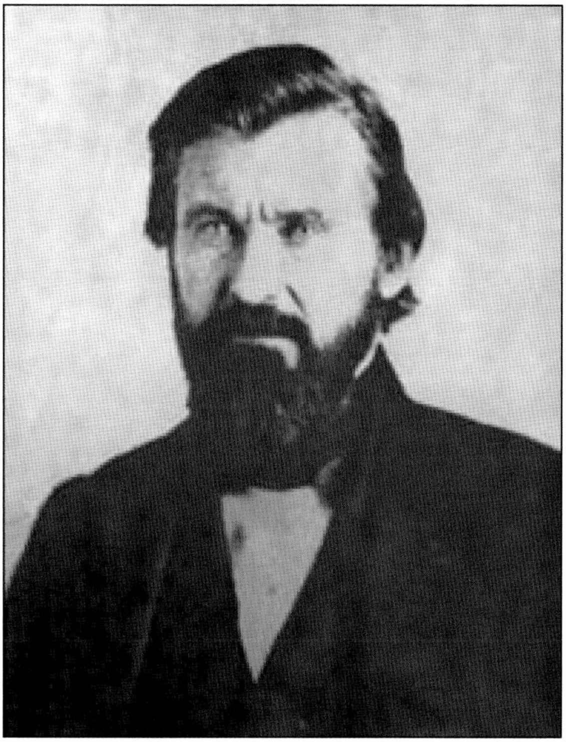

This photograph is of Orlando Davis in the mid-1860s. Orlando Davis was known as a lawyer that once tutored Thomas C. Hindman before he left Tippah County for Arkansas. Davis also wrote a diary during the Civil War, telling about Ripley and Tippah County's participation in the battles and visits by the Union Army.

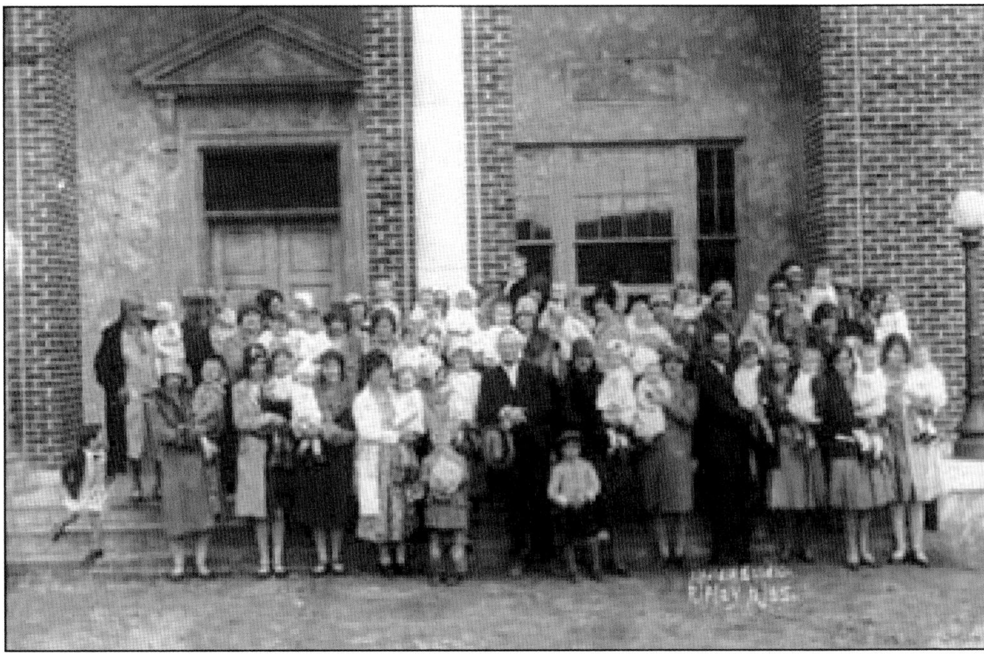

A countywide baby contest was held in the 1928 to 1929 timeframe. Mauldin Studios, a local photographer who did business in Tippah County for almost fifty years, took the picture on the courthouse steps.

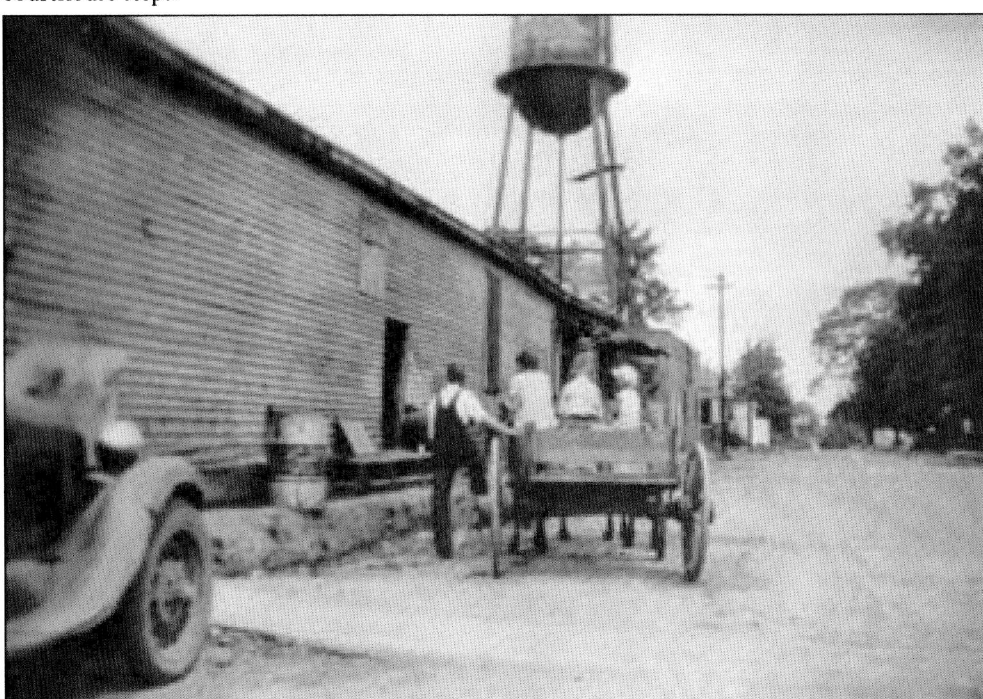

This is an early 1920s photograph of Commerce Street just north of the Ripley Square. The old wagon is on the dirt streets just outside the store of M.L. Finger and Son. The old Ripley water tank is seen in the background.

The massive ice storm of 1951 is still considered one of the worst in history. This street scene is located on South Main Street in Ripley with the steps to the high school located on the right side of the picture. Major tree damage and power outages consumed the area for more than a week.

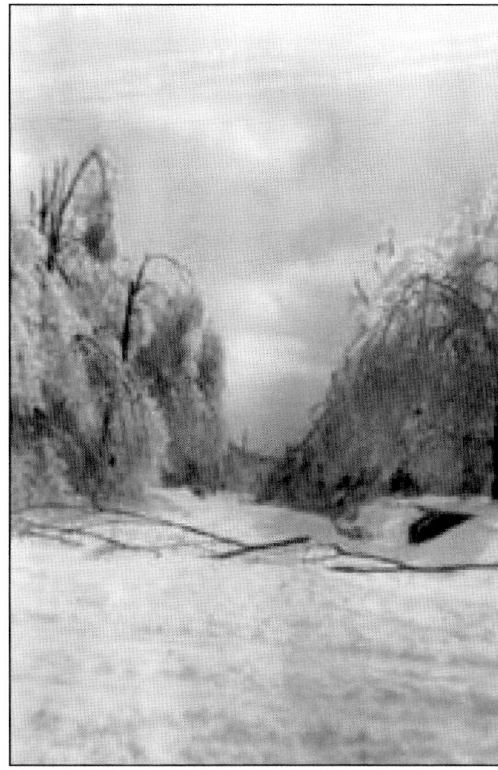

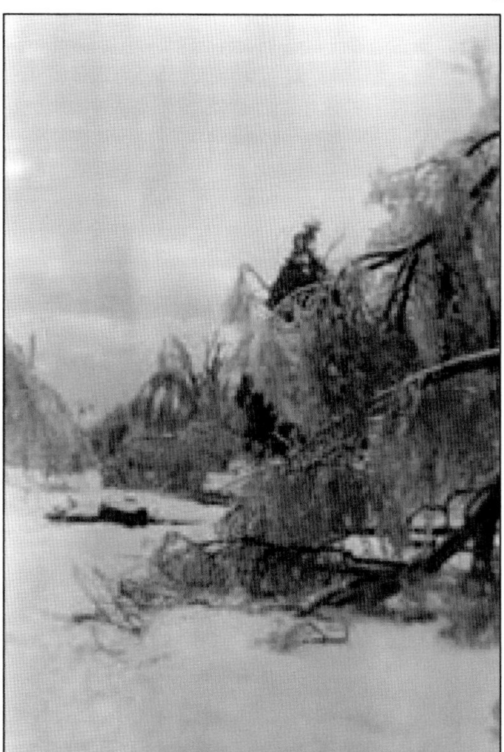

Tree and street damage can be seen looking south on South Main Street. The cold air stayed in our area for almost two weeks and kept the ice from melting.

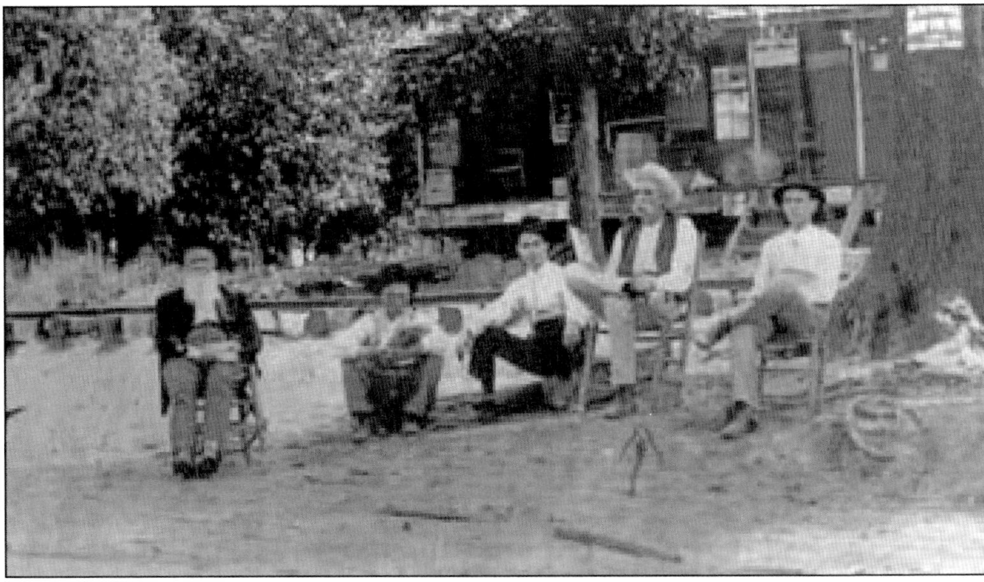

This photograph is of the 1906 Walnut mayor and board. Pictured here are, from left to right, ? Lafayette (mayor), C.A. Rowland (hotel manager), Luther Luna (depot agent), Edward Cossitt (postmaster), and ? Jones (jockey).

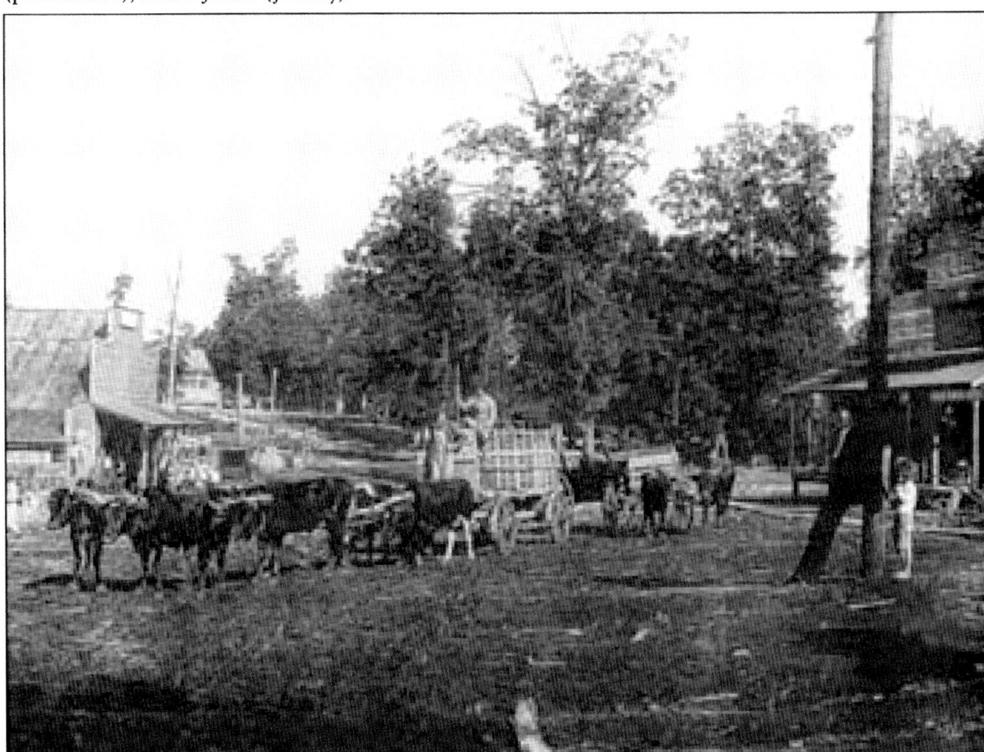

This photograph is of Chalybeate in the early 1900s. Clemmer Store is on the right and McBride and Wiggs Store is on the left. Chalybeate School is in the back view. Oscar Ray is pictured with the oxen and wagon and Percy Hollis is leaning by the pole. The young boy is Howard Giles.

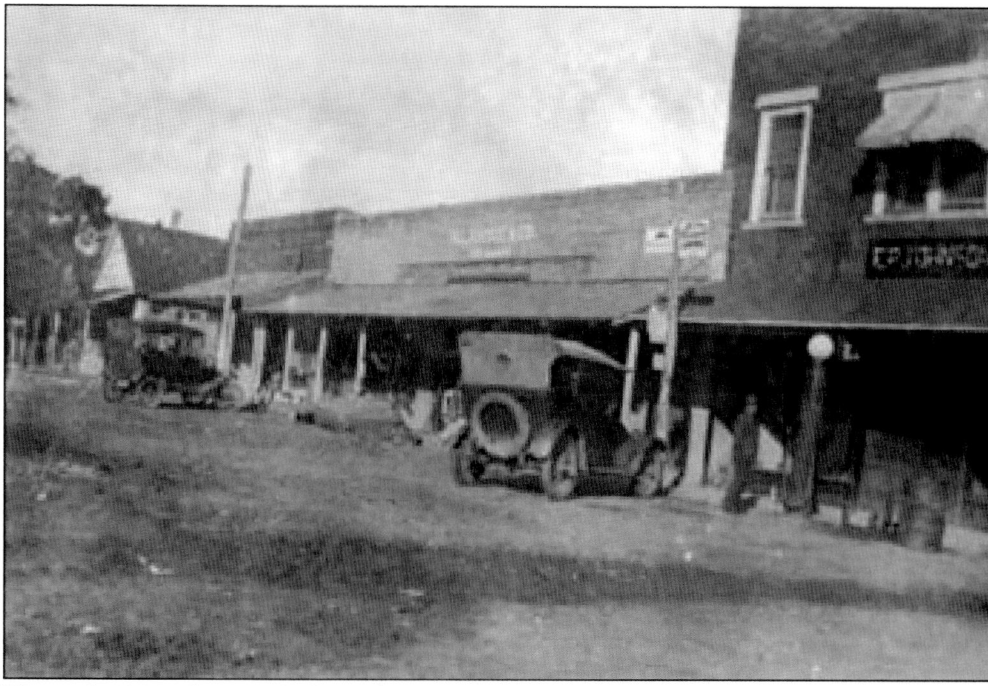

This early 1900s photograph shows the R.L. Nance & Company Hardware Store, which also sold furniture and caskets. R.L. Nance was also a funeral home for Tippah Countians. Notice the old gasoline pump in front of the gentleman at the right. The old *Southern Sentinel* office is located to the far left of the picture.

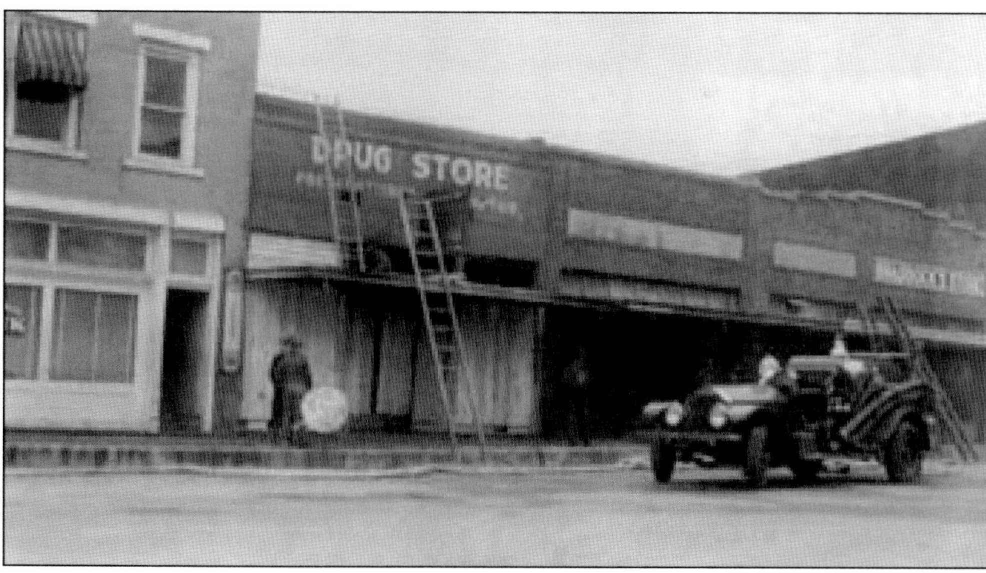

This 1940 view shows the west side of the square at the scene of a fire at Tate Drug Company. The old fire truck was used to protect the building and its surroundings during the fire.

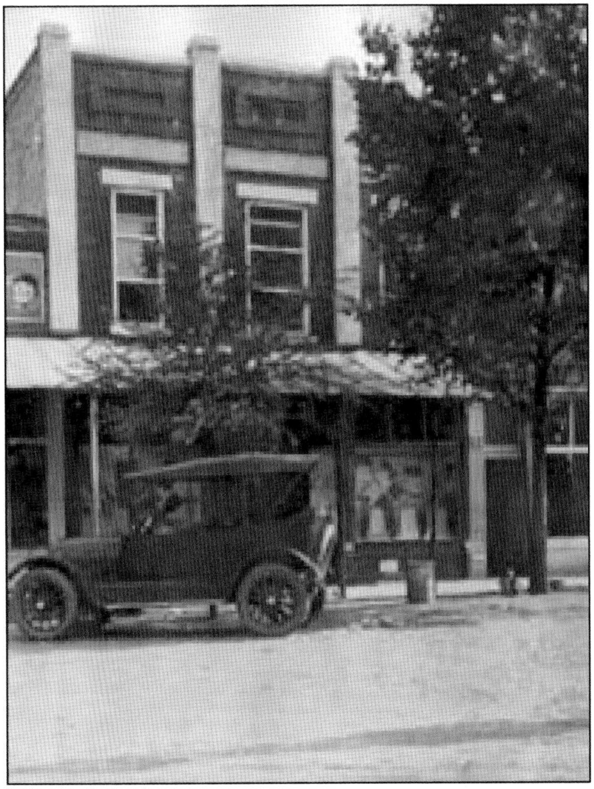

This is Brown's Store at the location of the present-day Akins and Adams Law Firm in 1920, located on the south side of Ripley Square.

This is an inside view of Brown's Store in 1920, which shows display cases and dry goods for sale. The floors were of wood slats and the ceiling was a tongue and groove slat ceiling.

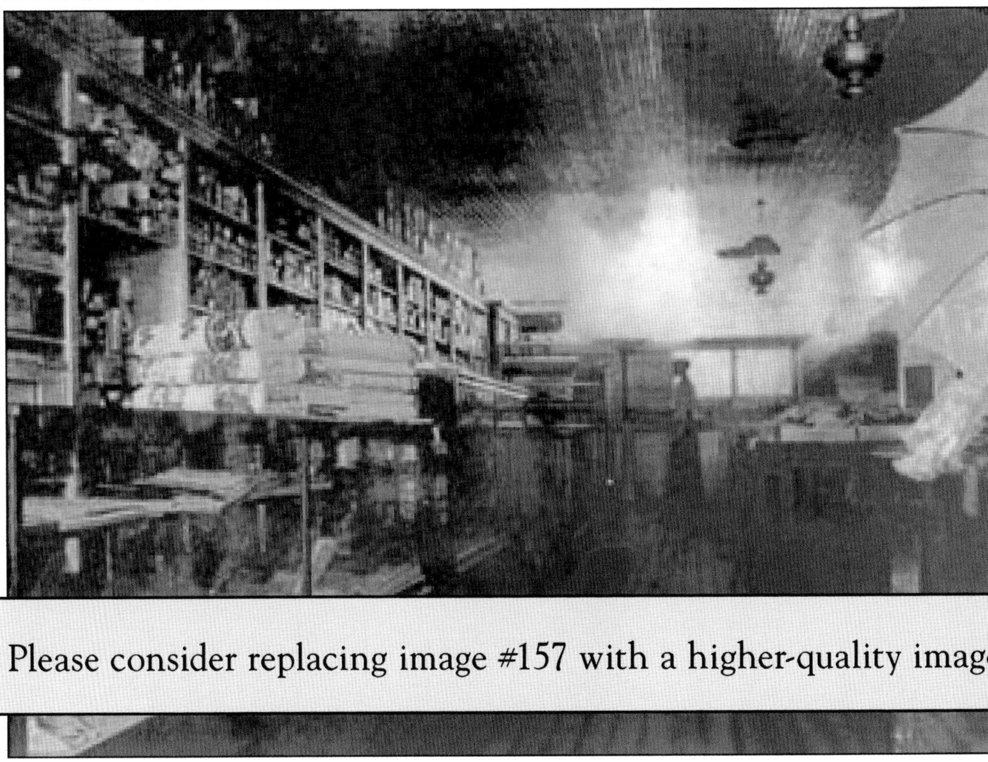

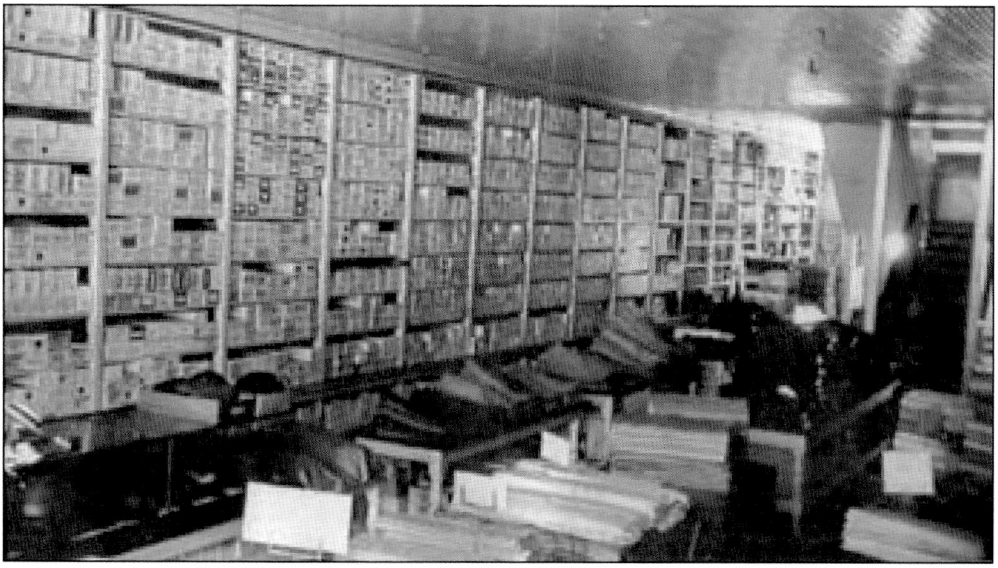

Brown's Store sold clothing and textiles in this early 1900s photograph. Fabrics are stored down the middle rows and the stairs in back lead to the upstairs area of the store.

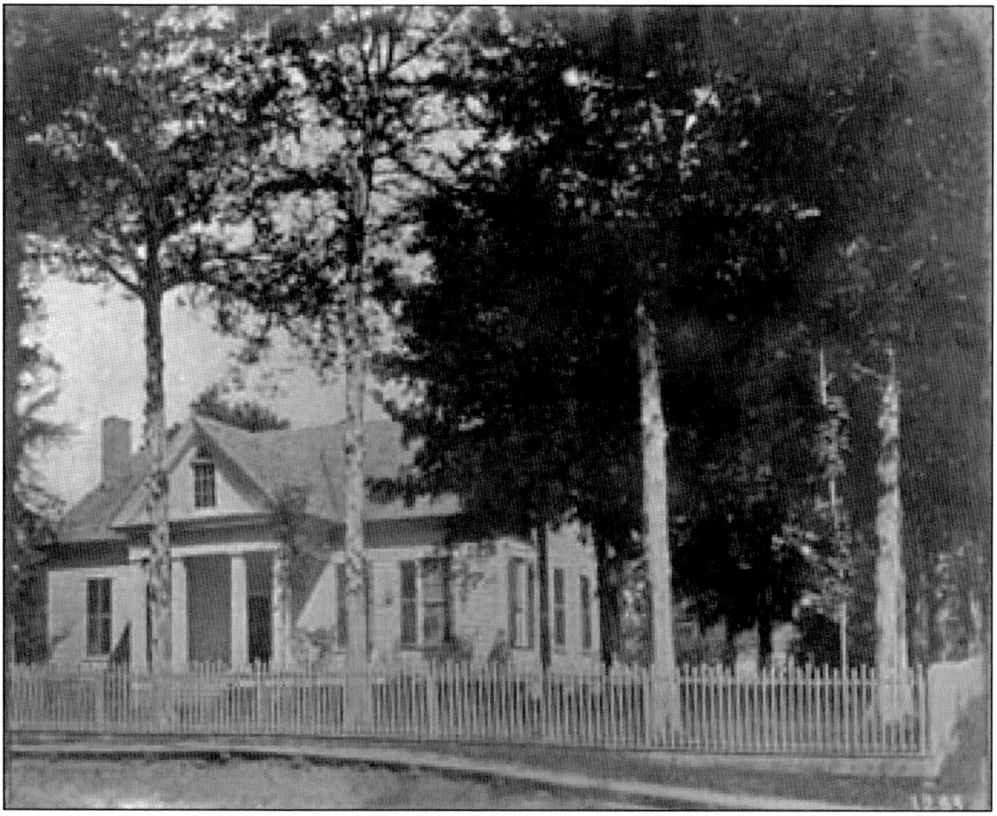

This is the Murry Falkner and Enoch Richey home that was situated on the corner of Cooper and Jackson Streets facing Jackson Street.

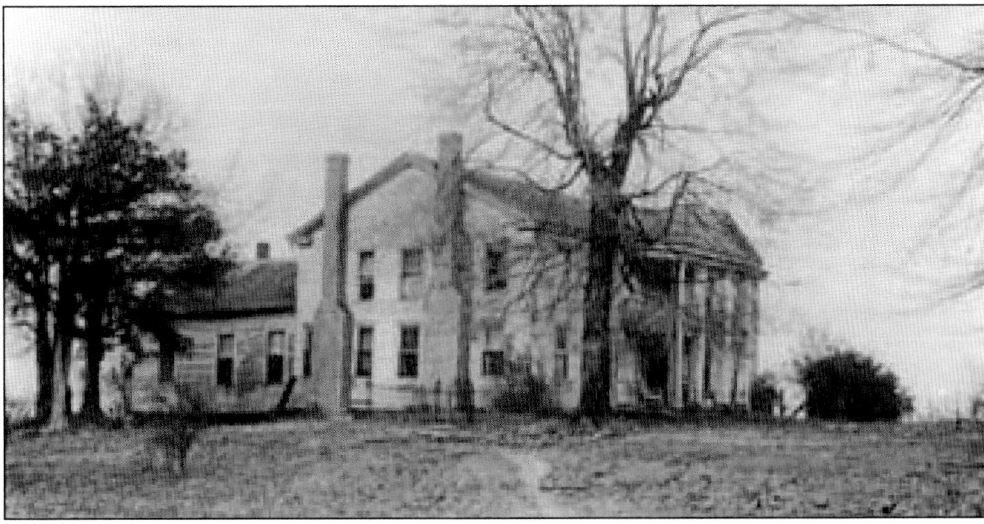

The old Hindman/Booker home was built in 1842 and was destroyed by a fire in 1938. Constructed out of logs covered with weatherboarding, the house stood on land east of Ripley. Hindman, a native of Knoxville, Tennessee, had been a Colonel in the War of 1812. He was later an Indian Agent under Andrew Jackson and assisted in the removal of the Cherokee Indians to Indian Territory. His son, Thomas C. Hindman Jr., was to become a major general in the Confederate Army. This photograph was taken in 1936.

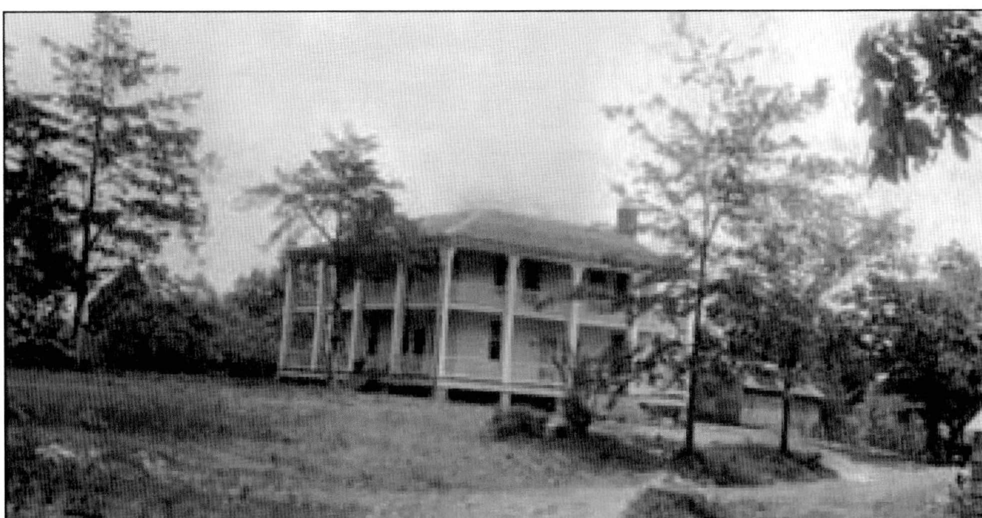

Known as the Rucker Place and located in Ruckersville, this house was built by Capt. A.C. Rucker, a noted Civil War leader of a regiment from Tippah County. This photograph was taken in 1936.

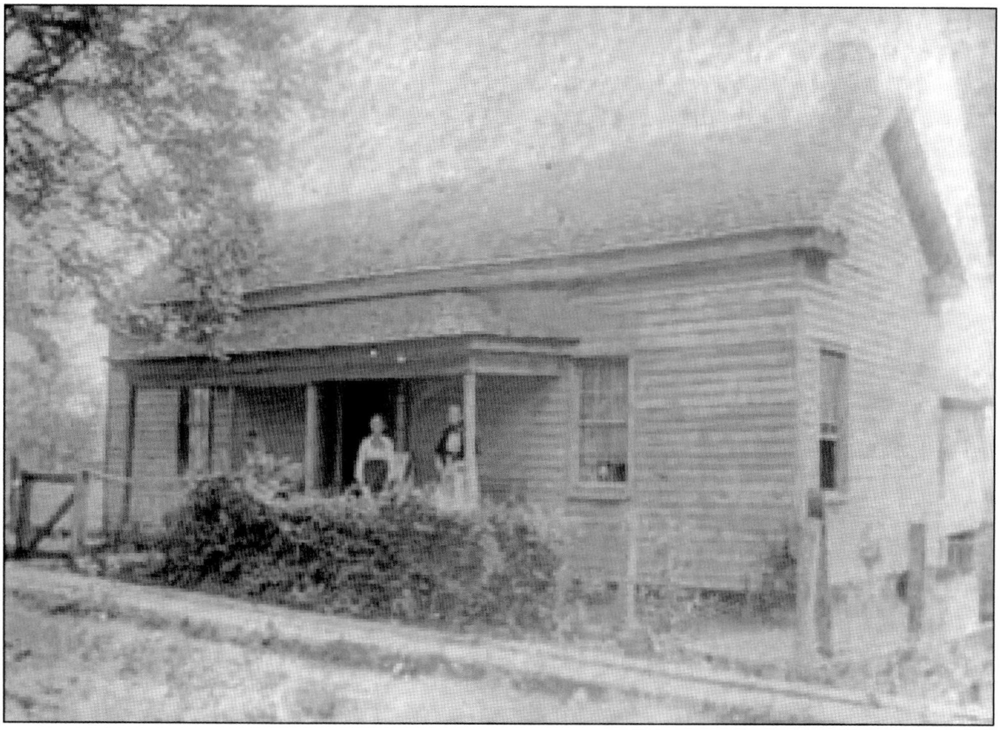

The James A. Gurney home was situated on the current site of McBride Funeral Home in Ripley.

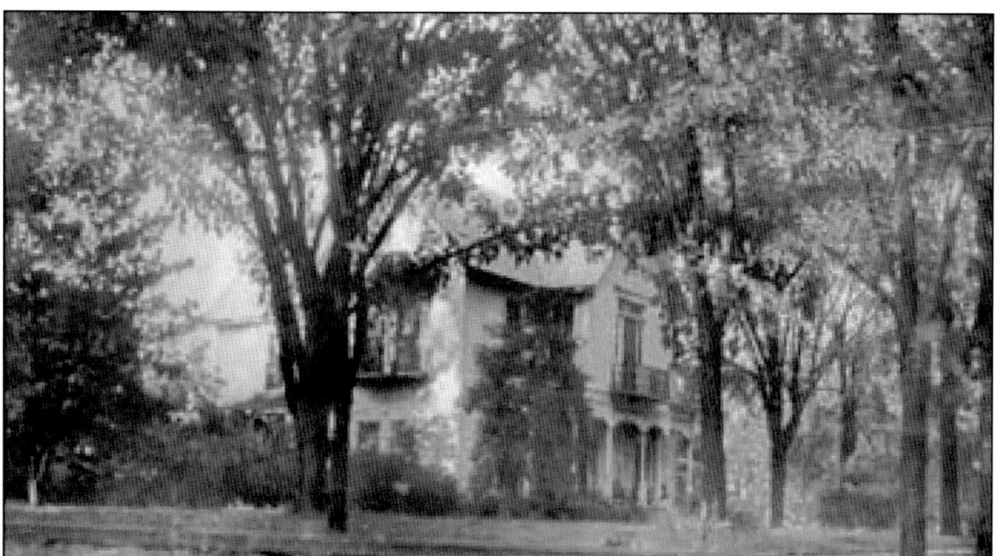

The William Hines House was also known to be the Dr. N.G. Carter home, or the home of the daughter of W.C. Falkner, Willie Falkner Carter. This house was located on Cooper Street just east of the railroad in Ripley. This photograph was taken around 1939.

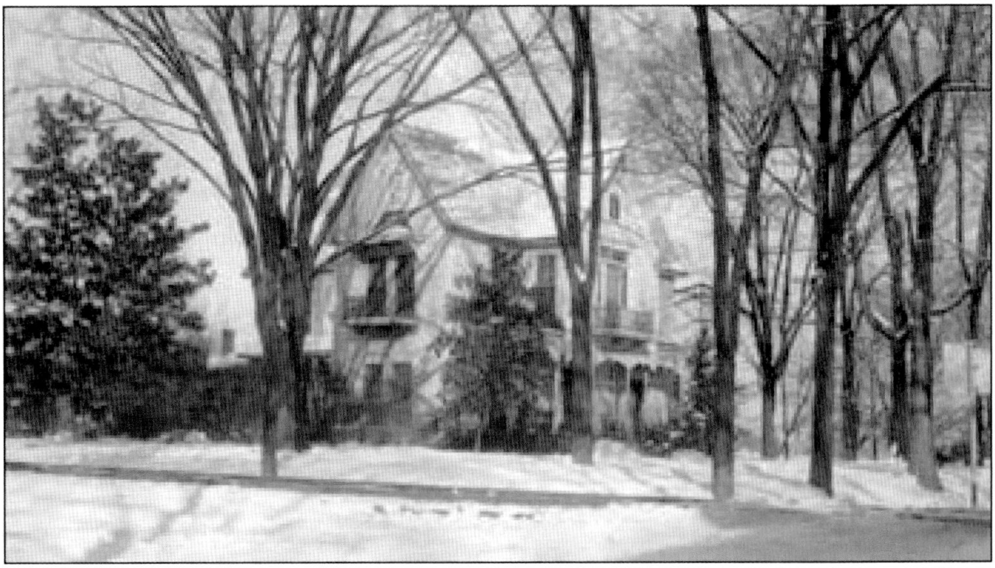

This is a winter photograph of Dr. Carter's house near the railroad tracks. Col. W.C. Falkner built the house for his daughter Willie Medora as a wedding present. This is a winter scene of the home where Col. W.C. Falkner died on November 6, 1889, after being shot by R.J. Thurmond the previous day. The home was later the home of William Hines and his wife, who was the daughter of Capt. Thomas Spight.

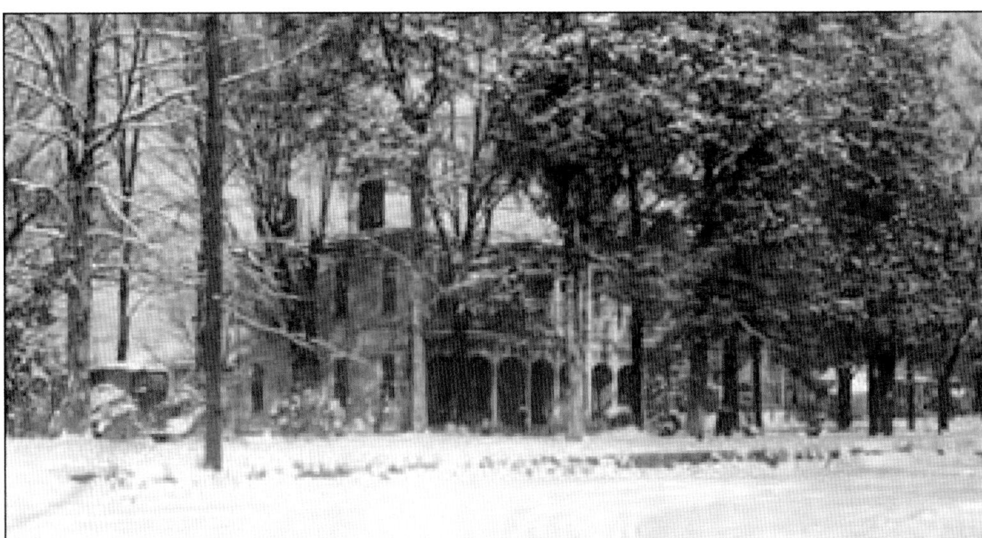

This early 1900s photograph shows the Andrew Brown Sr. home that was located on the northwest corner of Cooper Street and Jackson Street during a winter storm.

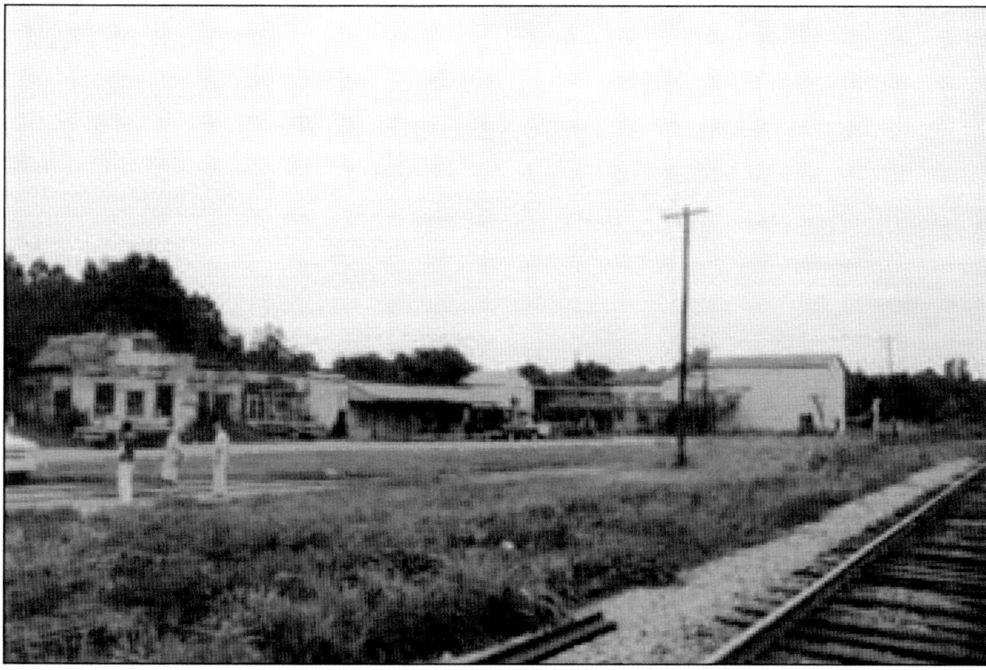

This photograph shows the row of stores and the cotton gin on the east side of the railroad tracks in Falkner, Mississippi. Most of the buildings were not being used at the time that the photograph was made and the railroad was taken up in the early 2000s.

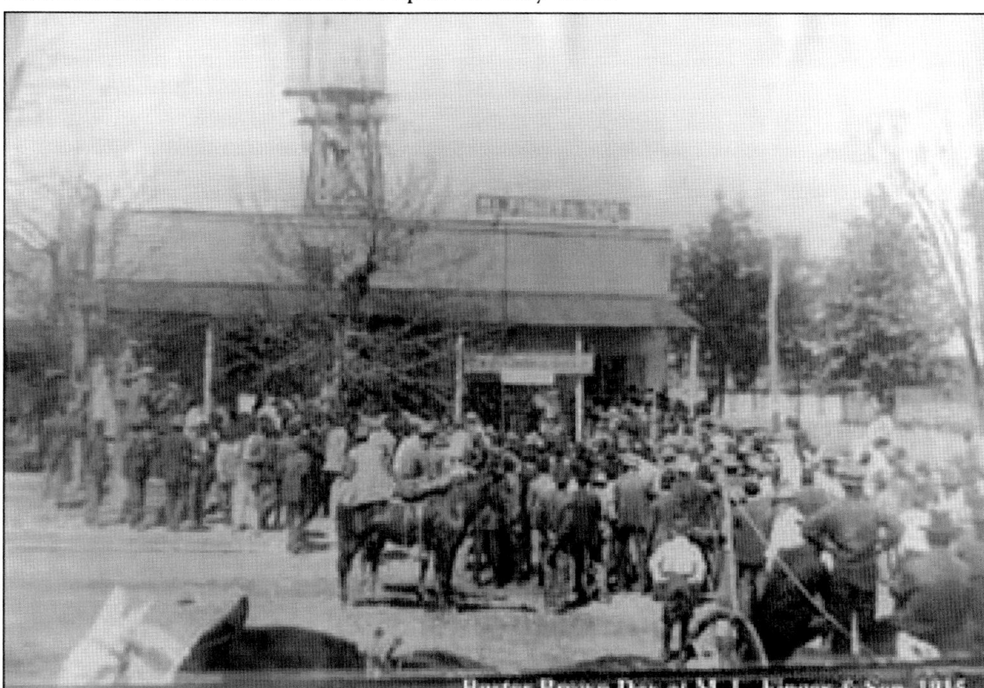

The M.L. Finger and Son Store was having their annual Buster Brown shoe day. Tippah Countians love a good event that provides great bargains, and this crowd of men was shopping hard during this day in 1915. The building was located on the northeast corner of the square.

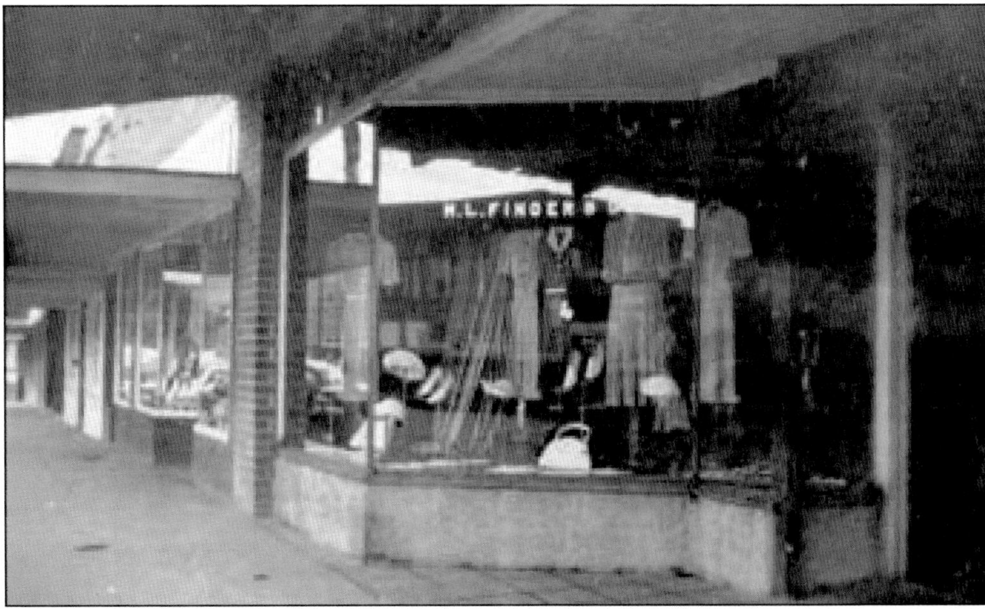

The main department store in Ripley with clothing for men, women, and children was M.L. Finger and Son. The store was located on the east end of the north side of the square.

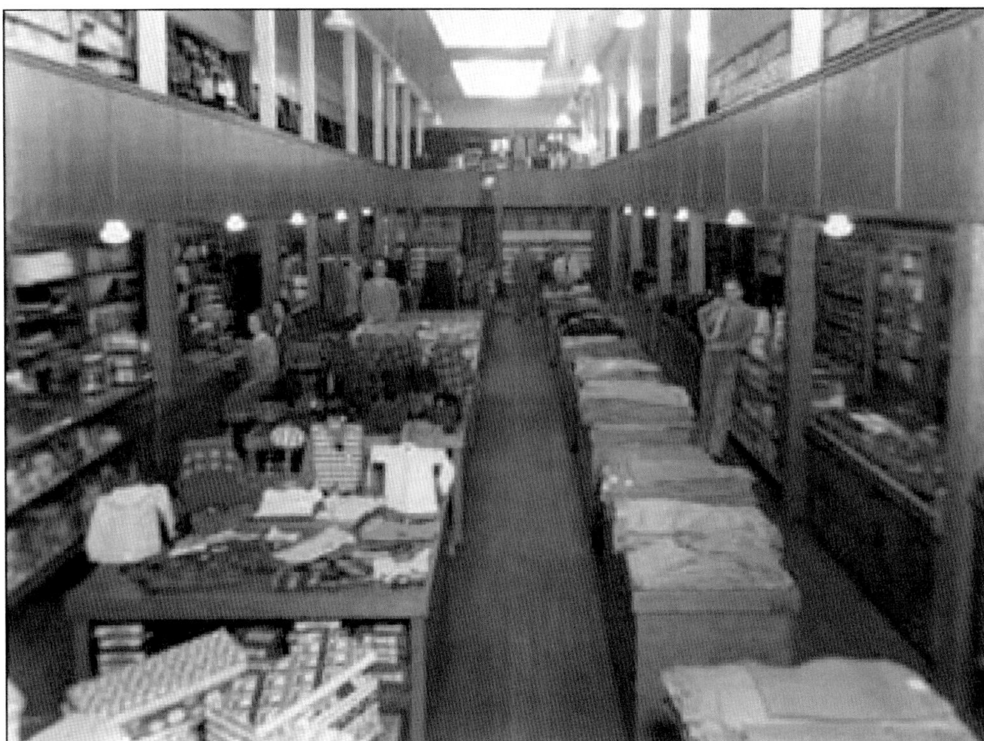

M.L. Finger and Son was a noted mercantile that provided fine men's and women's clothing, fabrics, and shoes for citizens from throughout Tippah County. Pictured above are, from left to right, Jo Malone, Leone Morton, unidentified, Mims Clayton, Lee Cox, Jennie Gaillard, Dewey Shelton, Ellis Finger, W.A. Finger, and Hays Wicker.

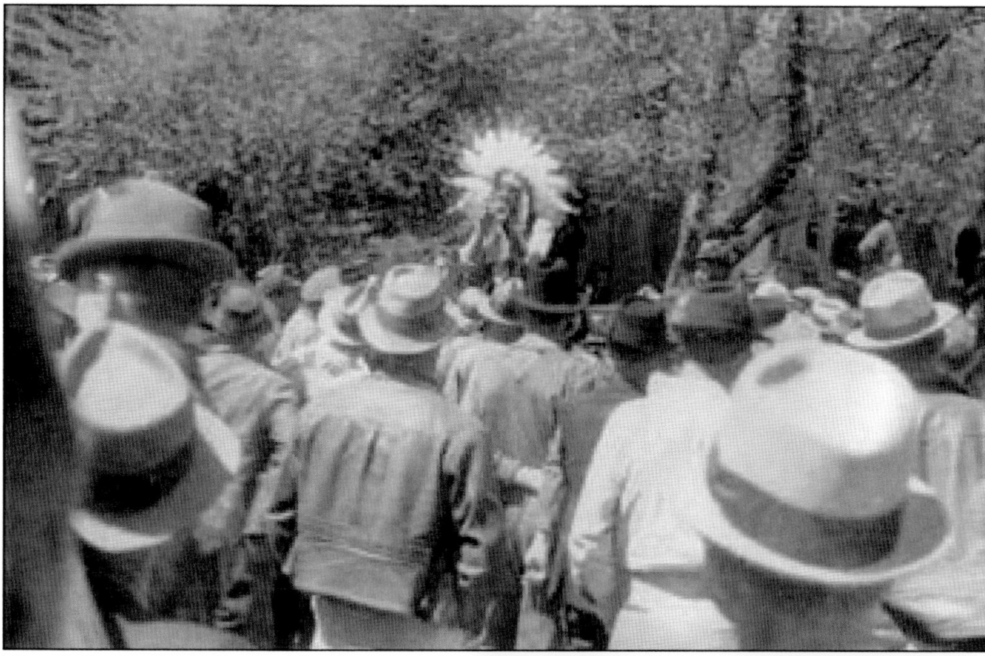

This 1939 photograph of a traveling medicine show shows an American Indian explaining the health benefits of elixirs and medicines.

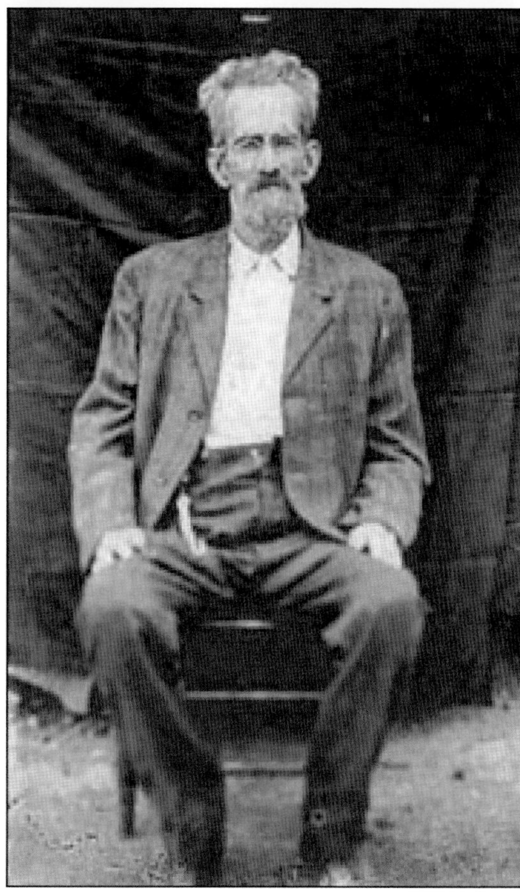

This early 1900s photograph is of Mike Reed, which is known to be the second white child born in Tippah County.

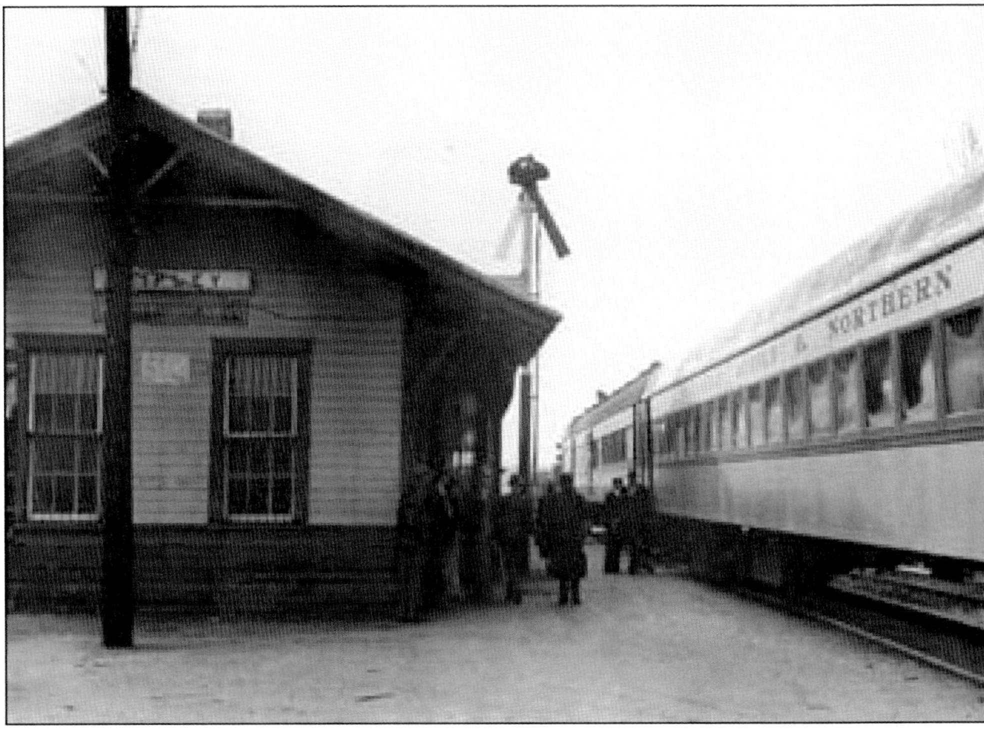

The Ripley depot was on the Gulf, Mobile, and Ohio Railroad, and was a major carrier of freight and passengers from the Gulf Coast to Chicago during its lifetime. This railroad was built by Col. W.C. Falkner in the 1870s and 1880s, and has served the area very well for many years. The depot was located southwest of the courthouse square along the rail. The First United Methodist Church was located to its south. The depot survived until it was torn down in the 1970s.

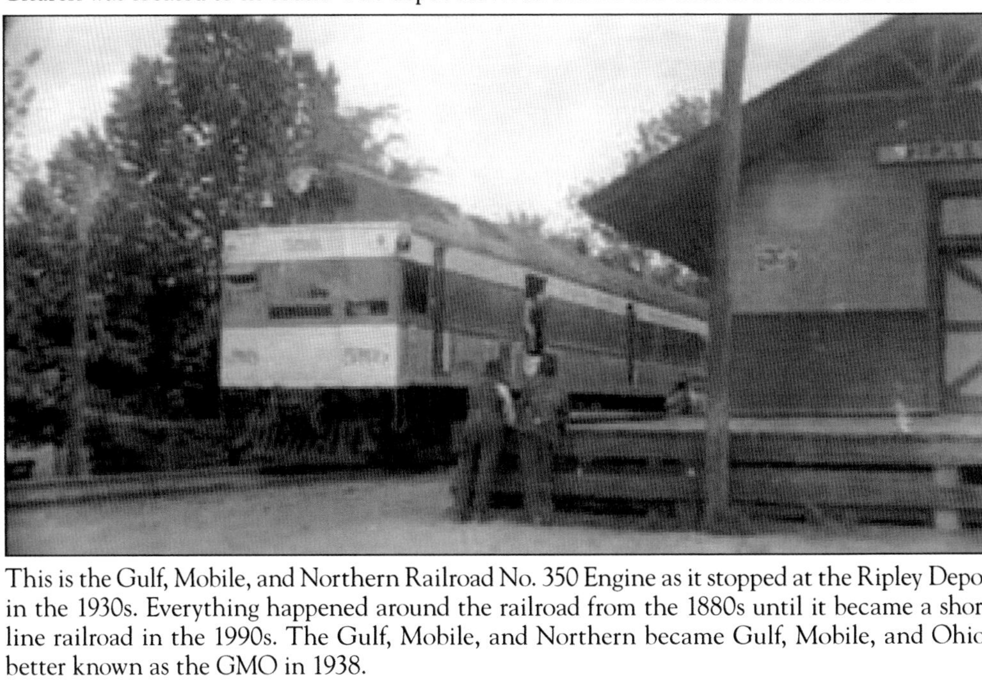

This is the Gulf, Mobile, and Northern Railroad No. 350 Engine as it stopped at the Ripley Depot in the 1930s. Everything happened around the railroad from the 1880s until it became a short line railroad in the 1990s. The Gulf, Mobile, and Northern became Gulf, Mobile, and Ohio, better known as the GMO in 1938.

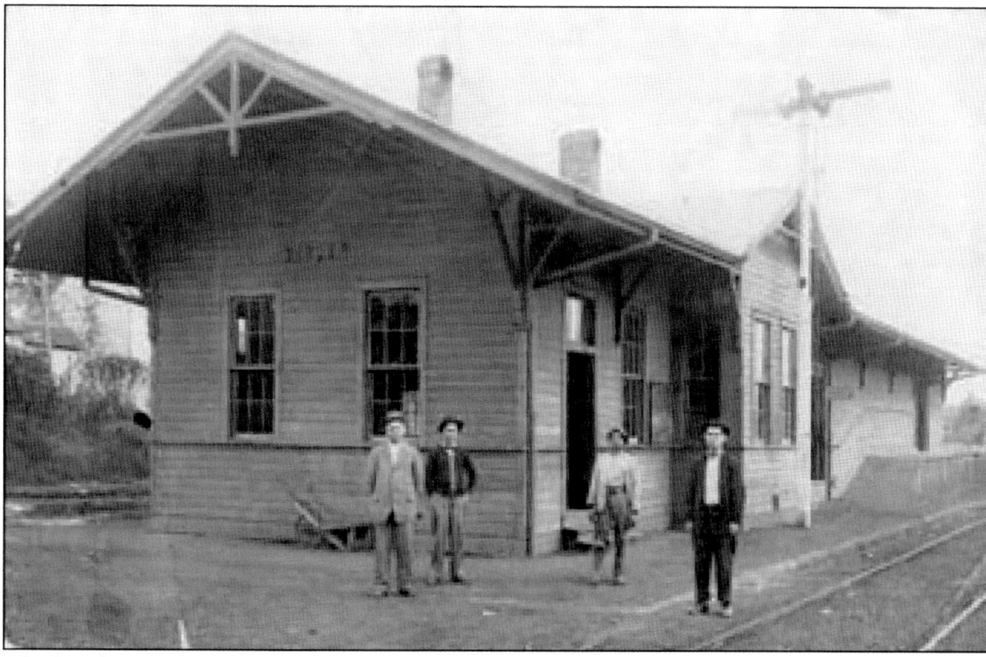

The Southern Express Company ran the Ripley Depot and all of its freight and passengers during this early 1900s picture. This view of the western side of the depot shows the depot agent, a telegraph operator, a ticket salesperson, and a freight laborer. The chalkboard between the two men on the right was a schedule of the day's trains coming through.

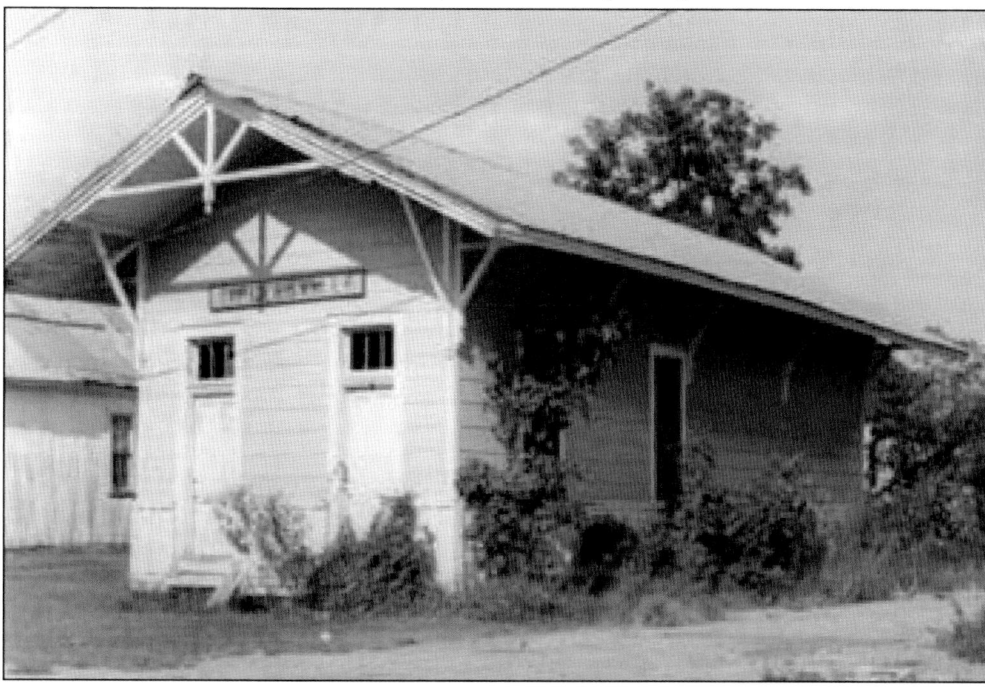

The Tiplersville depot was growing up in weeds in this 1950s photograph due to inactivity. The building was later moved and renovated at a location near the lake at Blue Mountain College in the 1980s, where it still stands today.

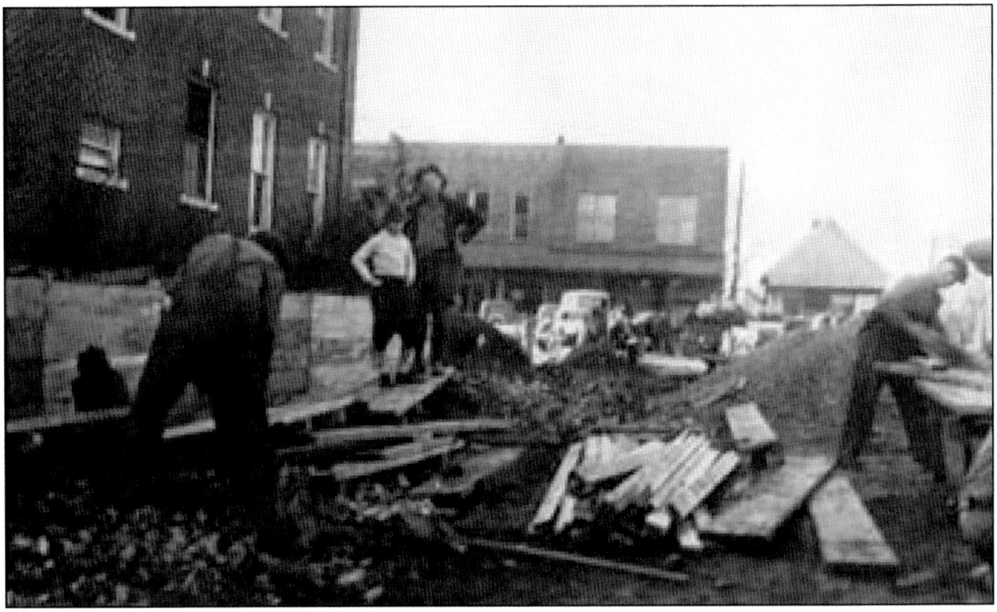

The courthouse curbing was being built in April 1937, with Doll Carr, Andy Brown, Howard Smith, and Bob Decanter as the builders. The curbing was done just before the downtown square was paved. The small building on the right is the law office of one of R.J. Thurmond's kinfolk. It is also where Renfrow's Café was located.

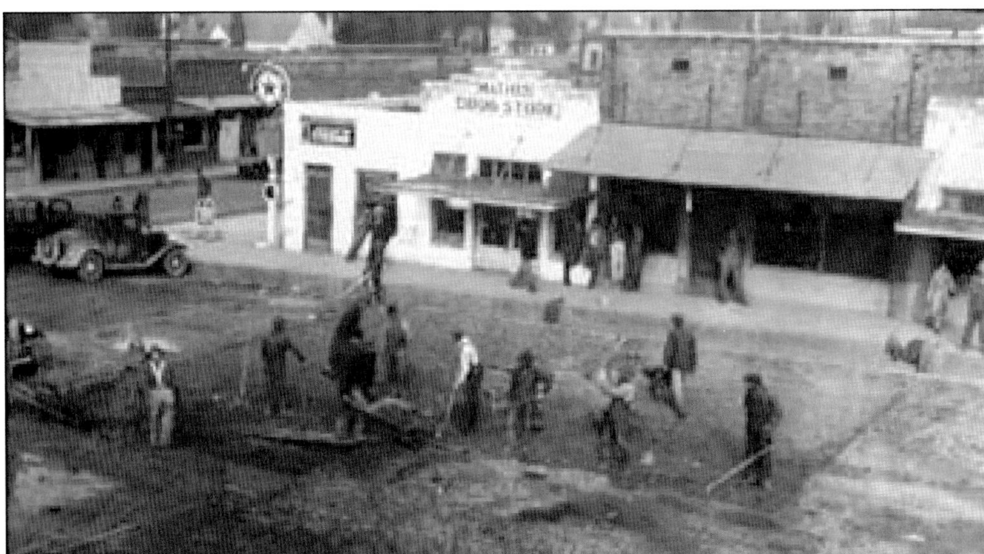

Pictured is some of the first days' work on the courthouse square in January 1937. The workers used only hand tools to smooth the surface for the first paving project.

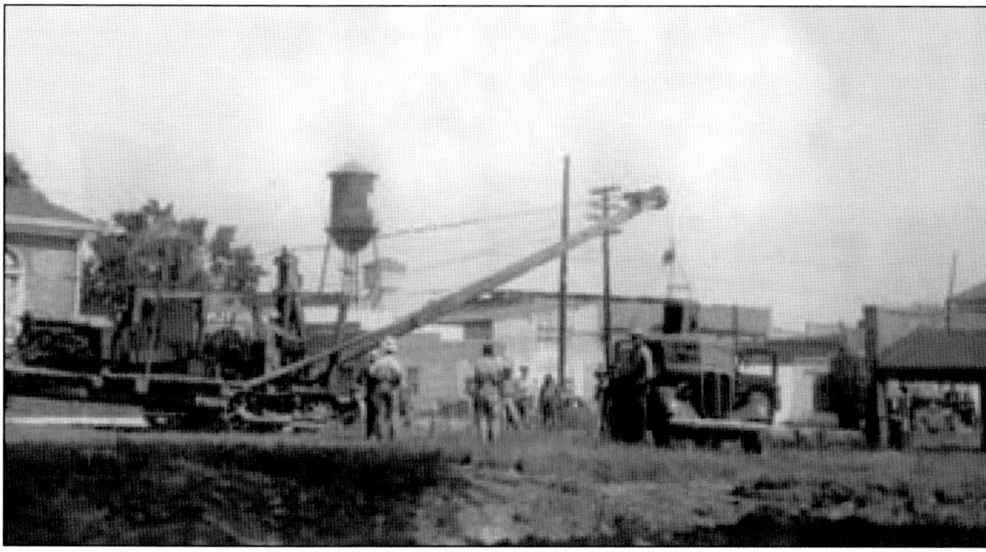

This is a great photograph of the homemade dragline that had been built and was operated by Alvie Goolsby. The dragline was being used in the digging of the basement for the new post office on North Main Street in Ripley.

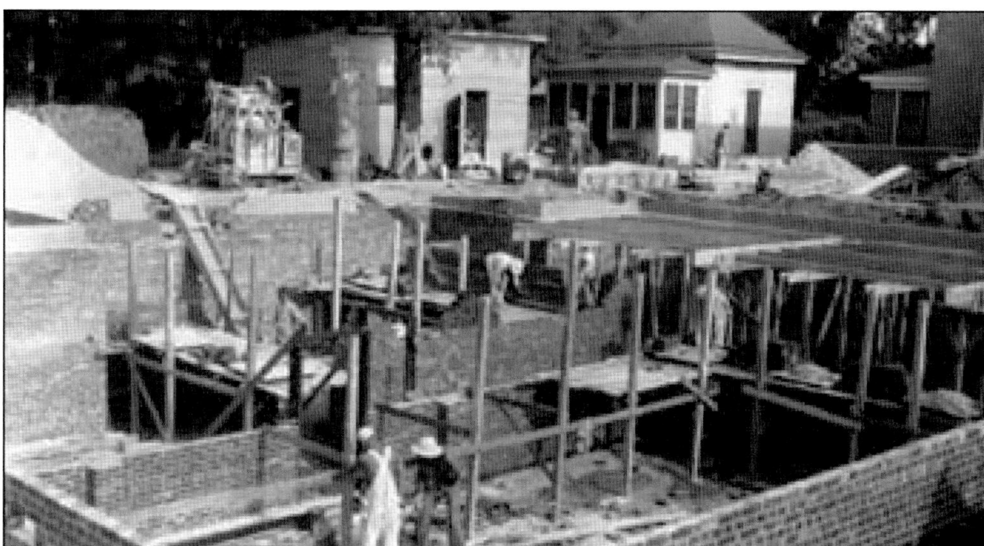

This is a photograph of the building of the new post office in Ripley, with 16-inch flooring and all of the re-bar added to the structure. This building was built in 1937 and used until 1999, when a new post office was built south of town. The Main Street building was sold to Dixie-Net in 1999.

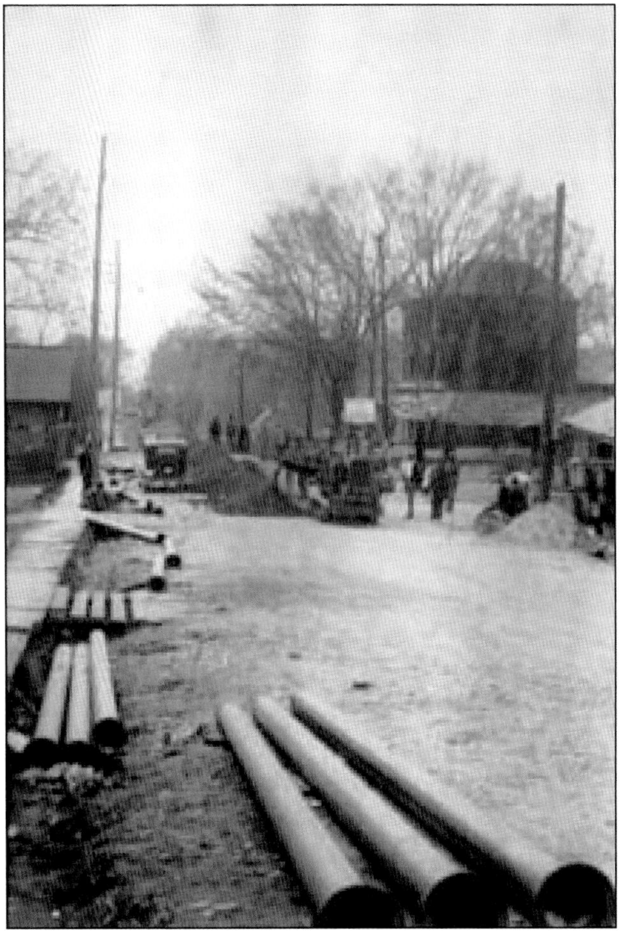

This is the scene of the first cut on the water works project on West Spring Street looking west from the square. The picture was taken from the corner of Renfrow's Café, looking across the railroad to include the old Tippah County Jail that was replaced in 1928.

This photograph shows the ending of the life of the Jamieson Store in Falkner with all of its aging characteristics. The right side of the store has farming supplies with seeds for planting a summer harvest. The old scales are located in the center and were used to weigh the seeds.

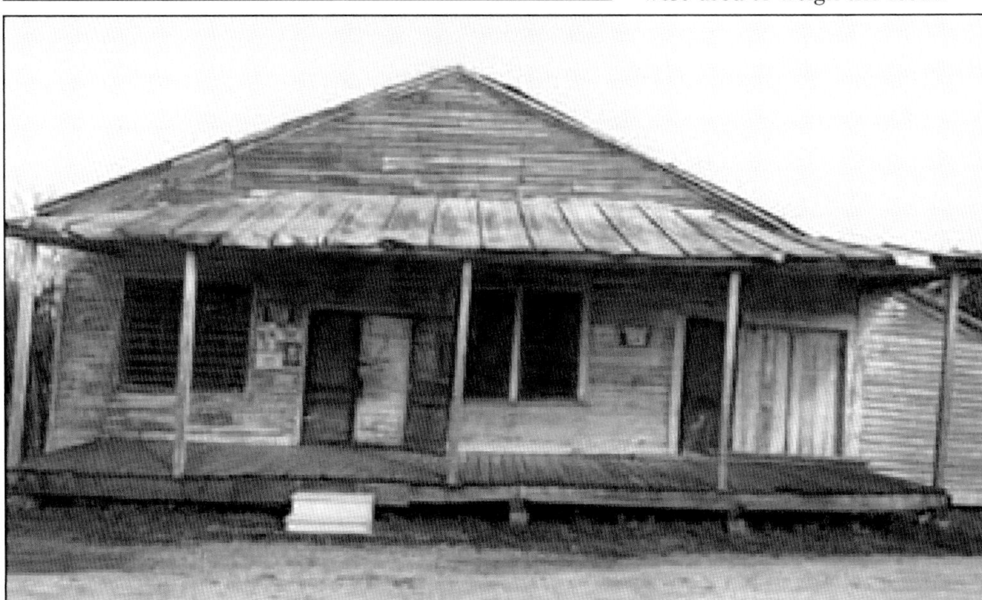

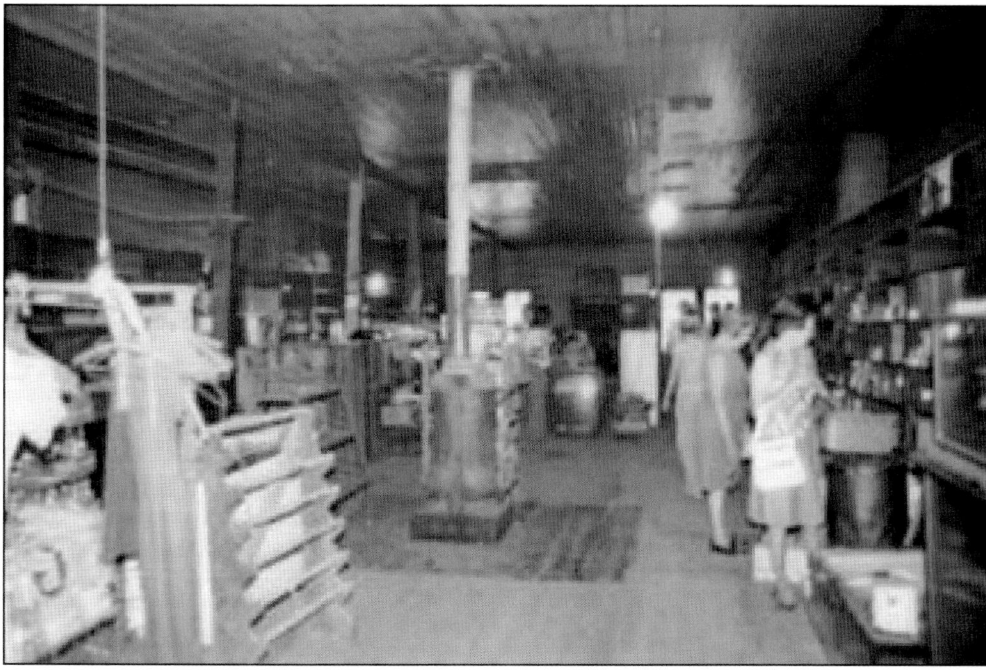

Pictured is the old Jamieson Store in Falkner. At that time, there was a line of stores located on the east side of the railroad, and a cotton gin across a road at the south end of the stores. This store served as a community grocery and dry goods store. The old stove sits in the center of the building and served as a gathering place during the winter months.

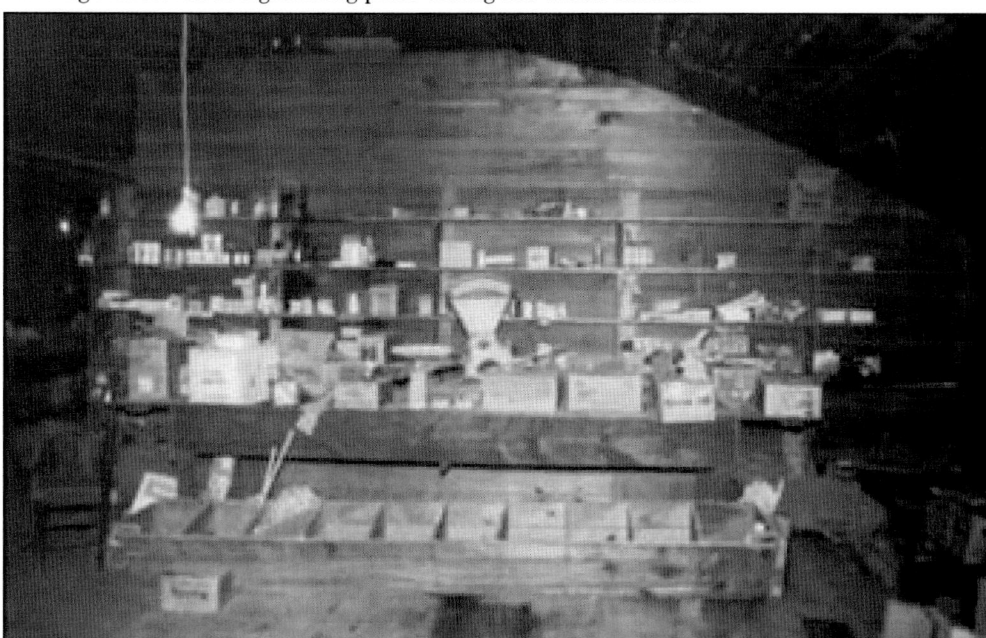

This photograph was taken in the 1940s and shows the old store with all of its aging characteristics. The right side of the store has farming supplies with seeds for planting a summer harvest. The old scales are located in the center and were used to weigh the seeds.

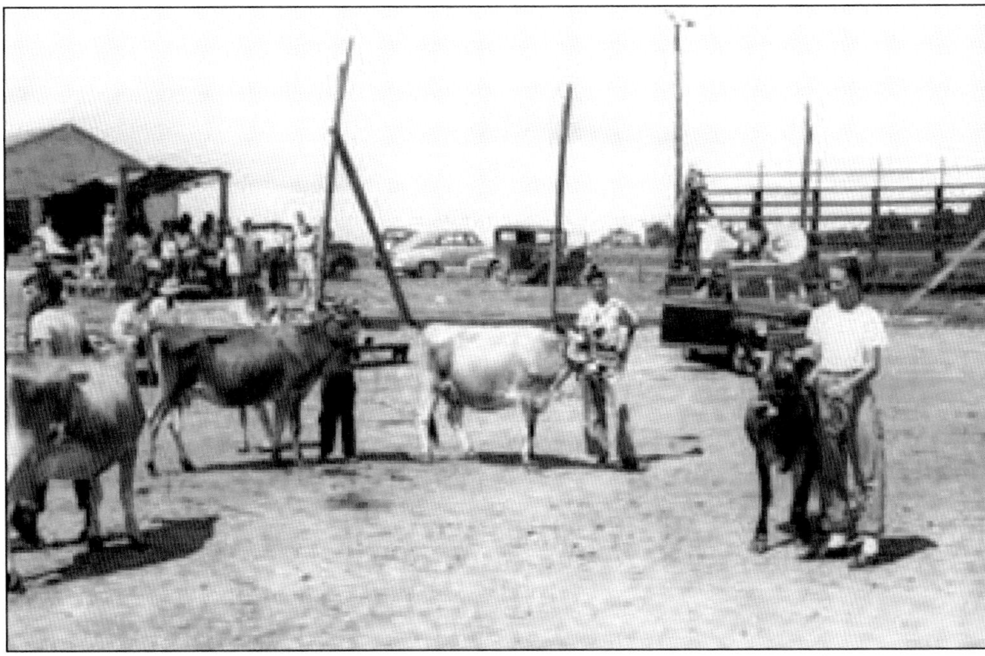

This 1940s photograph taken at the fairgrounds shows 4-H students at the Tippah County Fair, as they showed off and competed with their jersey milk cows. The fair was located on Highway 15, just south of Ripley. Notice the old car with huge loudspeakers ready to announce the contestants and winners.

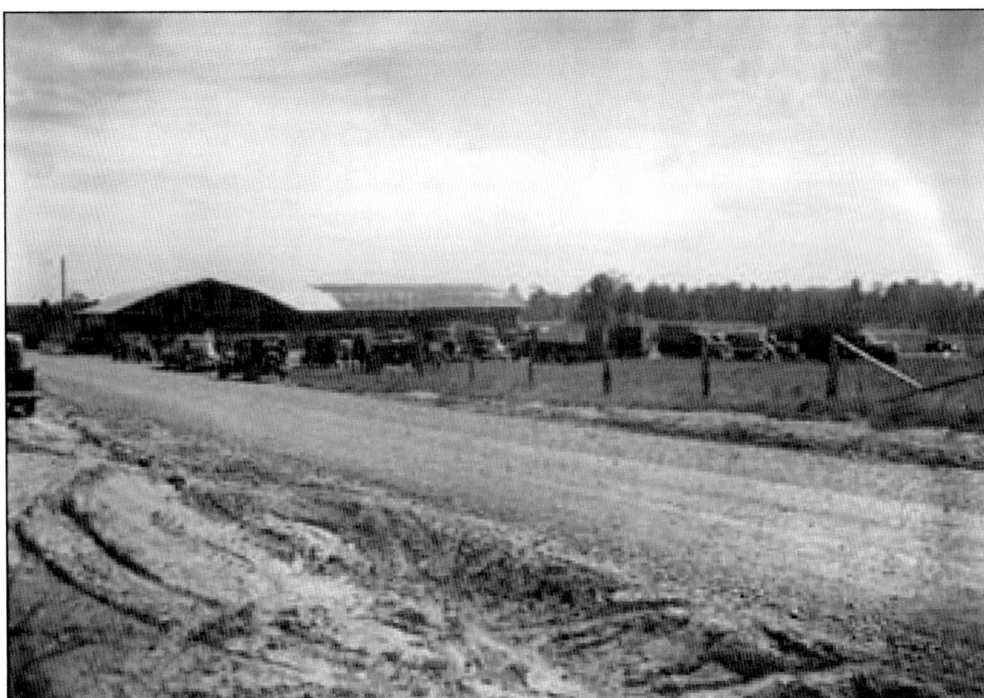

Martin's Sale Barn, located north of Ripley on Martin Road, was the location for cattle, horses, mules, goats, and sheep sales for the area. This sale still continues today and thrives as a goat sale.

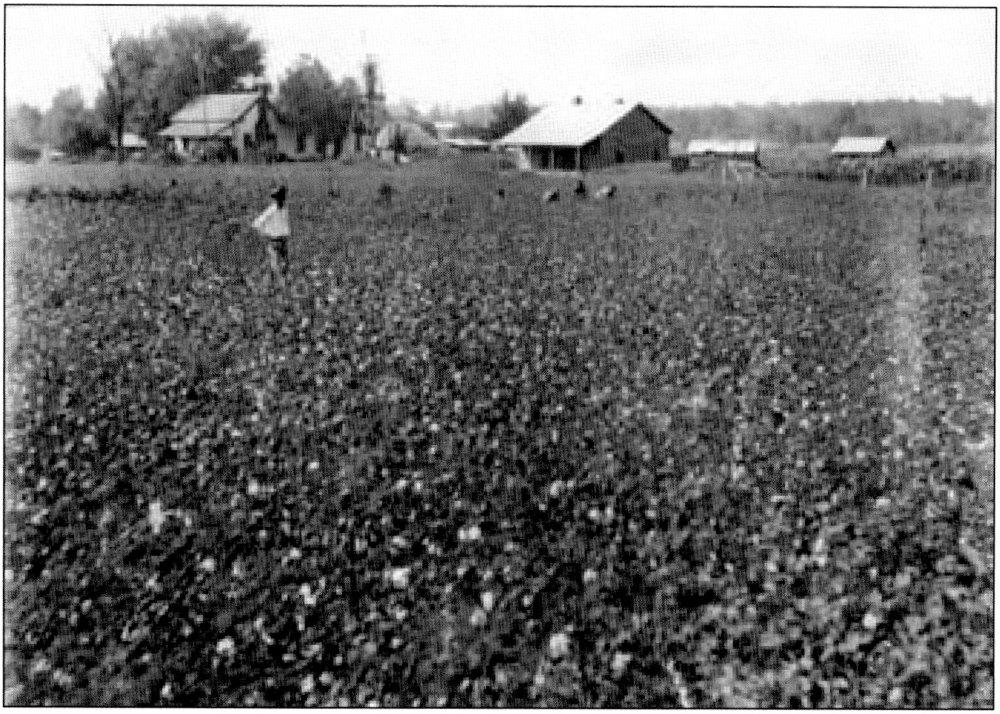

Shown in this photograph is a view of a cotton farm in Tippah County with the workers picking rows of cotton. Very little cotton was left on the plant once it has been handpicked.

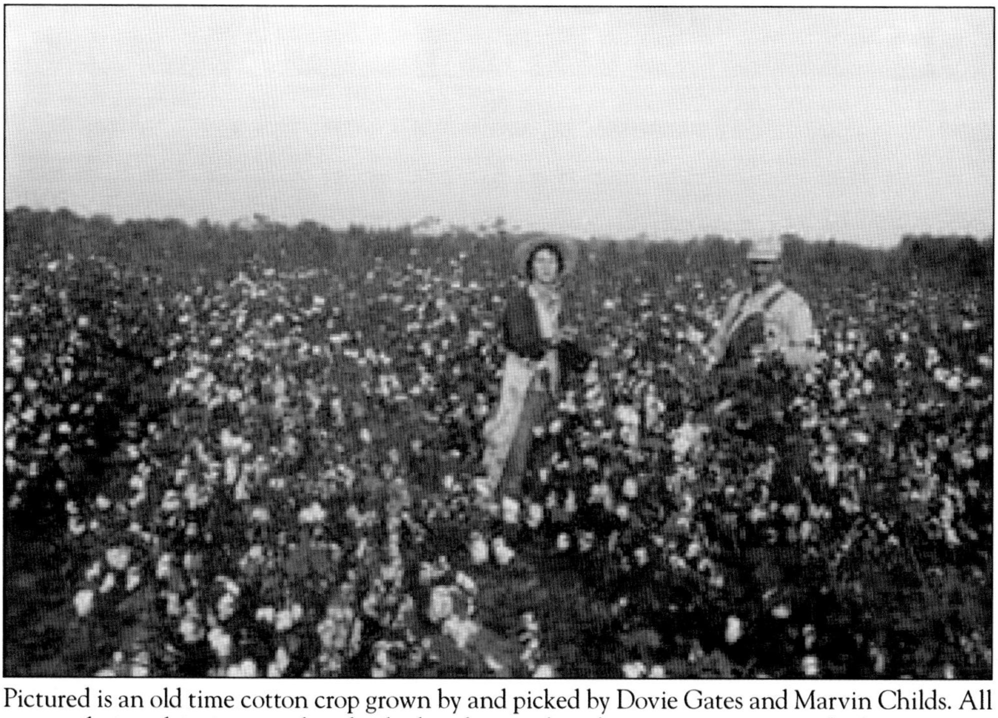

Pictured is an old time cotton crop grown by and picked by Dovie Gates and Marvin Childs. All cotton during this time was handpicked and carried to the cotton gin in a mule drawn wagon to be baled.

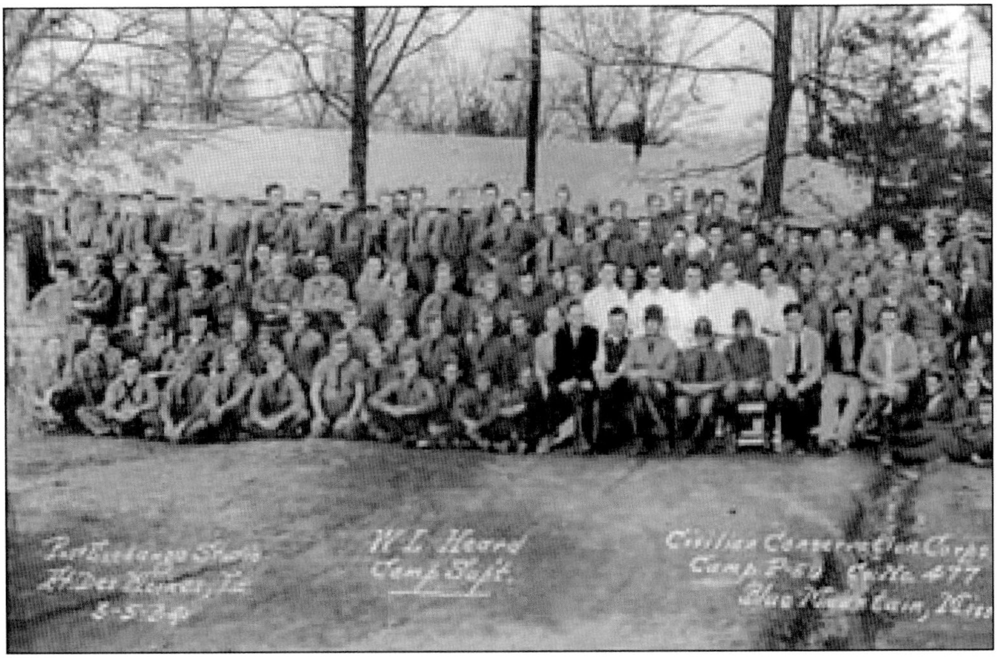

The Civilian Conservation Corps started in the 1930s by President Franklin D. Roosevelt. It made its way into Tippah County in 1934. Camp P-59 Co. No. 477 was located in Blue Mountain and worked to build and make life better, not only for the men, but for the area. The men were dressed much as they would for military service, but were used in work details.

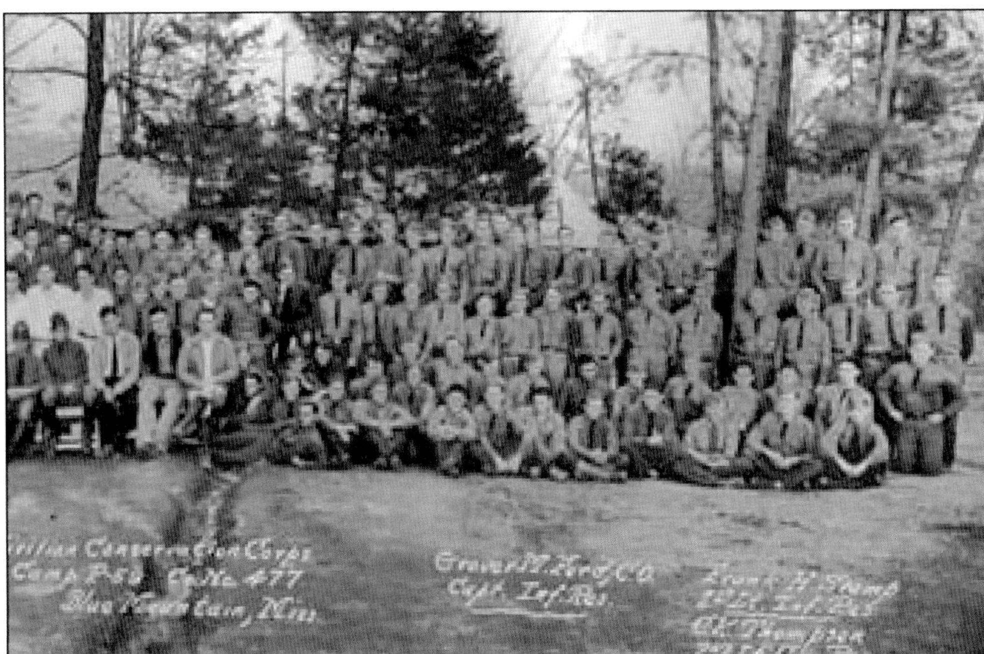

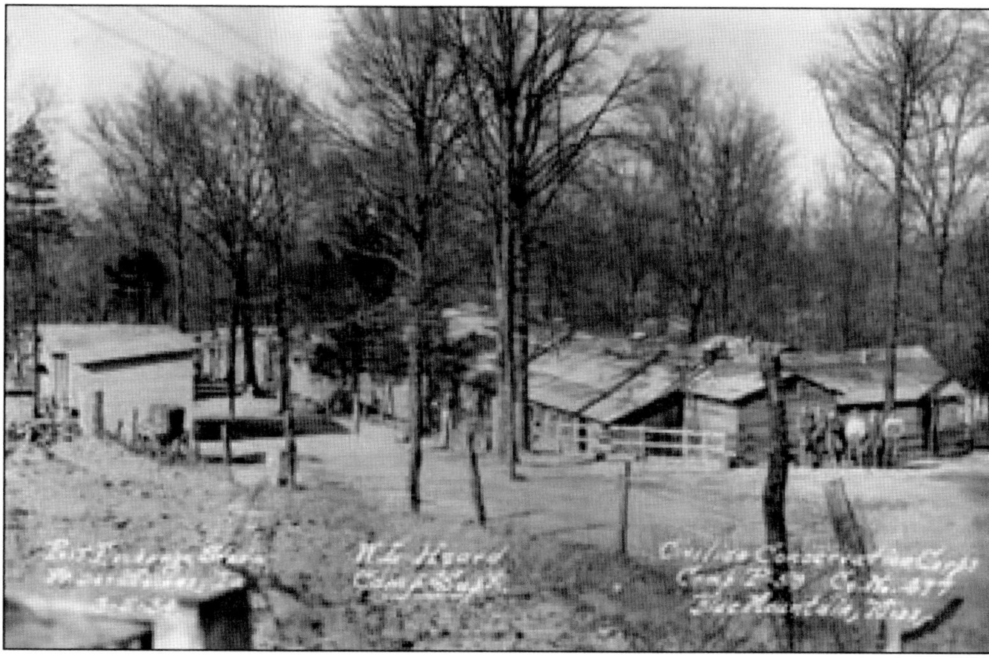

The Civilian Conservation Corps built barracks and buildings used to house and keep the men supplied with food and equipment needed for the men to live for a year or two. They were located in the Blue Mountain area and came from all over the United States. They worked on projects for the government that made parks, railroads, and facilities better for future use.

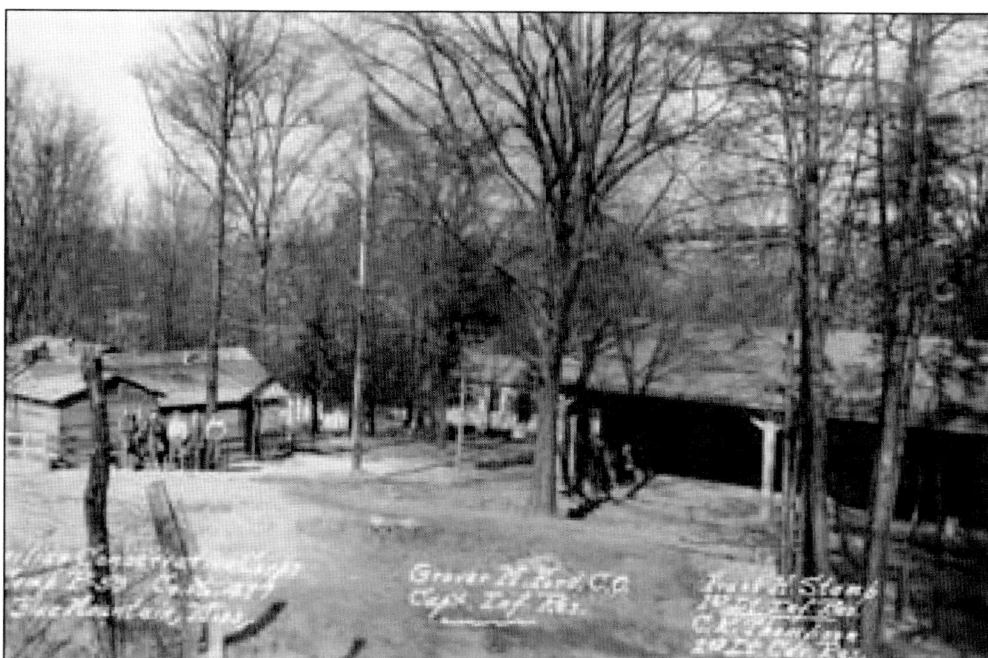

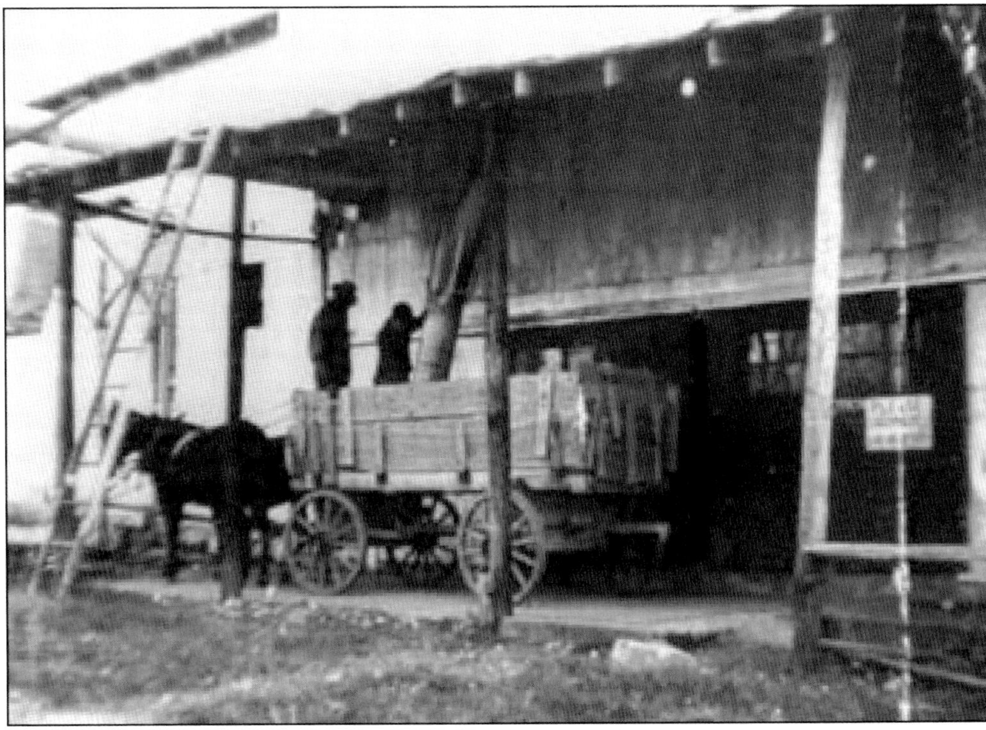

Employees at the Walnut Gin are seen removing the cotton from the wooden wagon with wooden spoke wheels during the early 1900s. Cotton gins were located throughout the county for almost 60 years before their need started to subside.

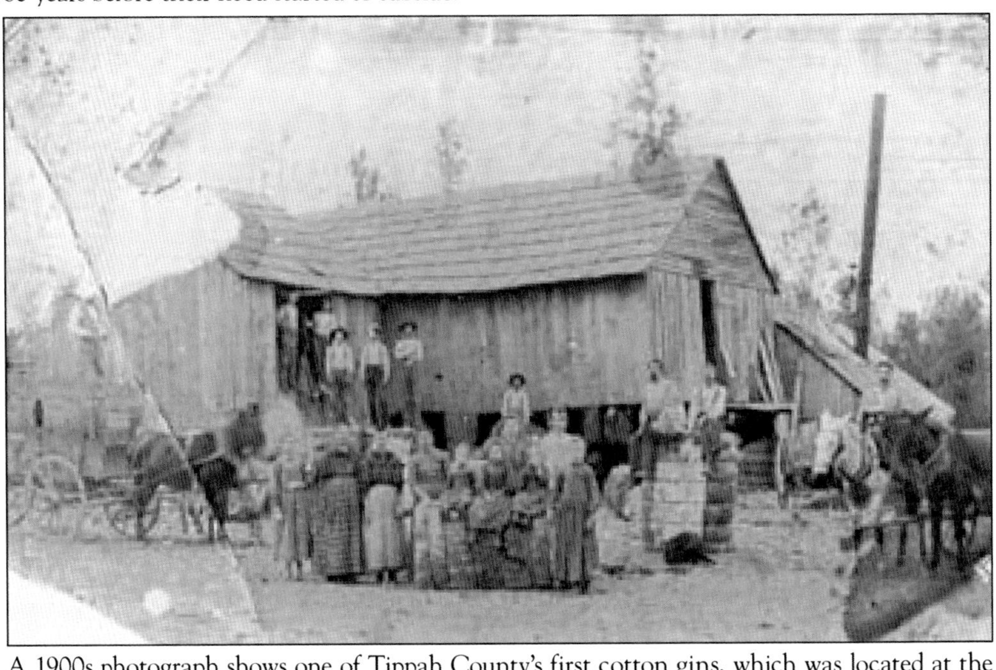

A 1900s photograph shows one of Tippah County's first cotton gins, which was located at the "old Charlie Elliott place." The gin was very small and was a family operated business. Bales were stored on the ground and were brought to the depot for shipping purposes.

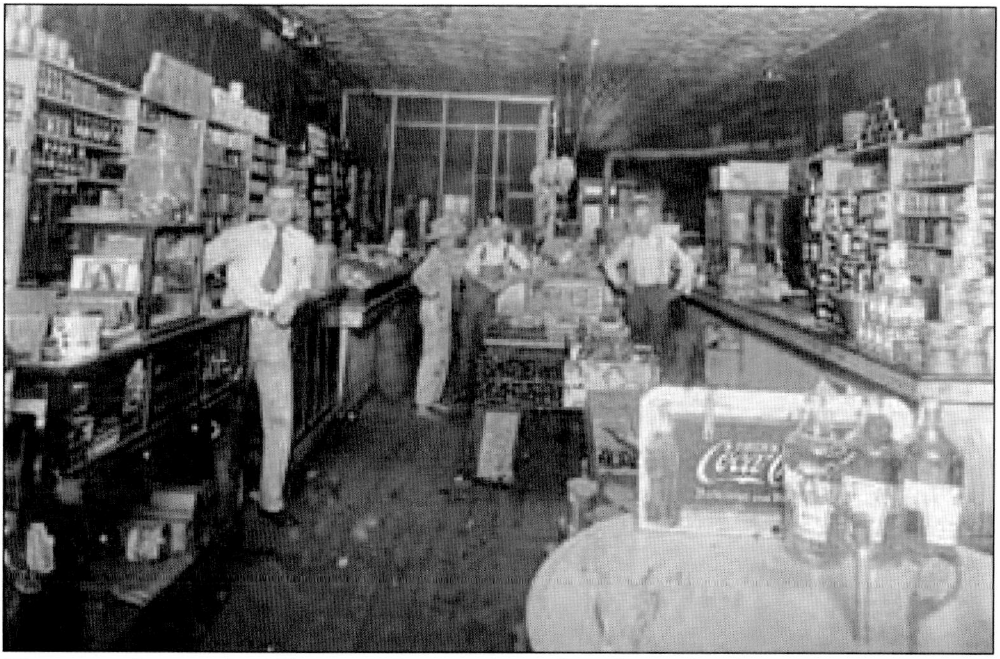

This great photograph of Shannon's Grocery, located on the south side of the square in Ripley during the early 1900s, showcases a nostalgic look at the inside of a grocery and seed store. This photograph includes one of the first Coca-Cola signs in the county. Pictured is Bob Shannon, owner, and J. D. Pugh (right).

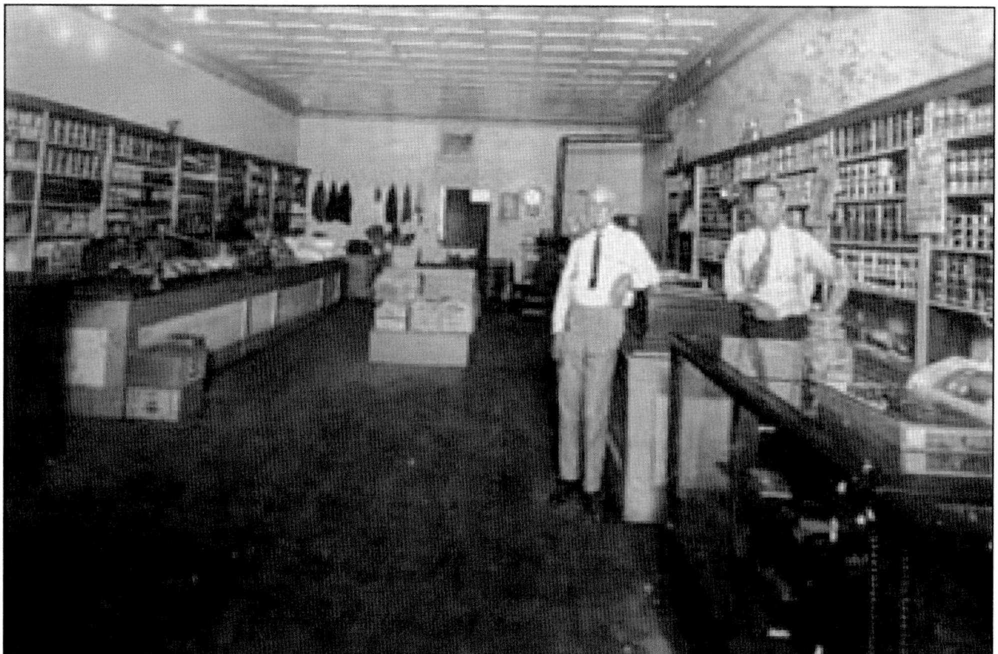

Henson & McBride was a grocery and general store in the early 1920s. It was located on the west side of the square and was owned by William F. "Birdie" Henson and Patton A. McBride. Later the store, next door to Renfrow's Café, was owned and operated by Mr. and Mrs. Bob Barkley.

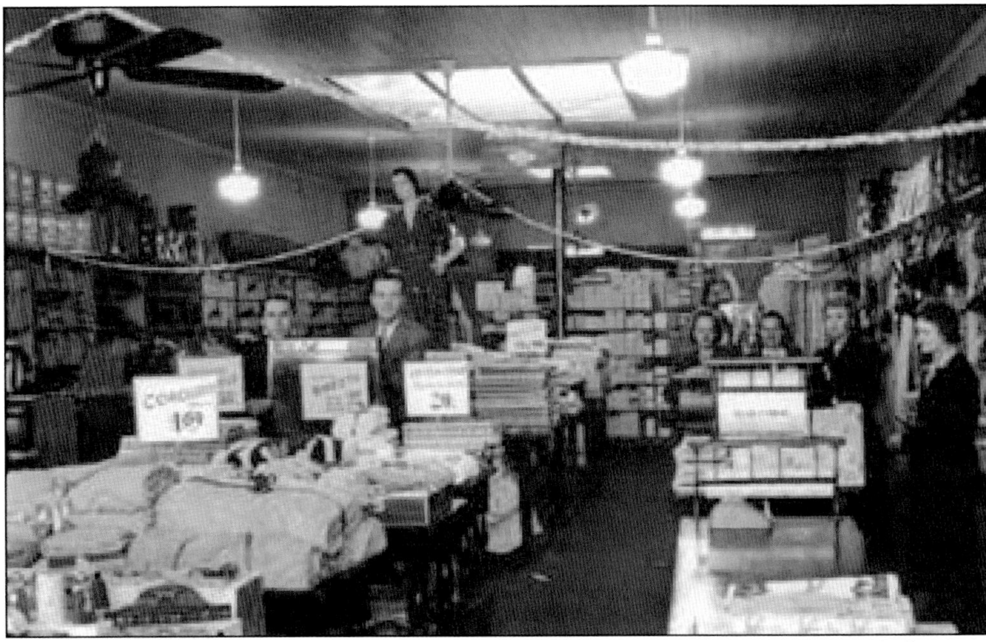

Ballard's Store was located on the square in Ripley during the mid-1950s. The store was a clothing and dry goods store with a number of employees. Pictured here are, from left to right, John Falk, Easley Ballard, Dimple Goforth Graves, Velma Clayton, Lula Hugh Clayton, and Velma McClusky.

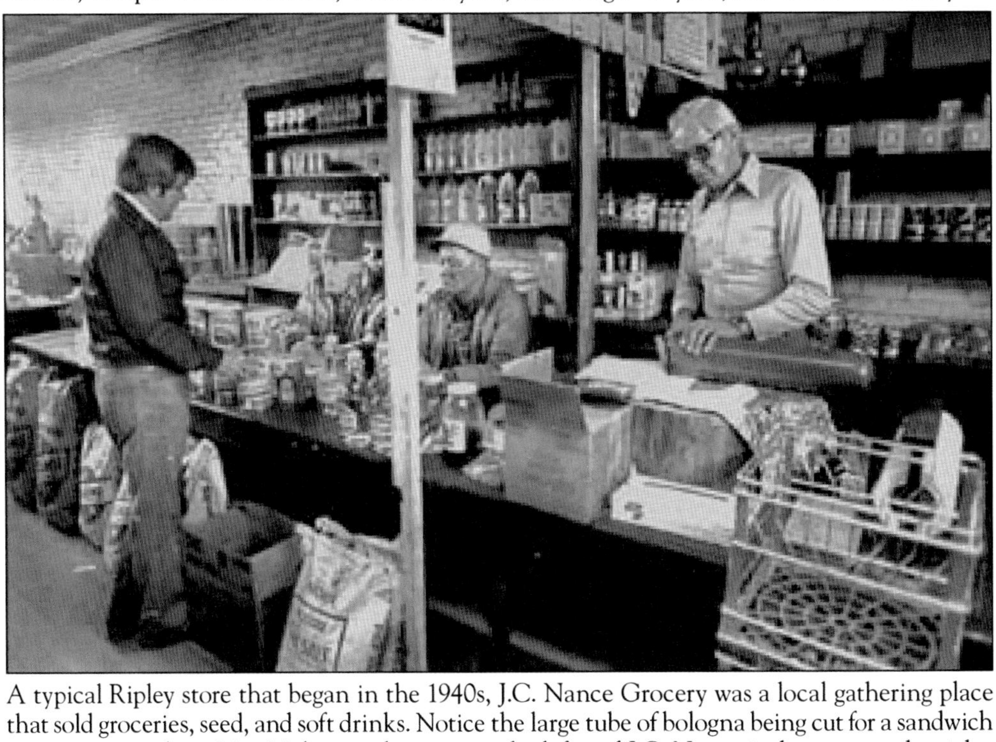

A typical Ripley store that began in the 1940s, J.C. Nance Grocery was a local gathering place that sold groceries, seed, and soft drinks. Notice the large tube of bologna being cut for a sandwich or to go on crackers. Van Malone is the man on the left and J.C. Nance is the man on the right. The store was located on the east side of the square, and for many years, it was located next to the *Southern Sentinel.*

The north side of the square in the late 1930s shows the location for people to leave their wagons while doing business in town. Even the curbing had signs that read "wagons." The wagons were backed up and in some cases the mules were unhitched to allow for room to get around them.

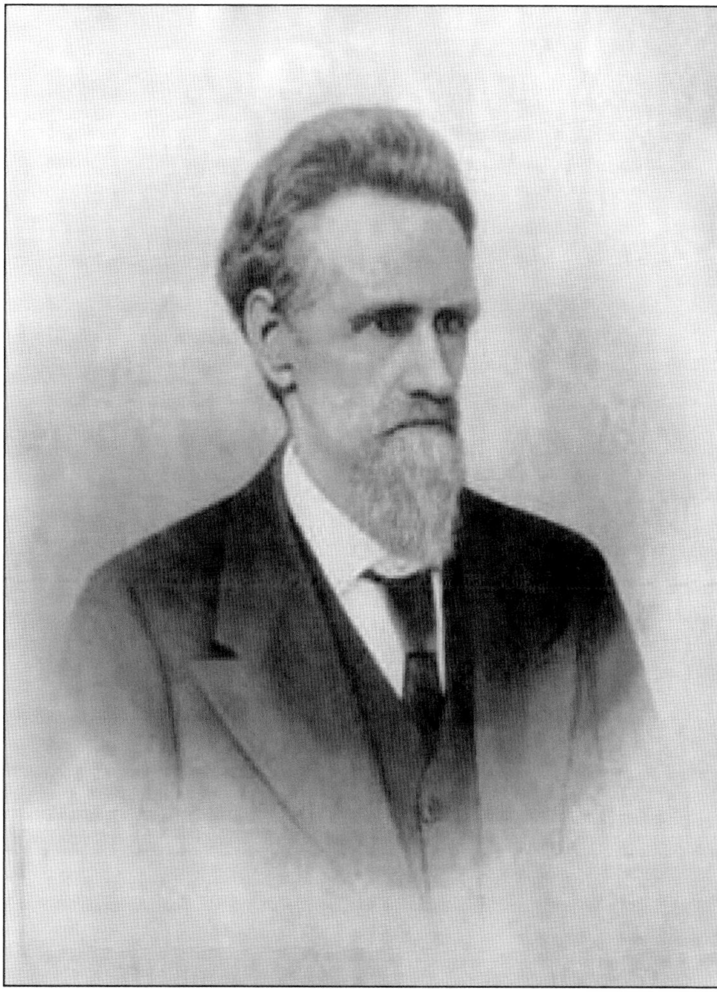

This photograph shows a very typical scene on a southern square during the late 1930s. Old trucks had flatbed bodies with covers for family to travel in and an old version of a tractor-trailer that delivered soft drinks. There is still a wagon on the square and everyone had to navigate around the Civil War Monument in the middle of the street.

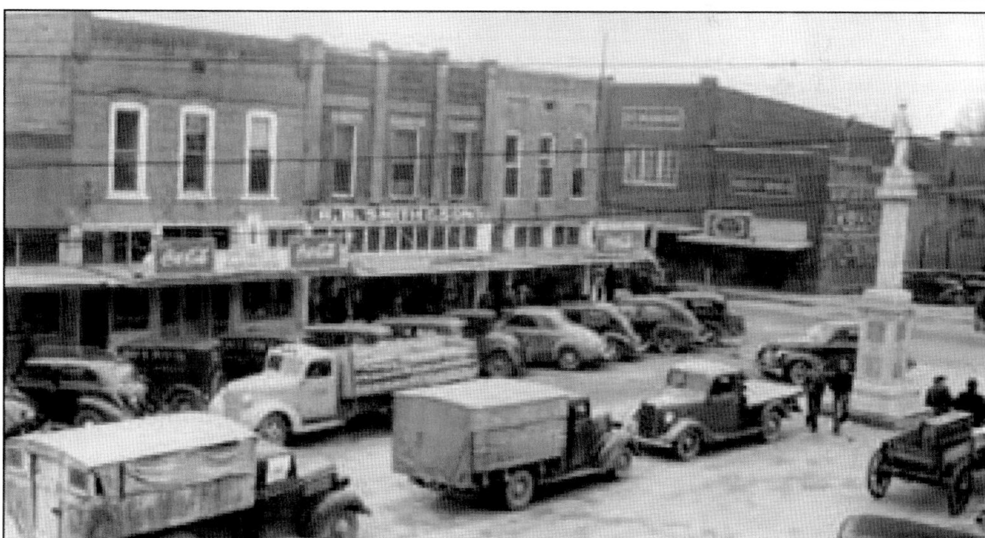

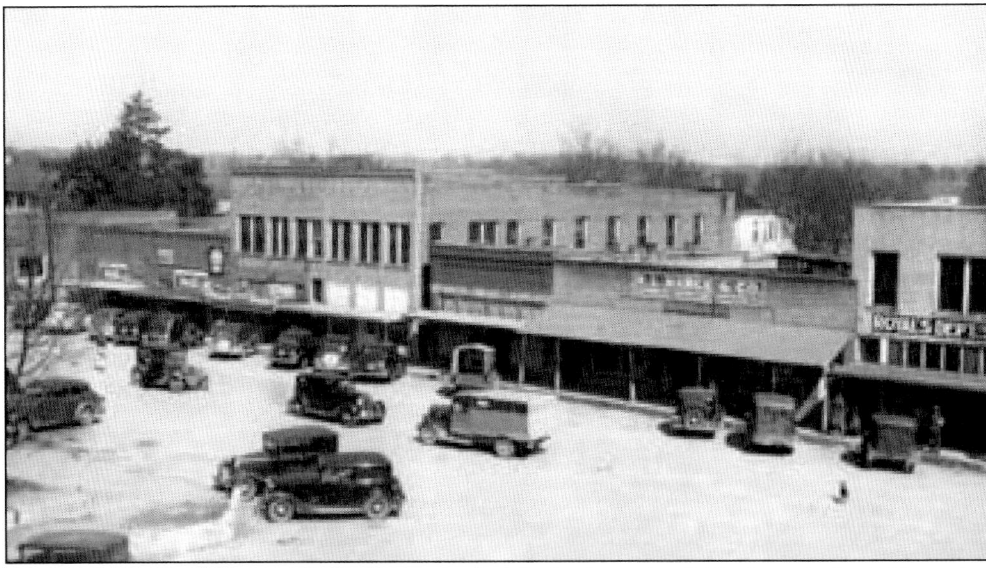

This photograph shows a view from the east with vehicles from the 1910s through the 1930s parked on the square. Notice that cars were allowed to park in the middle and could go any direction back then. Now, automobiles only travel in a counterclockwise fashion around the square.

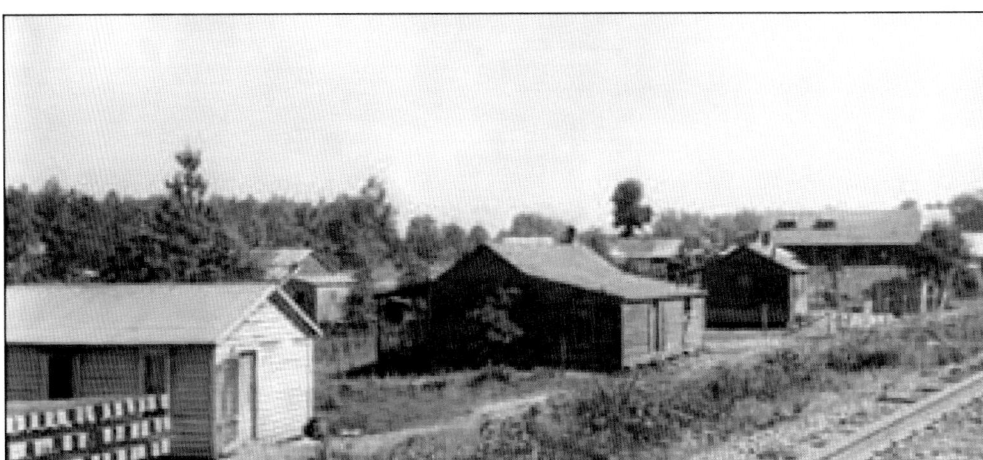

This photograph shows scenery of Tippah County dwellings along the northern route of the railroad inside of the Ripley city limits. This picture was taken in the 1930s during the summer months. Notice the crossties stacked on the left side of the picture.

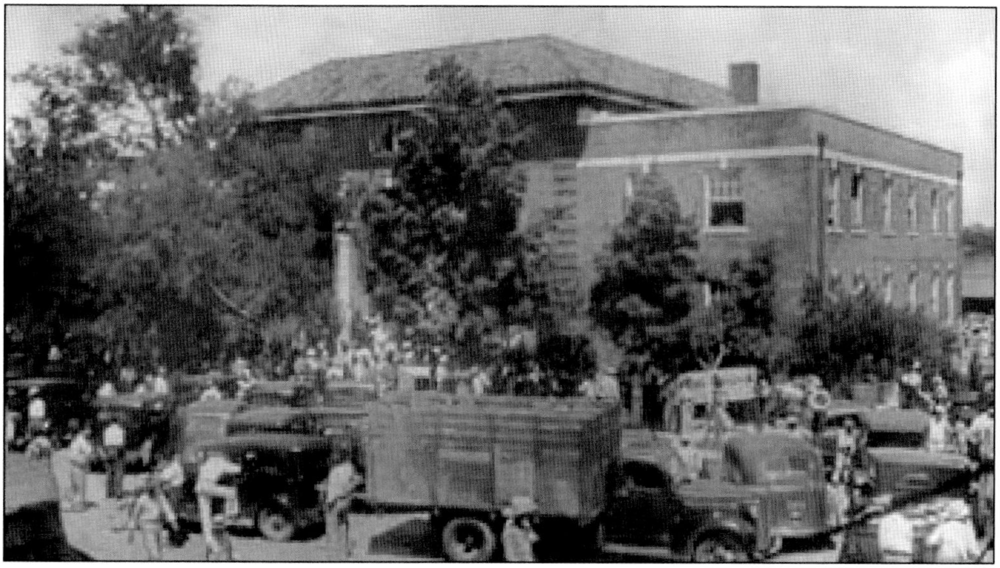

This was Election Day for Tippah County during August 1939. Southern election days were exciting and no one knew the outcome until the votes were in. This tradition continues even today.

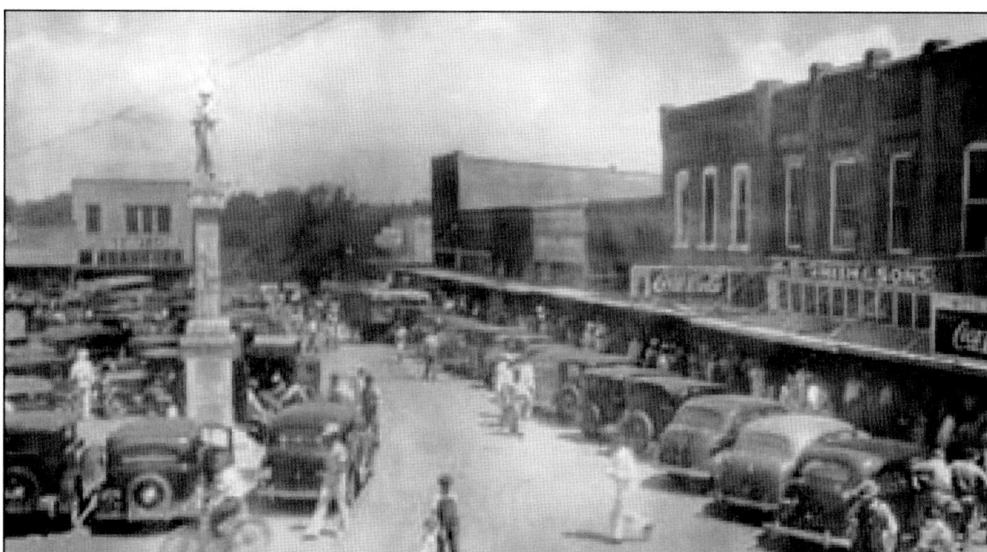

A south side view along Jefferson Street shows a vast crowd during the elections of August 1939. People were talking and deciding what direction their vote would be cast.

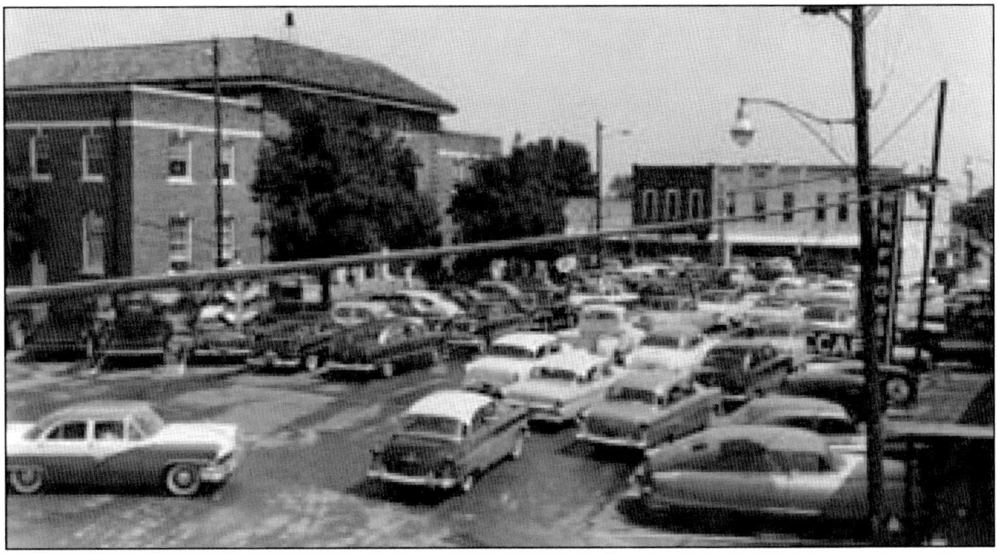

The Tippah County Singing Convention took place each year during the summer months at the Tippah County Courthouse. Traffic would be very congested throughout the weekend and vehicles should be parked in the same direction, but as you can see, it doesn't always happen that way. This photograph is from the 1956 convention.

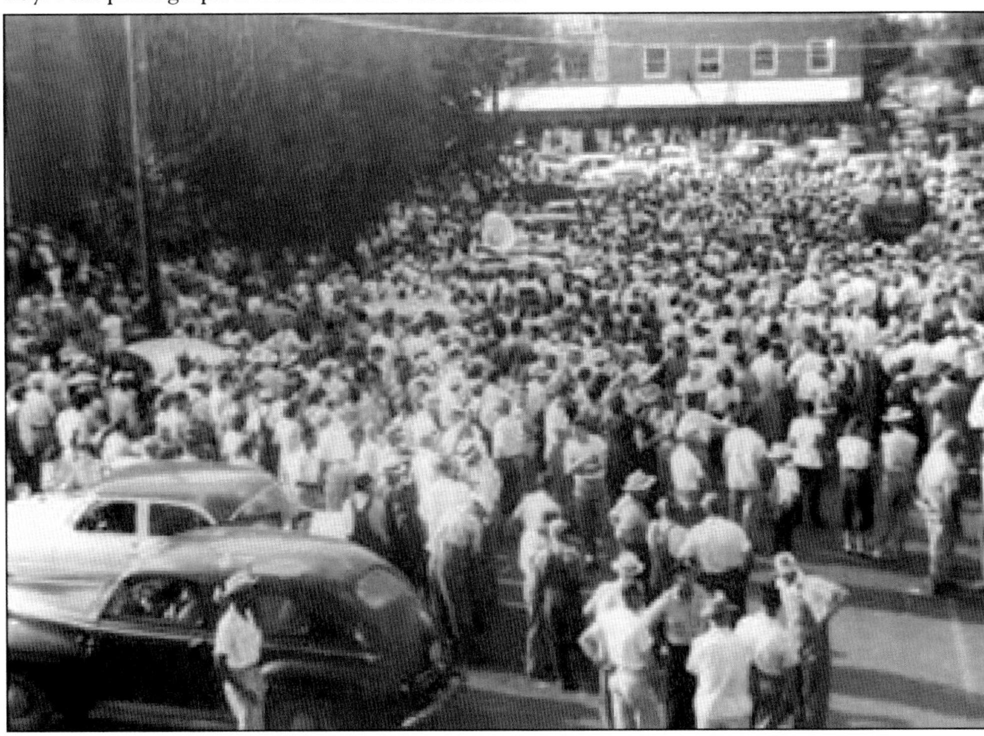

A Tippah County Election Day crowd is seen here during the early 1950s at the courthouse square. Town Marshall Clarence Witt can be seen wearing the dark cap in the semicircle group at bottom of photograph facing camera. Velma and Gordon "Dick" Clayton can be seen along the right edge of photograph with their backs to the camera. Velma is wearing a white blouse and a black skirt and Gordon is wearing a white hat.

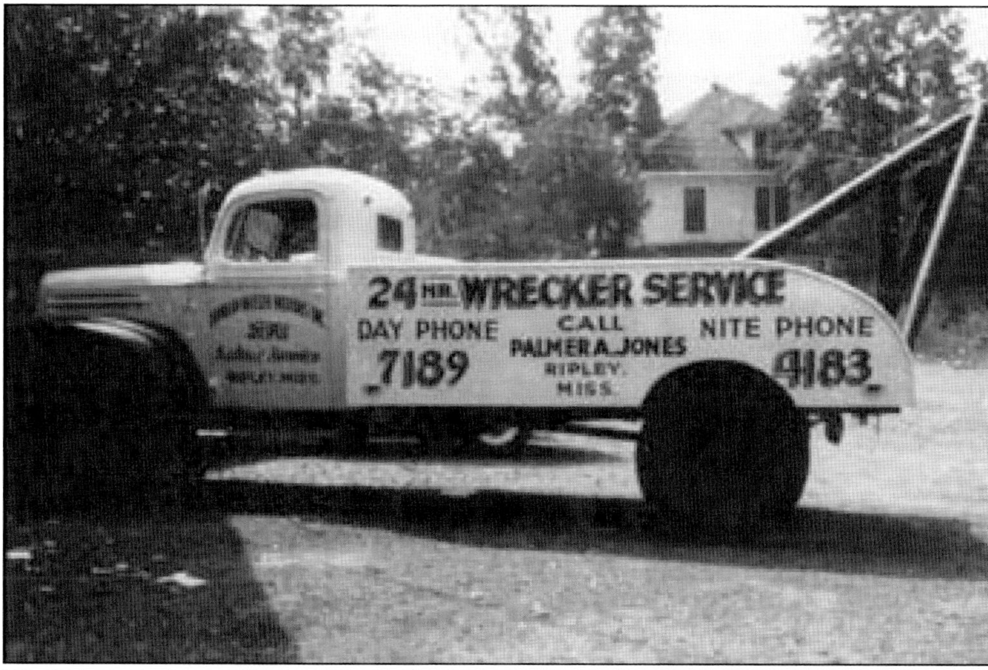

The Palmer A. Jones Wrecker Service has been in operation in Tippah County for the past 60 years. This old 1930s wrecker was used for all pickup service. Notice that the phone numbers are comprised of only four digits each. The Wrecker Service was and is located on Highway 15 just north of the Highway 4 intersection.

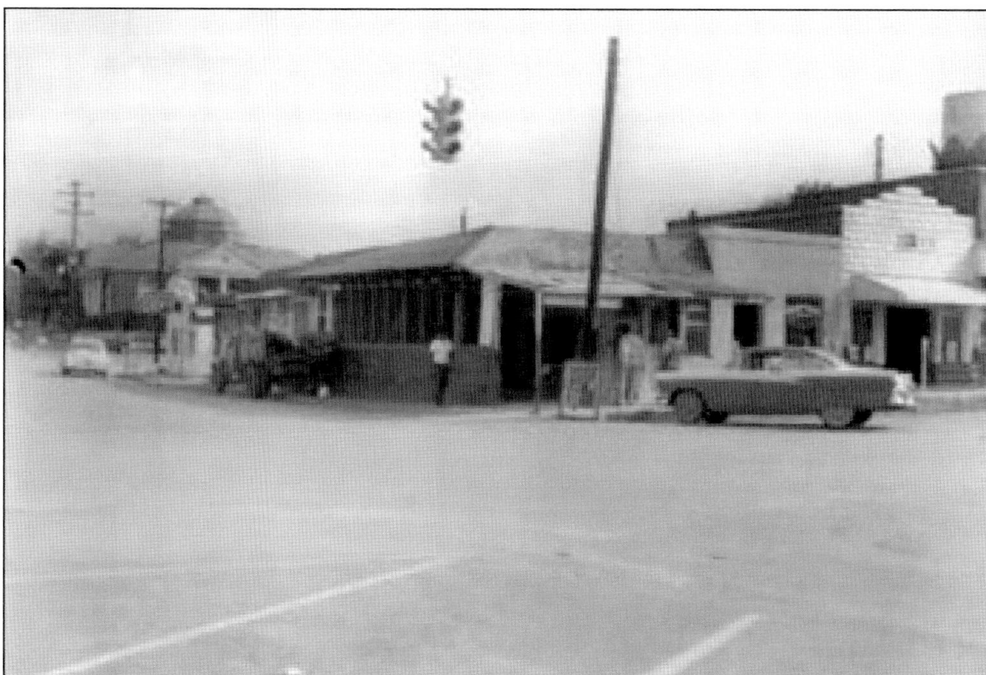

The northwest corner intersection of Main Street and Spring Street is shown with a café at the corner. First Baptist Church is shown in the background during this 1956 photograph.

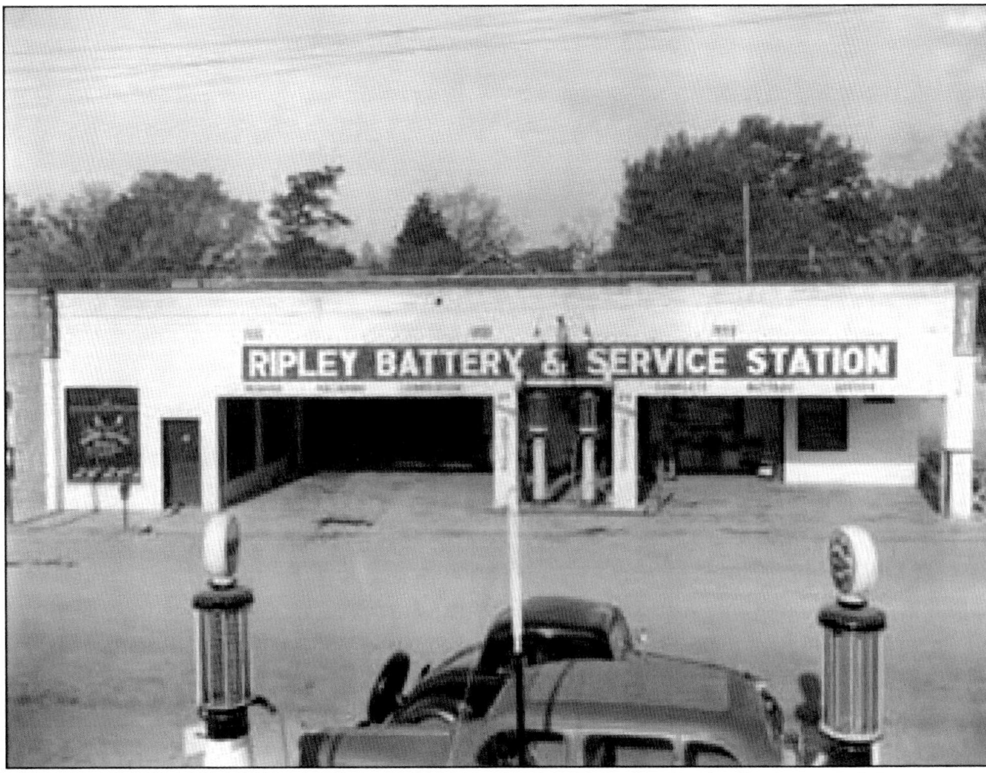

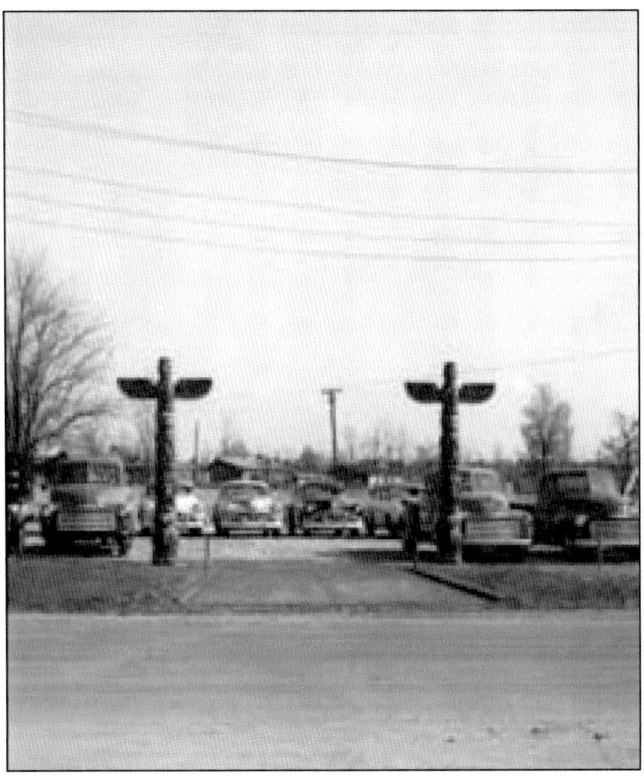

Ripley Battery and Service Station was well-equipped with everything they needed to maintain an automobile. With 24-hour service, gasoline, washing, polishing, lubrication, and complete battery service, the business located at the southeast corner of Main Street and Mulberry Street was ready for business. The old gasoline pumps have long since disappeared from our landscape.

This is local Pontiac dealership, located at the intersection of South Main Street and Highway 15 during the late 1940s, sold GMC trucks and Pontiac cars.

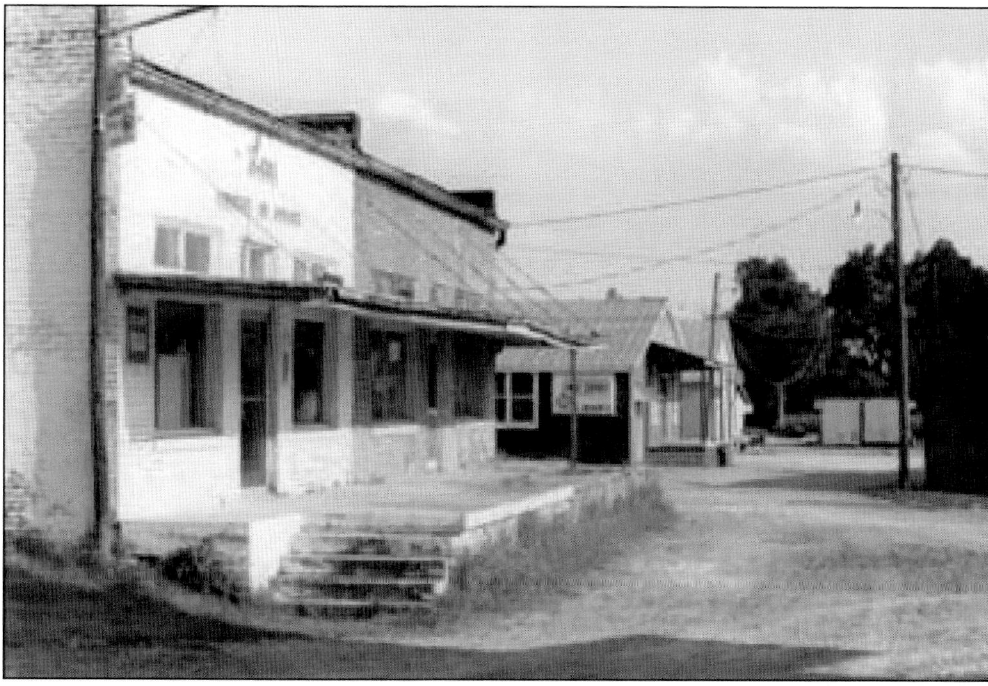

This is a photograph of the Luna Furniture and Appliances Store and the W.L. Tomlinson Company in Walnut. The Luna Furniture and Appliances building was recently torn down and Tomlinson's Hardware is still going strong.

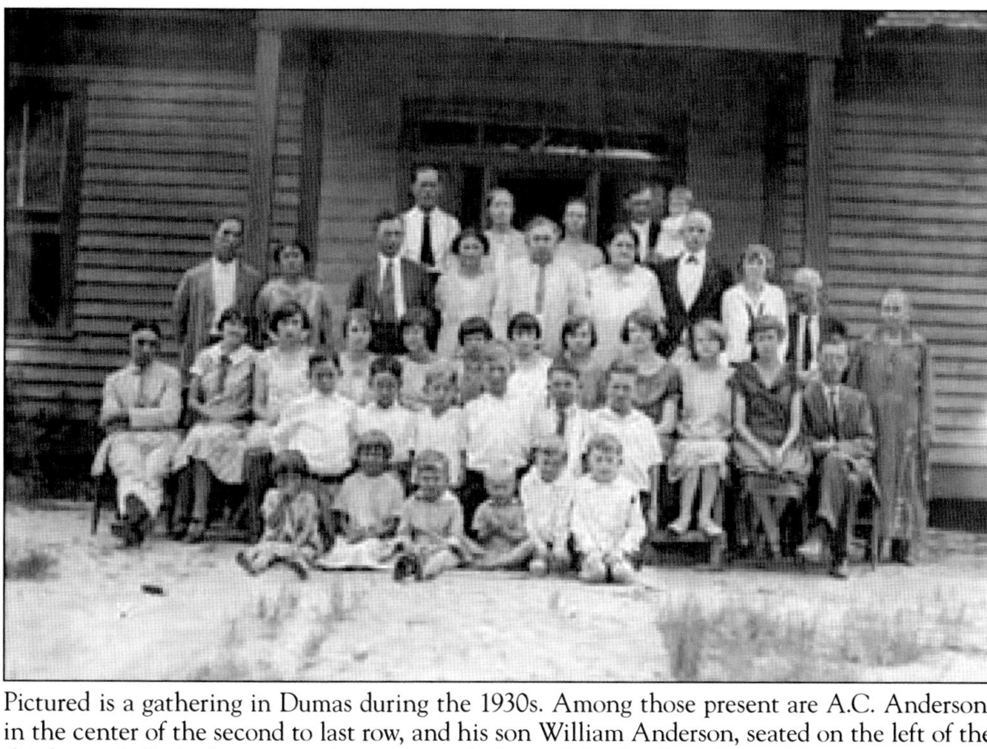

Pictured is a gathering in Dumas during the 1930s. Among those present are A.C. Anderson, in the center of the second to last row, and his son William Anderson, seated on the left of the third row. A.C. Anderson was the owner and editor of the *Southern Sentinel*.

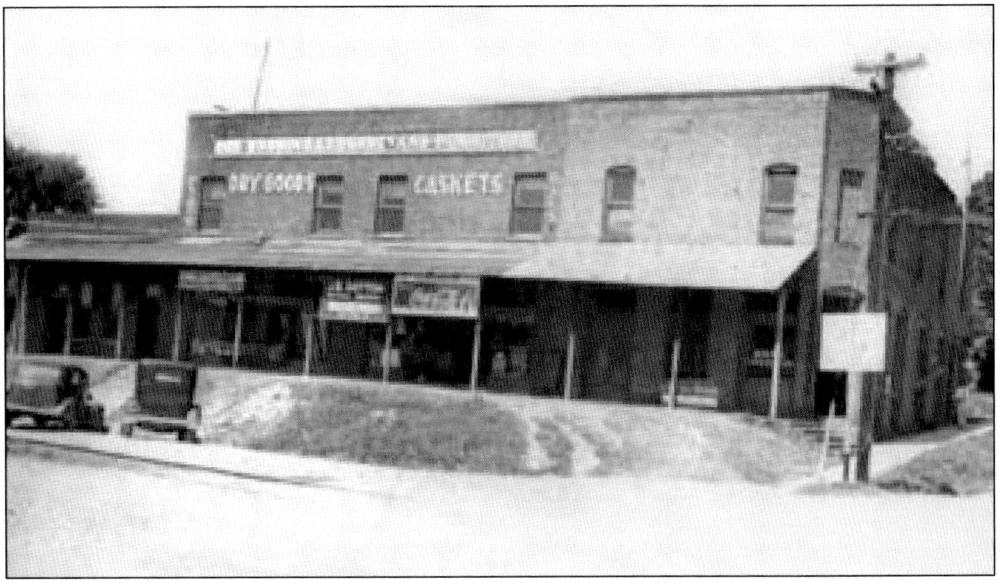

In 1938, Downtown Blue Mountain is pictured with the Bank of Blue Mountain on the right and J.B. Guyton Dry Goods and Groceries Store flanked by the City Dry Cleaners. The railroad is located in front of the buildings, with the Blue Mountain College entrance immediately on the right.

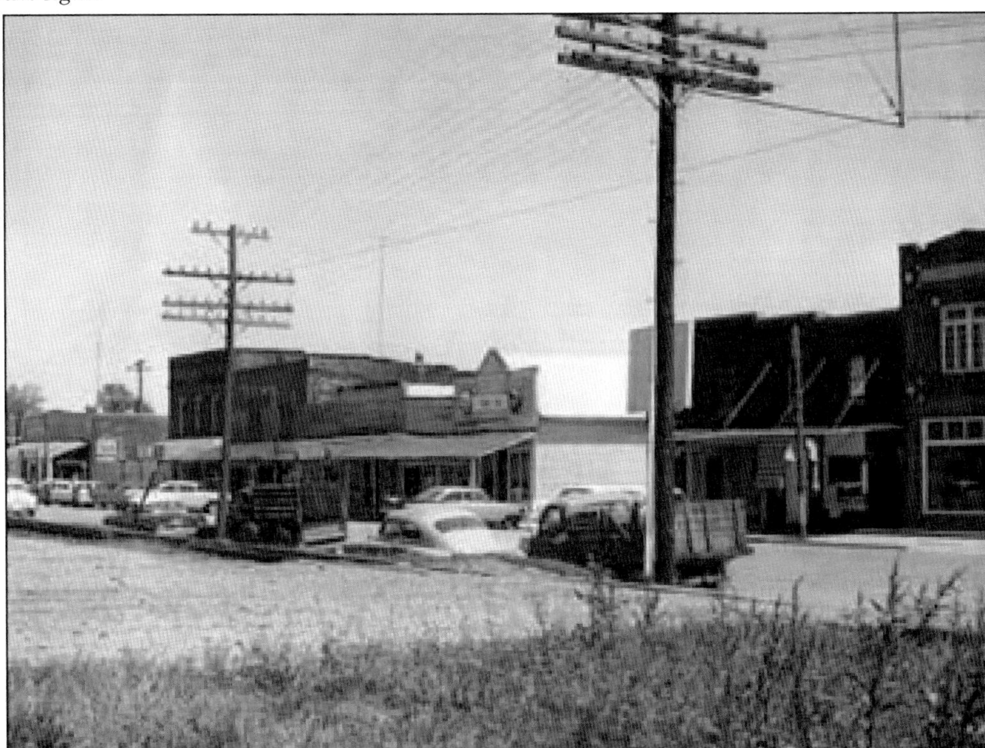
Pictured here is the Town of Blue Mountain, as it looked in 1959. The town had around 10 businesses located on the east side of the railroad. Blue Mountain College is located around 500 yards to the northwest of this picture.

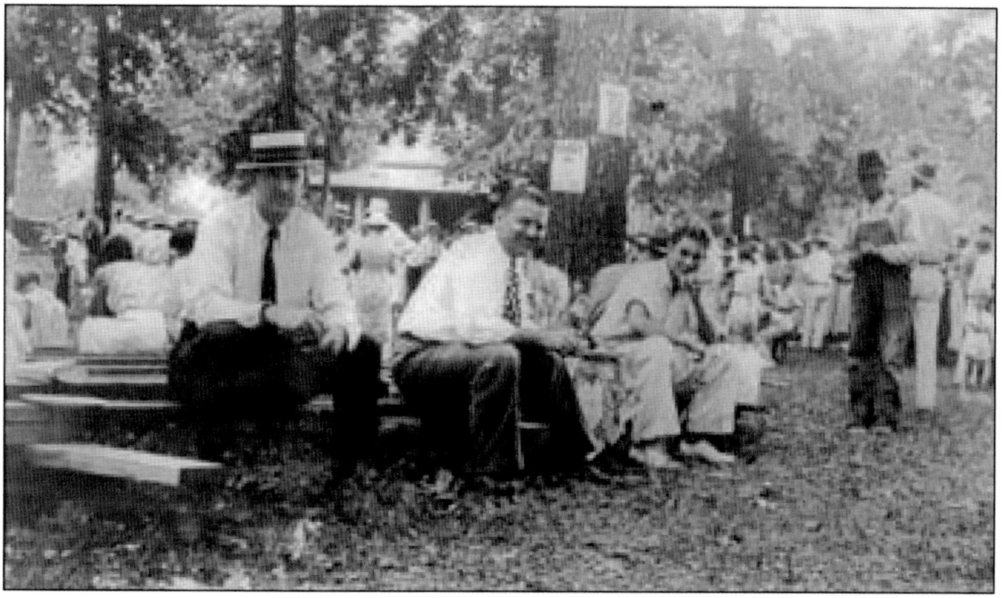

This photograph was taken at a political speaking event at Blue Mountain during the summer of 1935. Pictured is Oscar Shannon (center, seated), who was a candidate for Tippah County Superintendent of Education. A great wooded area provided shade and benches were provided for the people to relax.

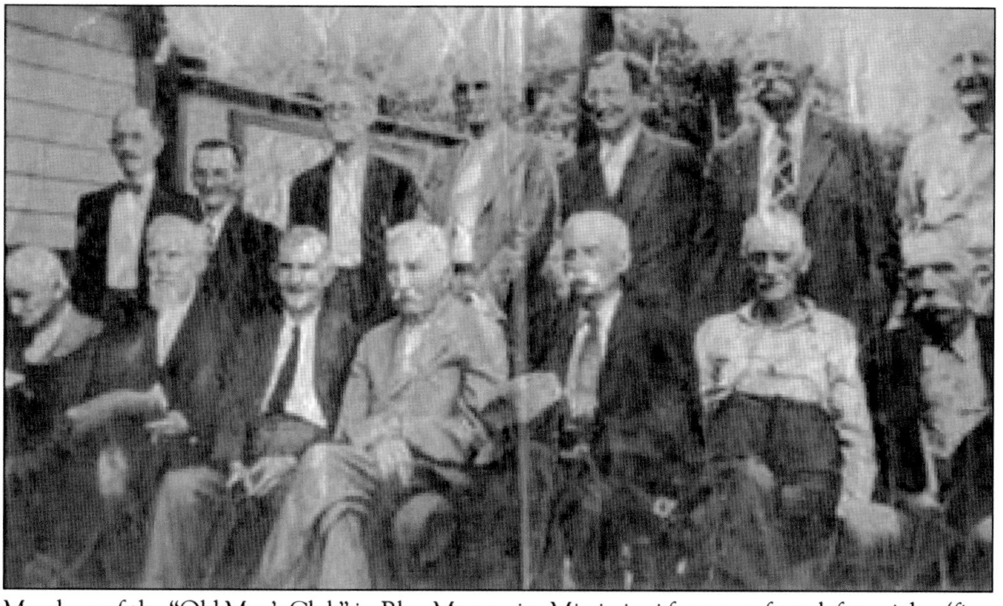

Members of the "Old Men's Club" in Blue Mountain, Mississippi from are, from left to right, (first row) Henry Mason (96), Dr. J.E. Buchanan (84), J.A. Skelton (82), E.L. Roach (82), G.W. Dean (80), J.A. Adair (80), and W.A. Roberson (77); (second row) J.R. Webb (78), W. Ezell (76), William Nance (71), C.A. Lequeux, R.S. Young, J.W. Clark (72), and J.A. Jernigan (71).

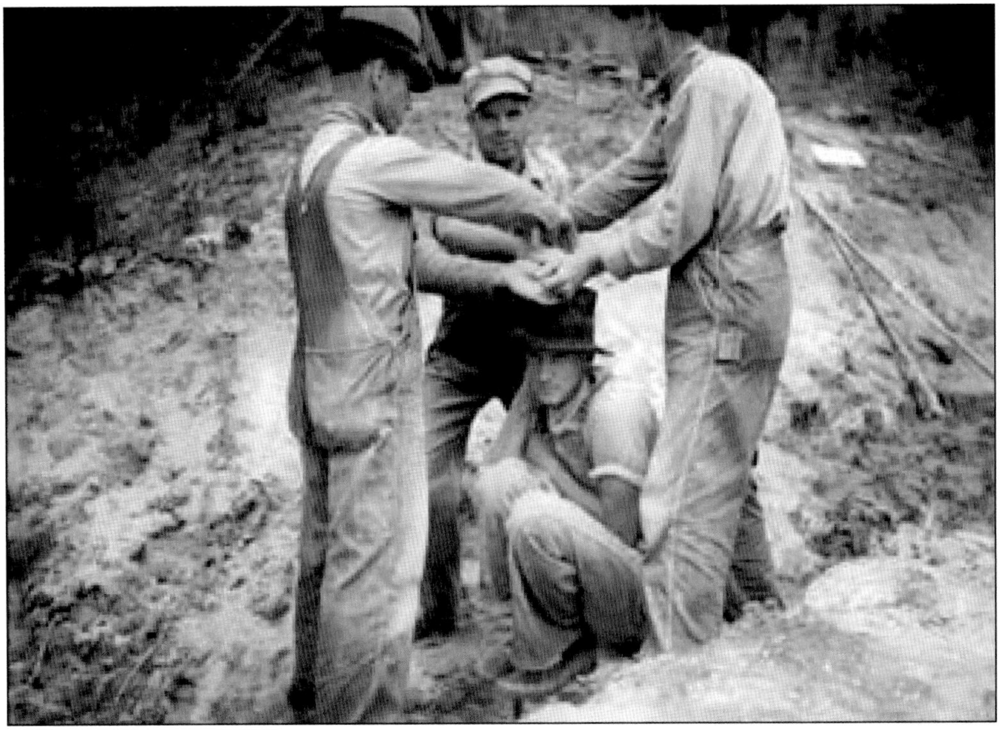

Tippah Countians that had been working on a construction site were seen clowning around for a picture in the 1930s.

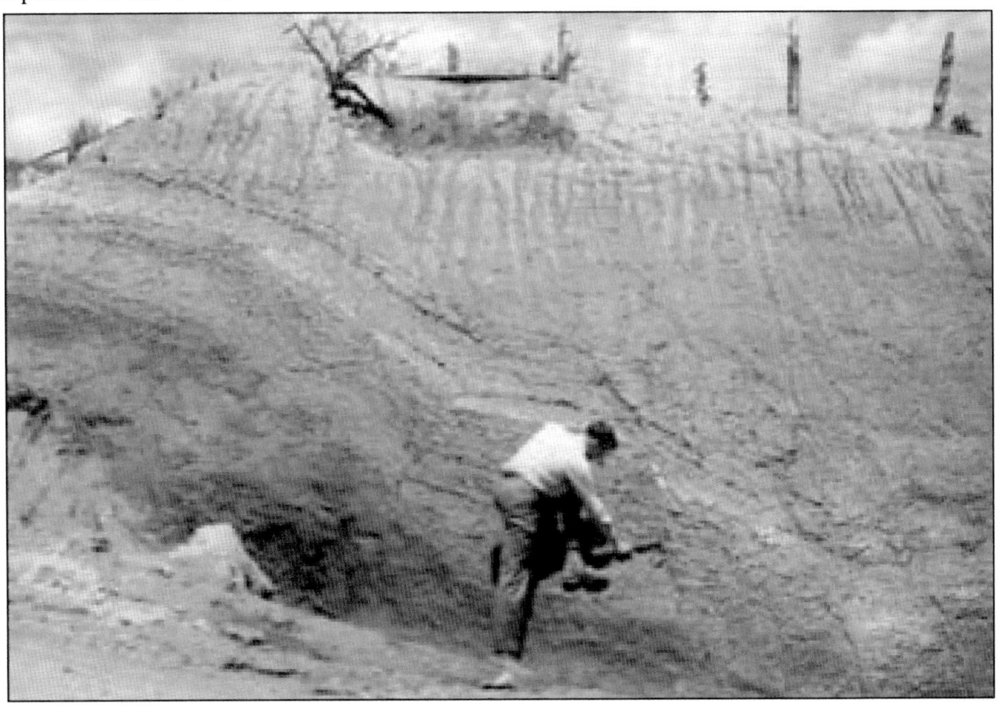

This is a scene on a county road near Eddins Hill and Ripley where an earthquake fault or a cave-in had occurred years ago. A worker is examining the layout for results.

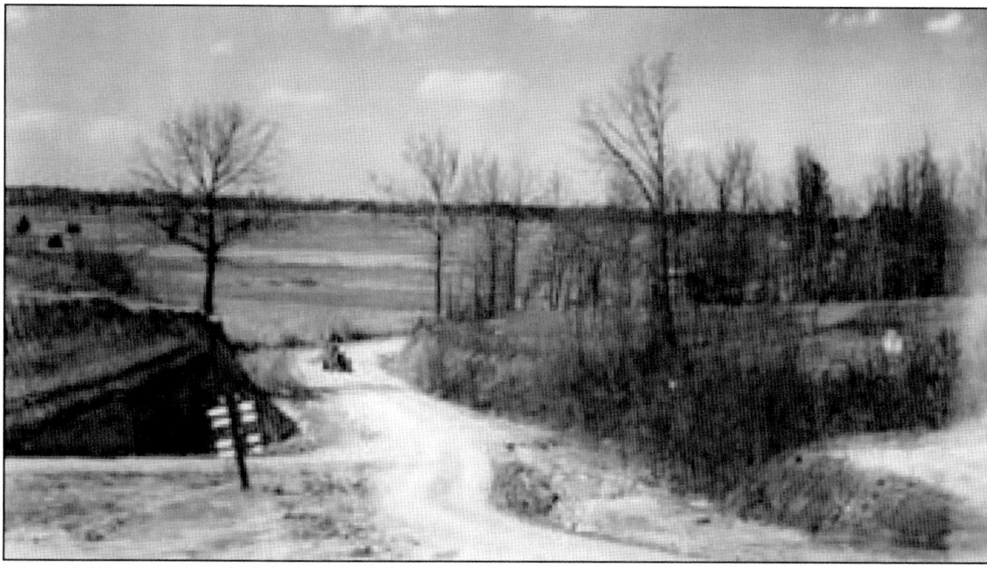

This 1940s photograph taken by Andrew Brown is of the top of Eddins Hill looking north.

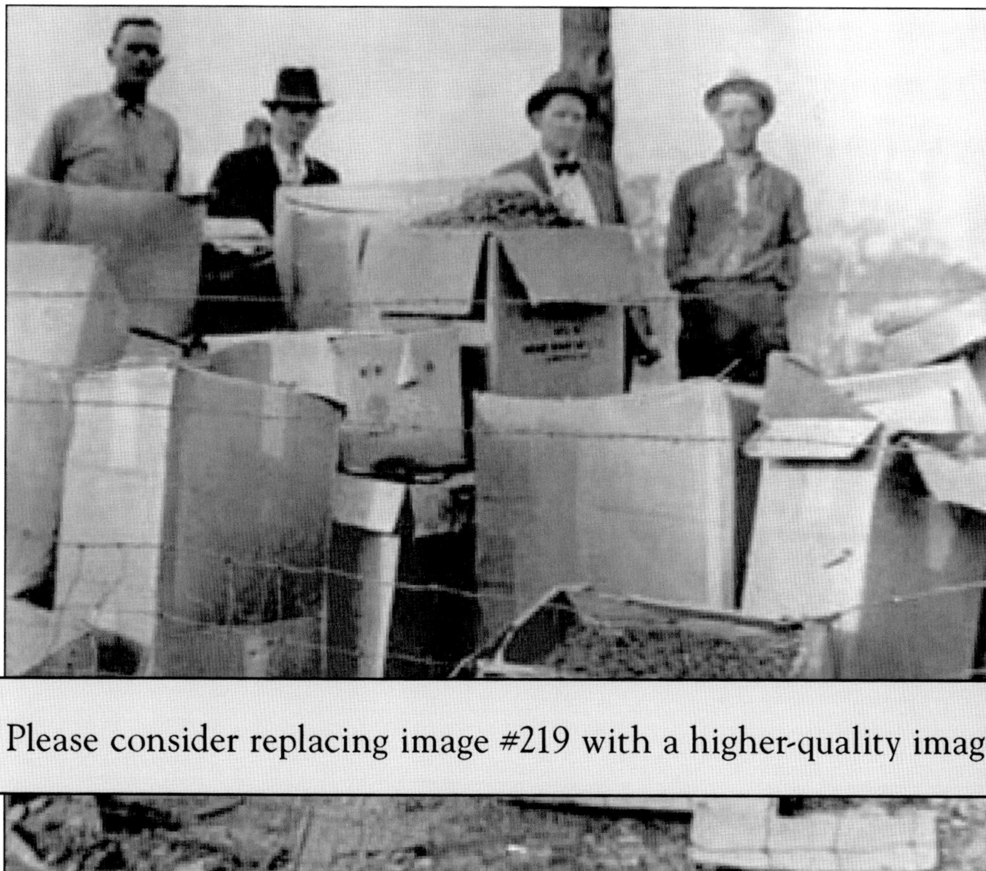

This 1936 photograph shows marijuana that had been grown by Herman Jernigan. The second man from the left was Benton Elliott and the man on the right was Herman Jernigan.

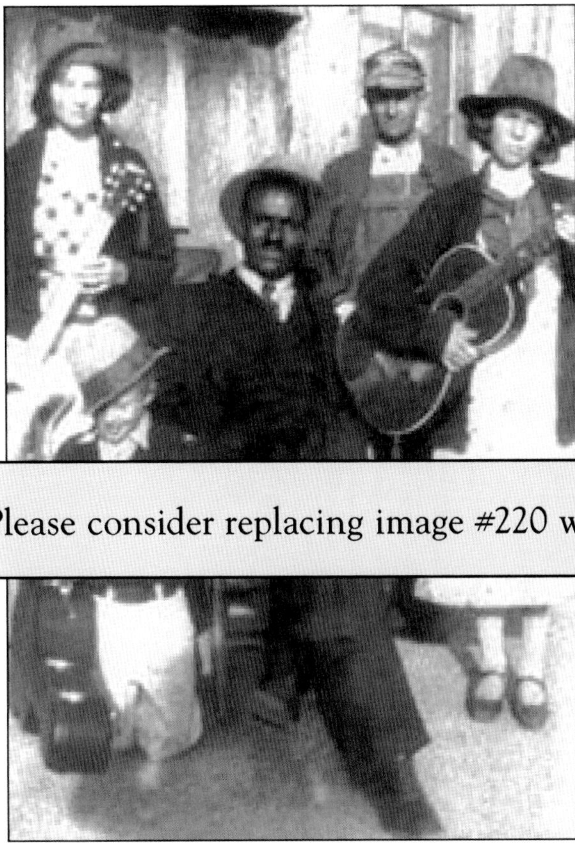

It is noted that this picture is said to have taken for humorous purposes. Roger Garrett (sitting) worked for the Roten family and also sang with them on the weekends at different functions. They all put on hats for this picture in the early 1930s. "Brud" Keener Eason Roten is kneeling and standing are Vernal Mae Roten (left), Archie Olin Roten (center), and Annie Ree Roten.

Please consider replacing image #220 with a higher-quality image.

Local talent from Tippah County that played at fairs and other functions were the Dixie Hot Shots. Those present for the picture are, from left to right, Rufus Jamieson, Troy Luna, Wayne Jamieson, Robert E. Jamieson, and Jessie V. Jamieson.

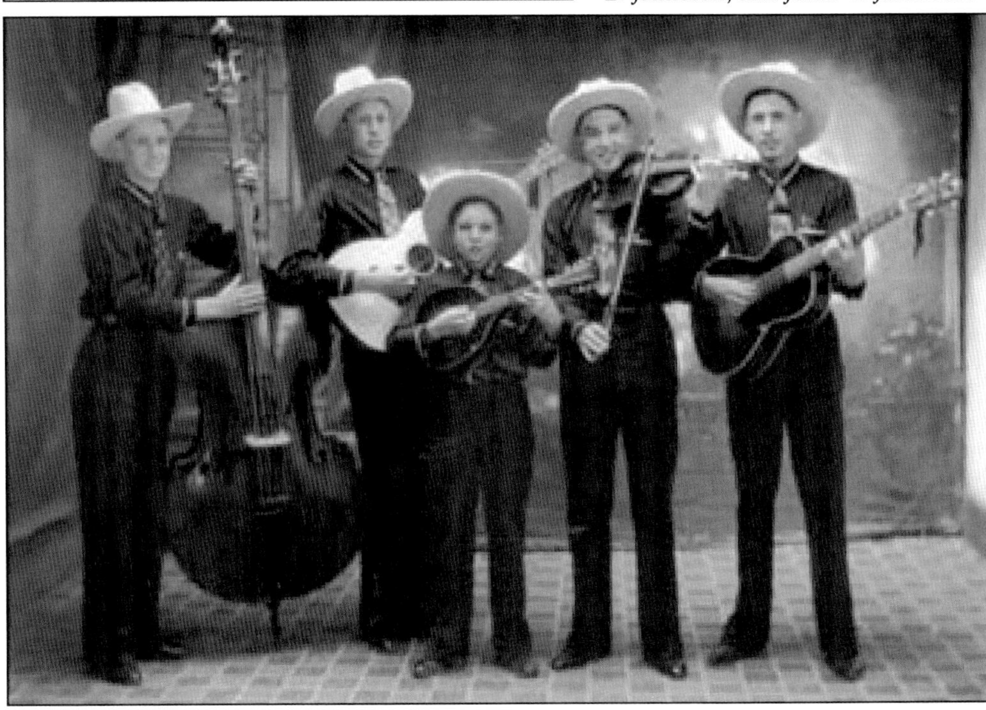

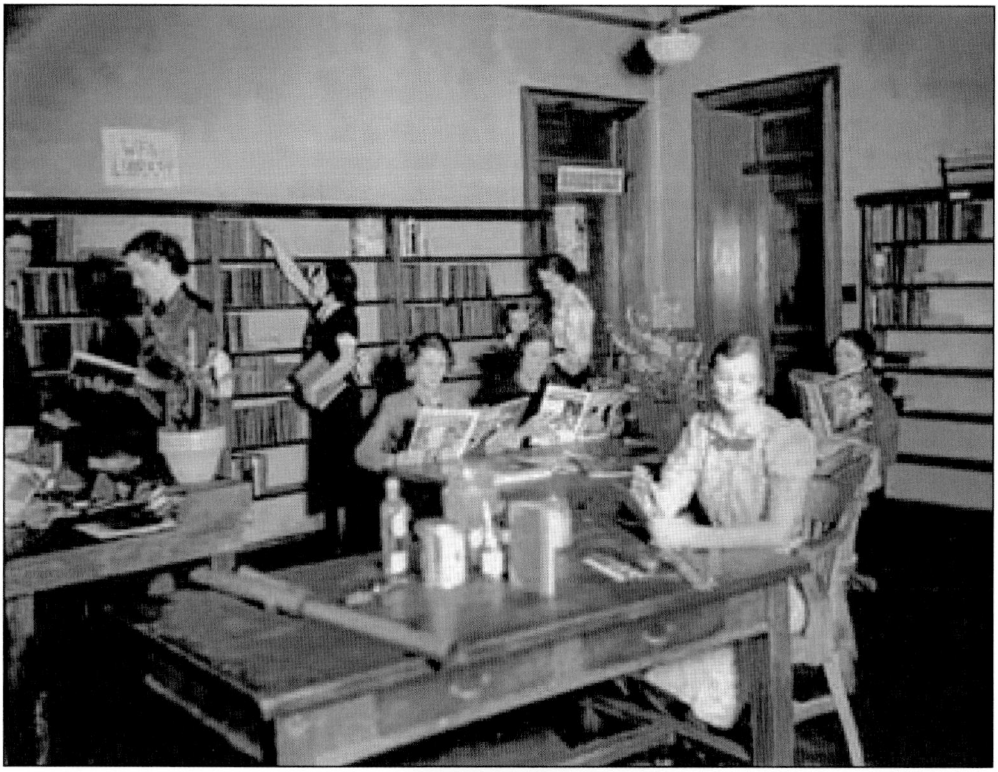

The WPA Library in the courthouse in the late 1930s is pictured here. Included in the picture are, from left to right, Bessie Mae Branyan, Blanche Bartlett, Julia Moore Luther, Bill Street, Maude Graves, and Clara Lee Gattis.

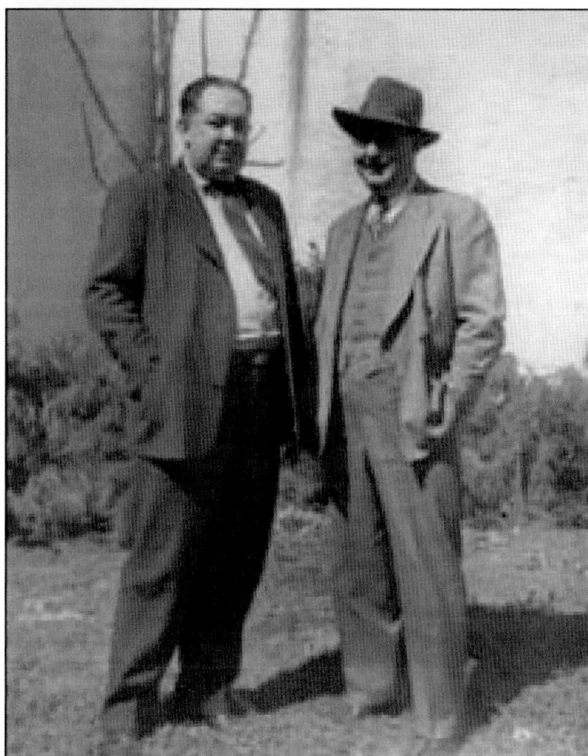

William Anderson and Dr. John Tate, noted newspaper owner and a leading doctor in Tippah County, are pictured here. It is a known fact that upon hearing of Dr. Tate's death, his office manager Mildred Martin and his janitor Mr. Storey put all of Dr. Tate's invoices in a trash can behind his office and burned them. Dr. Tate had asked them to do so, in order that no one would owe him a penny after he passed away. He was a very generous man.

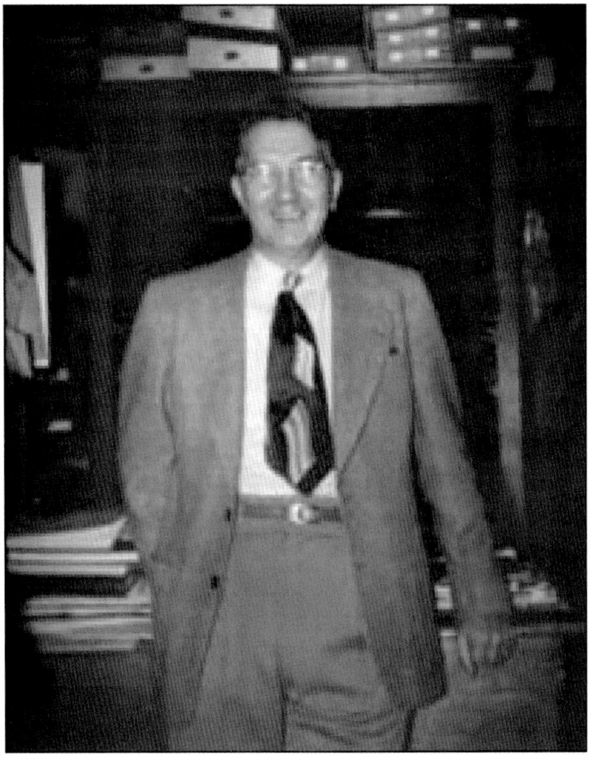

This is a photograph of Jimmie Finger, a noted storeowner of Ripley for a number of years. The store was located on the north side of the square and was in business from 1892 as M.L. Finger & Son until the early 1980s as W.A. Finger & Son. In the early years, they sold a wide variety of merchandise and later became a clothing store.

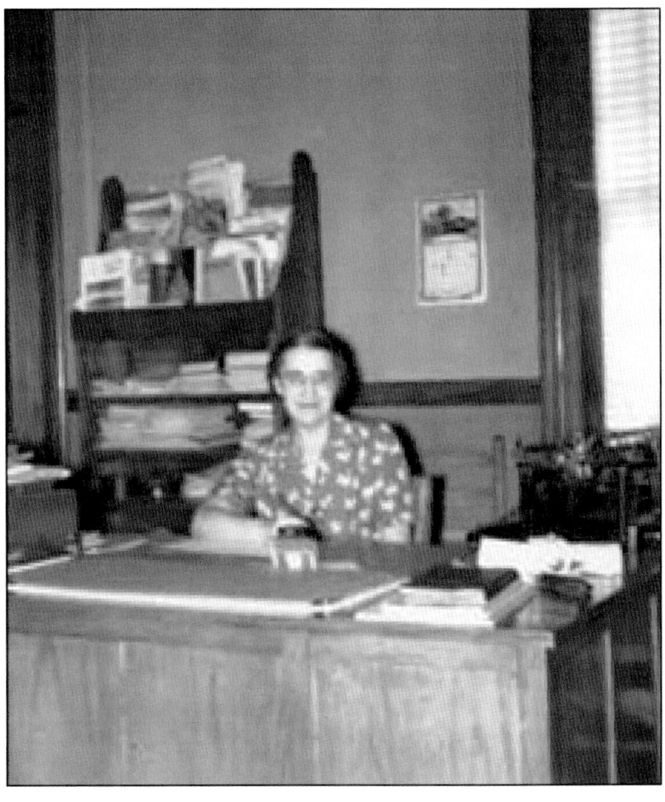

Eula Dees, a noted education specialist of Tippah County, is shown in her office during her serving as Superintendent of Education. Ms. Dees was never married and was later honored by the library at Northeast Mississippi Community College. The library was named the Eula Dees Library.

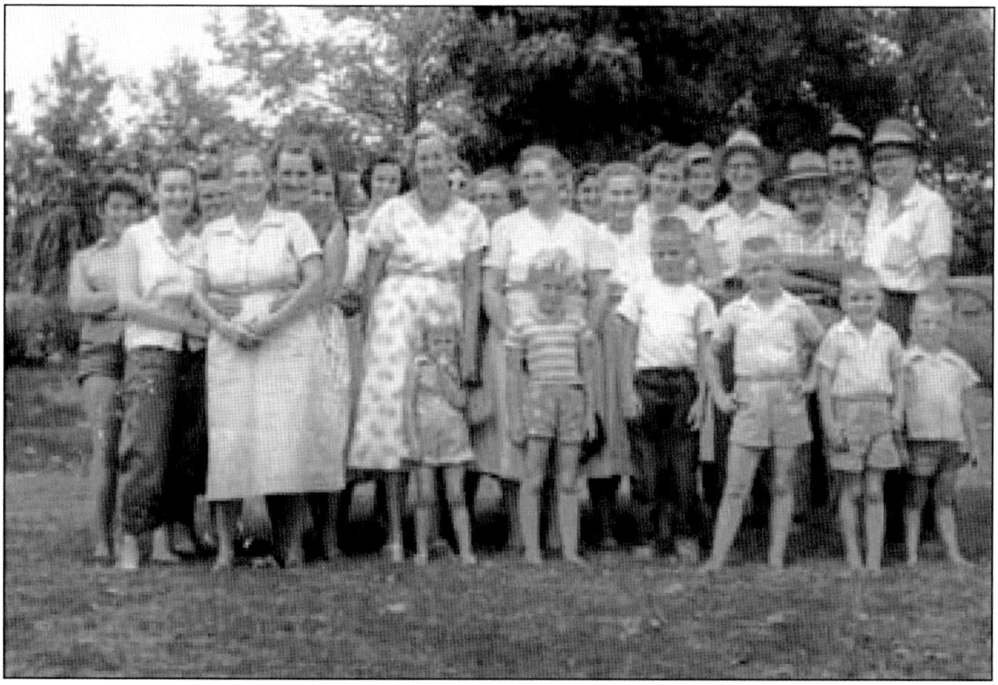

Pictured here are family members that belonged to the Mount Hebron TCDC. This club was started in the early 1950s and still continues today with eight other clubs in Tippah County. Tippah County is the last county that still sponsors clubs that help their communities prosper.

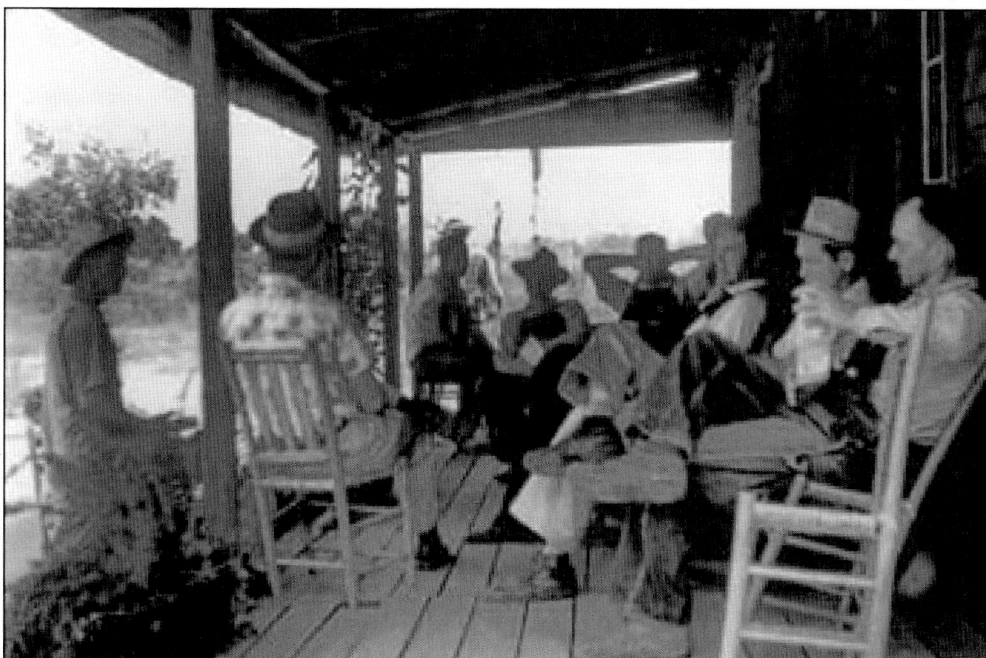

This early 1950s photograph is of a group of leaders discussing the business of the Tippah County Development Clubs. The old house with the plank floors and straight ladder back chairs in the shade make for an interesting conversation.

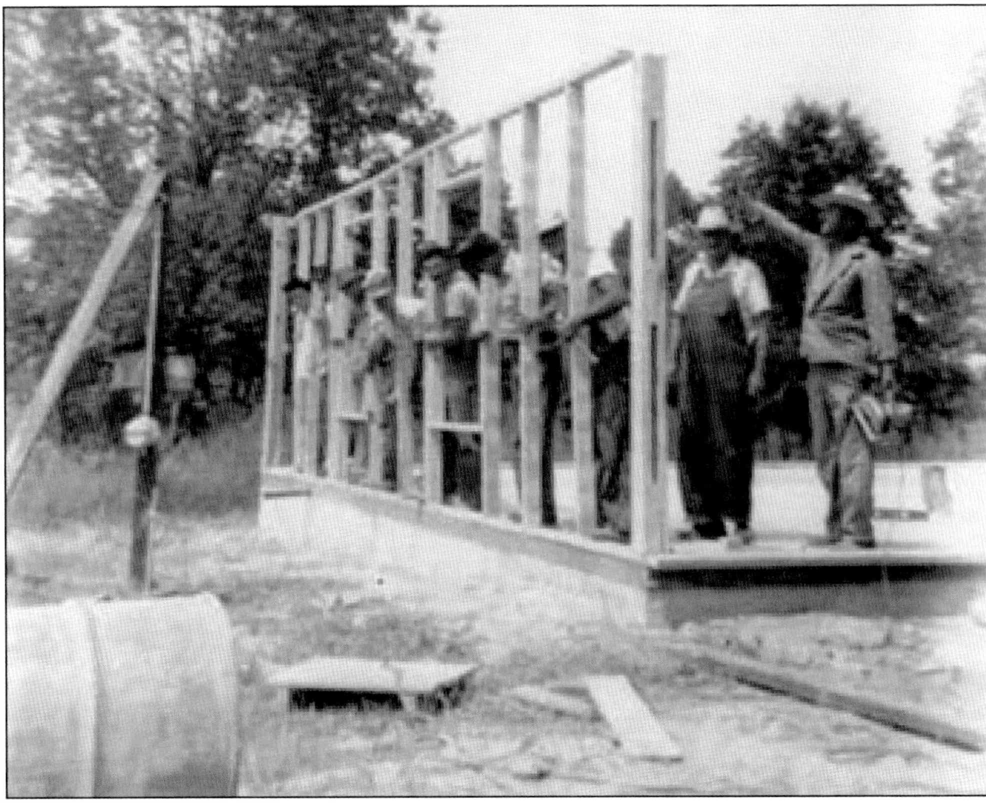

The Mount Hebron TCDC building was constructed by volunteer labor on land in northern Tippah County near Walnut. Herschel Terrell, one of the building committee members, is directing the installation of the frame.

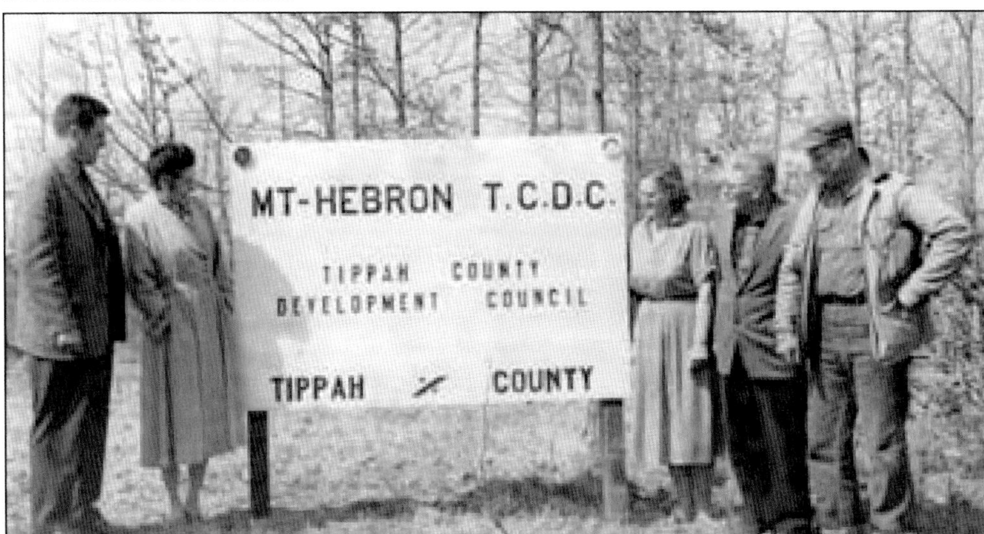

The Mount Hebron TCDC sign had just been installed and was witnessed by Ray Sartor, the county agent, and a TCDC member on the left, and Mary Dollar, Mrs. Hudson, and J.Y. Keith on the right.

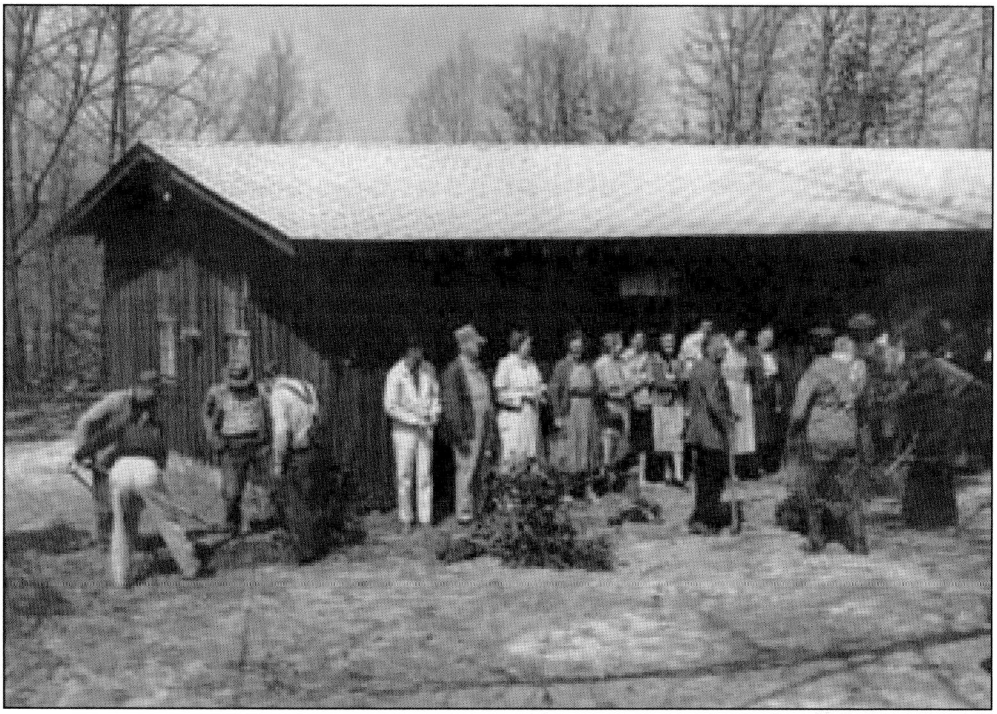

Shrubbery was being planted to landscape the front of the new Mount Hebron clubhouse near Walnut. This was built in the late 1950s for the club to conduct community business.

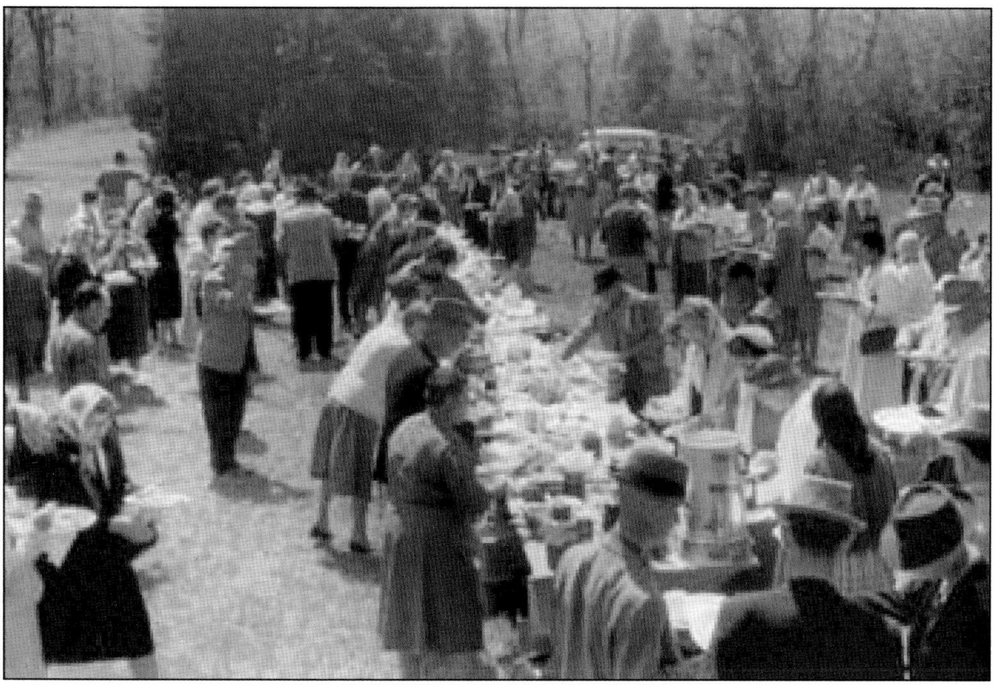

This picture exemplifies what the Tippah County Development Clubs were all about, with families getting together and having fun with food and homemade goods at the center of attention. This photograph from the 1950s is during an early spring.

Consistent with our mission to preserve history on a local level, this book was printed in South Carolina on American-made paper and manufactured entirely in the United States. Products carrying the accredited Forest Stewardship Council (FSC) label are printed on 100 percent FSC-certified paper.

MADE IN THE USA